"*Perfect Parenting* is full of no-nonsense, practical wisdom about many of the most common, and vexing, child-rearing issues. Parents will find solutions they can put into practice ri...

■ Pet...
Fa...

"*Perfect Parenting* is *the* dictionary for parents. No longer will parents need to thumb through all their books and magazines for answers to common questions. Parents will particularly appreciate the range of possible solutions. The author clearly understands that there is no right answer to any problem. I predict that *Perfect Parenting* will be the best-thumbed book in all parents' libraries."

■ Kathy Lynn
Parenting Today
Vancouver, British Columbia

"*Perfect Parenting* is good news, for parents and kids alike. Here's a wealth of wisdom about children's behavior, coupled with ingenious yet practical solutions to almost every imaginable problem. Pantley's approach puts parents in charge but lets children know they're respected and loved. And it's all wrapped up in one easy-to-access package."

■ Tamara Eberlein, author
Whining: Tactics for Taming Demand-
ing Behavior and *Sleep: How to Teach*
Your Child to Sleep Like a Baby

"*Perfect Parenting* is a must-have book for today's busy parents, who may not have time to read a complete book to find answers to their child-rearing problems. With *Perfect Parenting*, parents can quickly look up a specific topic and find several practical, easy-to-follow solutions, all of which foster a loving and respectful parent-child relationship."

■ Katey Roemmele, editor
Northwest Family magazine
Bellingham, Washington

"*Perfect Parenting* includes just about every issue that comes up for discussion in our parenting classes. The lists of possible solutions will appeal to a wide variety of parenting styles; there is something for everyone! The 'think about it' sections that appear after each realistically described situation help to establish a problem-solving perspective and allow the mind to open up to the numerous ways parents' and children's needs can be met. We are fortunate to have Pantley's experiences and humor to help guide us to better relationships with our children."

> ■ Connie Schulz, M.S., C.F.L.E.
> Family Outreach Specialist
> State College Area School District
> State College, Pennsylvania

"Some parents are lucky. They go into parenting with skills that they learned by observing effective ways their parents handled certain problems. We have all met them, or maybe you are even one of them. But any one person's experience is limited. Imagine trying to put together the collective skills of many of these people and then putting them into a package where all of us could easily access this accumulated wisdom for almost any parenting problem you would have. With *Perfect Parenting*, Pantley's latest book has given all of us such a wonderful resource."

> ■ Rona L. Levy, Ph.D..
> Professor, University of Washington
> Seattle, Washington

"*Perfect Parenting* gives sound advice and *more*. Parents and caregivers who follow through on the tips in this book will discover that they can be firm and consistent without being punitive or harsh. Loving guidance is the secret of this book. It is full of practical tips for almost any situation. It promises to make parenting more enjoyable and to help children become better behaved, more responsible and more successful . . . without tearing down their self-esteem."

> ■ Joan Comeau, Ph.D., C.F.L.E.
> President, Family Information Services

"*Perfect Parenting*, a parent-friendly compilation of choices and strategies, is practical, wise, and witty. It gives parents a pocketful of solutions to everyday conflicts."

■ Susan Beekman, co-author
Battles, Hassles, Tantrums & Tears

"This is *the* book to keep on your kitchen counter. It's packed with creative, practical solutions to all your everyday parenting problems. The dictionary format makes it easy to find quick, specific answers. Pantley's advice is based on common sense and sound parenting philosophies."

■ Dr. Len Fellez, author
Guerrilla Parenting and Your Child's Self Esteem

"*Perfect Parenting* belongs on every parent's *must read* list. Elizabeth's practical approach to parenting is a wonderful blending of sensitivity, common sense and humor. You'll want to keep this book in a convenient place so you can refer to it often!"

■ John Devine, co-author
Victory Beyond the Scoreboard

"Elizabeth Pantley has done it again! Parents are lucky to have her as a source of valuable, 'Why didn't I think of that?' information in dealing with the common difficulties we face in raising our children. Her easy, comprehensive layout of this wonderful new sourcebook makes it a snap to find a 'quick' solution when there's a matter at hand that can't wait for complete text reading. *Perfect Parenting* is an exceptional tool for finding the answers as we struggle to give our children the decent, moral lifestyle that they deserve. Thanks, Elizabeth!"

■ Janice M. Boyles, publisher
Choosing Home and *The HomeWork Network*

Perfect Parenting

The Dictionary of 1,000 Parenting Tips

ELIZABETH PANTLEY

FOREWORD BY WILLIAM SEARS, M.D.

CONTEMPORARY BOOKS

Library of Congress Cataloging-in-Publication Data

Pantley, Elizabeth.
    Perfect parenting : the dictionary of 1,000 parenting tips /
Elizabeth Pantley ; foreword by William Sears.
       p.   cm.
    Includes bibliographical references.
    ISBN 0-8092-2847-5
    1. Parenting—Dictionaries.   I. Title.
HQ755.8.P35   1998
649'.1'03—dc21   98-17024
                                     CIP

Cover design by Monica Baziuk
Interior design by Susan H. Hartman

Published by Contemporary Books
A division of NTC/Contemporary Publishing Group, Inc.
4255 West Touhy Avenue, Lincolnwood (Chicago), Illinois 60712-1975 U.S.A.
Copyright © 1999 by Better Beginnings, Inc.
Printed in the United States of America
International Standard Book Number: 0-8092-2847-5

  06 07 08 QF 24 23 22 21 20 19 18 17 16 15 14 13 12 11 10

To my God

For guiding me in my efforts
to help families everywhere
find more peace and happiness
in their homes.

CONTENTS

KICKING
See ■ Hitting, child to adult ■ Hitting, child to child

LATCHKEY RESPONSIBILITIES
See ■ Home alone, child is

LAZINESS
at home   159
See also ■ Carelessness ■ Sloppiness
at school   160
See also ■ Homework, how to create a routine ■ Homework, not getting it done ■ Homework, sloppy or rushed work ■ School, behavior problems at ■ School, not wanting to go

LISTENING, not   161
See also ■ Arguing, with parent ■ Cooperate, won't ■ Introduction ■ Respect, teaching

LOSING   162
See also ■ Athletics, poor sport ■ Competitiveness ■ Self-esteem, low

LOUDNESS
See ■ Noise, excessive ■ Roughhousing ■ Yelling and screaming

LYING   164
See also ■ Promises, doesn't keep ■ Self-esteem, low

MANNERS
at home   166
See also ■ Arguing, with parent ■ Back talk ■ Disrespect ■ Interrupting ■ Respect, teaching ■ Tantrums, at home

TABLE MANNERS

FOREWORD

In my years of raising eight children and advising parents through my pediatric practice and through twenty-three parenting books, I have learned as much as I have taught. I have discovered one parenting dilemma that arises repeatedly. This dilemma is the arduous process of deciding on the right course of action when confronted with a discipline or behavior issue.

In my conversations with parents, one type of question invariably arises; "What do I do when my child . . . whines . . . talks back . . . hits her sister . . . won't cooperate . . . ." Parents often struggle to find the right answer and then experience frustration when that one right answer fails to solve the problem.

Parenting educator Elizabeth Pantley presents here a multitude of valuable ideas to answer your everyday questions. She gives practical suggestions on a diverse selection of topics that likely cover every parenting dilemma you'll encounter. The beauty of this simple dictionary format is that you can review all the suggestions for any one dilemma and then use whatever method best fits your child and your family situation to create your own solution. If that suggestion doesn't work, you've got in hand several others from which to choose.

Perfect Parenting will give you the tools you need to feel confident as you raise your children. This handy reference book may become an indispensable part of your family's life.

William Sears, M.D.

Dr. Sears is one of America's most respected pediatricians. He and his wife, Martha Sears, R.N., have been counseling parents for more than twenty years. They appear frequently on national television, are extensively quoted in the media, and have collaborated on twenty-three books on parenting, including *The Discipline Book*, *The A.D.D. Book*, *The Baby Book*, and *The Pregnancy Book*. William and Martha Sears are the parents of eight children, and grandparents of three.

ACKNOWLEDGMENTS

I am very grateful for the wonderful support of the many people who have made this book possible.

I would like to express my sincere appreciation to

- Susan Schwartz, at Contemporary Books. An editor with vision, patience, and wisdom.

- Meredith Bernstein, of Meredith Bernstein Literary Agency. An agent with incredible energy and enthusiasm.

- Dr. William Sears. An extraordinary man who has enhanced the lives of millions of parents, myself included.

- Susan Beekman, Janice Boyles, Joan Comeau, John Devine, Tamara Eberlein, Len Fellez, Peter Herbst, Rona L. Levy, Kathy Lynn, Katey Roemmele, Connie Schulz. People who believe that the ideas presented in this book will be helpful to families everywhere.

- Barbara Quick. A friend whose insight led me in the right direction.

- Michelle Feldman and Renée Strumsky. With appreciation for a lifetime of irreplaceable relationships—sister to sister.

- Dolores Feldman. My mom. With sincerest thanks for teaching me that love is the most important gift you can give your children.

- Angela Pantley. My cherished daughter, who opened my heart to all the joy and wonder of being a mother and who teaches me wondrous things about life.

- Vanessa Pantley. My precious daughter, who brings music, laughter, and serenity to my life with her gentle presence and soulful depth.

- David Pantley. My delightful son, who continually fills our home and my life with zest, enthusiasm, and a very special love.

- Robert Pantley. My perfect husband.

INTRODUCTION

WHAT IS PERFECT PARENTING?

Perfect parenting is parenting with a plan. It is based on action, rather than reaction. Knowledge, rather than chance. Thoughtfulness, rather than anger. Common sense, rather than nonsense.

Just as labeling one the "perfect marriage" doesn't mean that both partners are perfect human beings, perfect parenting doesn't imply that a parent can, or should even strive to, be "perfect." Perfect parenting is a *process* whereby parents, in all their human flaws and weaknesses, do their personal best to raise capable, responsible, happy children.

This book is a dictionary of ideas. It is meant to inspire you to find the right answers for the many discipline and behavior issues that arise in your family. It presents you with options and methods that can help you be thoughtful in your approach to raising your children.

READ THIS FIRST!

Raising children is a complicated job. There are times when every parent and caregiver can use some help and a few fresh ideas. This is a book packed with ideas. It will help you get through the day-to-day issues you face with your children. What you'll find here are practical, commonsense solutions that will make your life easier.

You should be able to find ideas here for just about any problem or issue you are currently encountering. Every child is different, and every parent is different. Because of this, there are no cookie-cutter solutions that will work for everyone. I suggest that you review all the solutions and take a few quiet minutes to think about them. Modify the suggestions to best suit your family, and don't be afraid to try out more than one until you discover your best answer.

Keep in mind that following a few important rules will make every situation with your child easier to handle, regardless of which solution you choose to implement. I call these the "Perfect Parenting Keys."

PERFECT PARENTING KEYS

 Take charge.

If your child doesn't clearly understand that you are the boss, even minor issues can cause you major headaches. Your first response to this statement may be, "Oh, but my children know who's the boss in our house." You may *think* they do, but there are many ways we give mixed messages and confuse our kids over this issue. The keys presented here will help you identify the areas where you can make some changes.

The first step to taking charge is simply to give yourself permission to be in charge and begin expecting your children to obey you.

With this solid foundation, you will build a loving, trusting relationship with your children. And, perhaps even more important, you will be able to lead your children into adulthood with values, wisdom, and life skills that only a strong, supportive parent can impart.

2 **Tell, don't ask.**

One popular mistake parents make is *asking* instead of *telling*. The way you phrase your words determines whether your children see your request as optional or required. Banish all wishy-washy phrases from your vocabulary.

When you want your child to do something (or stop doing something), make a clear, specific statement that leaves no room for confusion.

Take a look at the difference between these two types of requests:

Optional	*Required*
It would be nice if somebody cleaned up this family room.	Steven, please put all the toys back in the playroom. Amy, please gather the dishes and put them in the dishwasher.
Kids, don't you think it's time to get ready for bed?	It's eight o'clock. Time to shut off the TV and put on your pajamas.
I sure wish you'd get down from there.	That's not a place to climb. Please get down.
Gather up your stuff now, OK?	Please get your backpack, jacket, and shoes.

3 **When you say it, mean it. The first time.**

Some parents are in the habit of repeating a request over and over and over (and over!) before taking any action to see that a child complies with the request. Do you know anyone like this? (Perhaps intimately?)

Children have radar that tells them exactly when adults *really* mean what they say and when they don't. Some parents *really* mean it only after repeatedly ignored requests. This is usually highlighted by a red face, a tense body, a child's middle name spoken through clenched and gnashing teeth, and a fist pounding the table to the tune of "and I mean it, young man!"

Make yourself a promise to mean what you say—the first time you say it. What this means is that after you've made a clear statement of what is *required* (*see* Key 2), you take action. For example, if you call your child in from the yard and he doesn't immediately respond, you will have to put forth the extra effort to go out to the yard, take him by the hand, and announce, "When I call you, I expect you to come."

The beauty of this style is that you only have to "prove" yourself once or twice for your child to understand that, indeed, when you say it, you mean it. The first time. (For those with older children who have already learned that they can ignore you the first few times with no repercussions, it may take more "proving" before they believe that you have really changed. Your children *can* learn to believe that when you say it, you mean it. Hang in there. Be consistent. It's definitely worth the effort.)

4 **Be brief and specific.**

There is a disease that is rampant among parents. It's called lecture-babble-itis. The most obvious symptom is an emotional run-on sentence that goes on forever, punctuated by highlights of previous award-winning monologues. For example, you send your children upstairs with a polite request to get ready for bed. Half an hour later, you discover that they're having a pillow fight. The parent infected with lecture-babble-itis says,

"I sent you kids up here thirty minutes ago to get ready for bed and nobody's even *starting* to get ready and it's after eight o'clock and it's a school night and *why* do we have to go through this *every* single night, couldn't you just *once* get ready for bed without my getting angry about it and why is this room such a *mess* again, can't you ever . . ."

(Is it any wonder why kids roll their eyes?)

There is a cure for this dreaded disease. It involves making an effort to talk less but say more. In other words, be very specific in your description, but use as few words as necessary. Even when the kids have ignored the first polite request, the above disastrous speech can be transformed into something like this: "Kids, it's eight thirty. Pajamas. Now." As you can see, this statement is clear and short. It is easy to understand. The advantages of using this technique are twofold. Your kids will cooperate more frequently with a brief, specific statement than they will with a lengthy tirade. And, it's fun and easy for you to do this!

5 **Don't give in to nagging, whining, and pressure.**

Many parents start out on the right track but are derailed by an incredibly persistent child. It seems that when children couple their youthful energy with an extraordinary ability to pinpoint their parents' weak spots, the result is disaster.

If you're doing your job as a parent, there are many times when your decisions won't be popular with your kids. When your child is nagging, whining, and pleading with you, it's a sure sign that you've made the right decision. It's also a sign that you need to disengage from your youngster and teach her that you won't be swayed by her persistence.

Your most important goal as a parent is *not* to make your children happy on a short-term basis. It's to raise capable, responsible human beings. There are many times when your children will be unhappy with your decisions. Usually, this means you've made the right decision! We have an incredible amount of information and knowledge at our fingertips, more than any other generation of parents in our history. Take advantage of this information. Read. Think. And be confident in your actions.

6 Give choices; ask questions.

A primary goal of all children is to become independent. Instead of fighting against this very natural process, a wise parent will use it to his advantage.

For example, let's look at the very common problem of a child's messy bedroom. A parent can rightly expect that a child's room be neat and clean. A typical mistake is for the parent to demand that the child clean it—on the *parent's* time schedule and to the *parent's* exact specifications. The typical child responds with a full-blown temper tantrum, which ignites the parent's adult-sized temper tantrum, which results in a lot of anger and a still-messy room.

A better choice is to engage the child's decision-making skills and utilize his desire to be in control of his own room and his own life. A parent might offer several well-thought-out choices, such as, "Would you like to clean your room after school today, or would you prefer to do it after baseball practice tomorrow?" Another choice might be, "What would you like to do first—change your bedding or vacuum your carpet?" Yet another choice would be, "Would you like to clean your room yourself, or shall I help you?" It's clear that a child will respond better to any of these choices than he would to the statement, "Clean your room and do it now."

Another way to approach this problem is to ask helpful questions and direct the child into coming up with solutions on his own. Therefore, you might ask, "I notice that your homework is scattered all over your room. Do you think it might be easier to keep track of if you create a 'homework place'? How can I help you solve this problem?"

Yet another example of this approach is to take the time to discuss the issue with your child and ask for his ideas. "I know the mess in your room doesn't bother you, but I find it difficult to change your bed or put away your clothes. Can you help me come up with some solutions?"

As you can see, any of these techniques provide the parent with a variety of ways to encourage the child to become involved in solving the problem.

7   Use rules and routines.

Chores, homework, mealtime, bedtime, getting out the door in the morning. These are the things life is made of. If you have very specific rules and routines, you will find that things flow. If you don't—chaos. It's well worth the time to establish family priorities, rules, and schedules for the usual daily routines.

The first part of this key takes more than a few minutes of thought. You'll need to sit down and take time to ponder your daily activities. You'll need to make some decisions about priorities and what's most important in your family. Once you've done this, create charts to cover the steps involved in each major task, such as the morning routine, the after-school routine, or the bedtime routine. Purchase and post a large family calendar to show all the family activities and commitments. (This helps the adults in the family stay organized just as much as it helps the kids!)

A second part of this key is to evaluate your expectations for your children. Create a list of rules. These rules should cover expected behavior by clearly identifying two things: what is *not* allowed and what behavior *is* expected. In other words, listing "No fighting" as a family rule is only the first part of the equation. "Be kind and respectful to each other" clarifies the important concluding concept.

When everyone knows what to expect, you'll find yourself nagging and complaining much less and the kids cooperating much more.

8   **Build a foundation of love, trust, and respect.**

Imagine that you've been invited to a friend's home for dinner. Your friend welcomes you at the door and you step inside. Suddenly, your host shouts, "What is the matter with you! Your shoes are all muddy, and you're getting my carpet dirty!" Embarrassed, you mumble, "Sorry," and remove your shoes. As you do, you notice the hole in your sock, and so does your friend, who announces, "Geez. Don't you think you could have dressed properly for dinner? You look like a slob." As you take your place at the table, your host knocks your elbow off the table with a whispered "Tsk, tsk." The dinner conversation is primarily your friend's story about a guest who joined your friend for dinner last night who had *lovely* manners and no holes in her socks. The story is sprinkled with your friend's occasional corrections to your table manners. When you finish your meal, you stand up only to hear your friend say, "It sure would be nice if *somebody* helped clear the table."

I'm sure you get my drift by now. Many parents treat their children in ways that they would never treat a friend. In their efforts to raise respectable children, they become so focused on the end goal that they don't realize that the primary message coming though to their children is not a pleasant one.

Take a close look at your daily interactions with your children. Make sure that the primary message to them is, "I love you, I trust you, and I respect you." Children who are confident that they are loved, trusted, and respected by the important adults in their lives will respond overall in a much more pleasant way.

How do you get this message through to your children? First, give them what they want most from you—your time. It's much more effective to give small chunks of time every day than to try to pack in a "quality" experience once a month. Second, give them your ear. Children thrive when they have someone who really listens to them. It's not as important to give advice and solve problems as it is to just plain listen. Third, praise and encourage your children daily. Look for reasons, both big and small, to give your children positive feedback. Fourth, tell them you love them. Tell them you trust them. Tell them you respect them. Use your words and your actions to convey this most important message of all: "I love you, I trust you, and I respect you."

9 Think first; act second.

The times when you *act* before you *think* reflect the worst moments in parenting. Those are the times when you lose your patience—those horrible moments when you screech, bellow, threaten, or hit. These moments occur most often to parents who are unprepared for the parenting job.

None of us are born knowing how to be parents. We can love our kids with our whole heart and soul, but we aren't born with a gene that gives us an instinctual knowledge of the right consequence to impart when our children misbehave, nor do we automatically know how to solve daily child-rearing problems.

We won't learn a perfect-parenting process by chance. It takes research, thought, and planning to decide upon the best solution to any problem.

I don't think any chef, no matter how skilled, could enter my kitchen and without any direction, recipe, or ingredients create a four-course meal with a five-star dessert. It would increase the odds of our having a delicious meal if that person had access to my best cookbook and passage to the local grocery store. In much the same way, you will be a much more successful parent if you have access to ideas and solutions whenever you come across a parenting problem.

Perfect Parenting is your guidebook to a multitude of ideas. Use it as your basis to create thoughtful, purposeful solutions to your parenting problems. Whenever you come across a situation that baffles you or creates strife in your family life, take a few minutes to look up the ideas for that entry and any others that are similar. Contemplate how the ideas fit into your parenting style, how they match up to the personality of your child, and how they might work for you. Then, create a plan of action. And follow through.

Enjoy the benefits of this handbook of knowledge. Enjoy the benefits of thinking before you act. Enjoy the benefits of *Perfect Parenting!*

Perfect Parenting

ALLOWANCES

See also ■ Chores, money and ■ Money

SITUATION

Should my children get an allowance? How much should I give them? Should it be tied to chores, performance, or behavior?

THINK ABOUT IT

The purpose of allowance is to teach kids how to handle money. They can learn from early experiences how to make money decisions when the amounts are small and the decisions are simple. Children from kindergarten age on can begin to understand the significance of money and its value to them. Given this opportunity, children will be less likely to grow into adults with empty bank accounts and an alphabetical assortment of credit cards.

SOLUTIONS

1 It's best not to tie allowance to chores. If you do, there may come a day when the child doesn't need or want your money and can logically pass on the chores. How would you respond if your child says, "I don't need my allowance this week, Dad, so I won't be doing the dishes or taking out the trash." (*See also* Chores.) From this, I shudder to think why you would tie allowance to performance or behavior!

2 How much allowance to give a child has little to do with how much you *have* to give and more to do with what the child's money *needs* are. Does the child buy lunch at school, school supplies, or clothes? Or is allowance purely "pocket money"? Does the child receive money from other sources, such as from relatives? It's a good idea to give a child enough money to purchase his necessities and just a little more for extras.

3 Help your child create a budget. Discuss the value of having a set amount for spending, short-term savings, and long-term savings. Ask your child if he has a particular item he would like to save for. Find out the cost of the item and divide the total cost by the weekly (or monthly) amount he's willing to put aside for it. Make a graph to show the steps toward reaching his goal. Celebrate success!

4 Let your child open a bank account for savings. Look for a bank that offers a special child's program. Typically, these programs include a newsletter and special incentives. Shop around for the best program. Encourage your child to set a goal for a savings amount, and plan a reward to celebrate when the goal has been reached.

5 A junior- or senior-high-school-aged child can have allowances deposited directly into a personal checking account. This gives a young person practice in using and managing a bank account. At first, give the child one or two checks at a time and teach him how to balance his checkbook. Over time, and with practice, he'll be able to take charge of the account. A big caution: Until a parent is sure the child can handle this responsibility properly, the account should be in both names, and the monthly statements should be reviewed together.

ALLOWANCES, and raises

See also ■ Chores, money and ■ Materialism ■ Money

SITUATION
My child wants a "raise." How can I make the decision of whether to increase her allowance?

THINK ABOUT IT
When your child asks for more money, it's easy to give a knee-jerk yes-or-no response. Instead, use this as a golden opportunity to teach an important lesson about money.

SOLUTIONS

1 Ask the child to provide you with a written budget of what the money is needed for, along with a written request for a raise explaining why it's desired. If the child is able to present a logical, well-thought-out request, it's safe to say she's ready for a bigger allowance.

2 Ask the child to create an extra "job" for which she can be paid. This should not be a regular household chore but something extra. Some ideas might include baby-sitting younger siblings, taking over one of the parent's current chores (such as doing the laundry), or providing a service for a parent's business (such as envelope stuffing, sorting, or filing).

3 Suggest that the child look outside the family for work. The neighborhood is typically a fertile ground for children's fledgling businesses. Some ideas are car washing, yard weeding, baby-sitting, housecleaning, pet sitting, pet walking, or pet-poop pickup (a good choice because the neighbors are very willing to let someone else do it!).

4 Often the child is actually receiving sufficient allowance but is unskilled in money management. Help the child create a budget and an accounting log to record and monitor spending.

ANGER, child's

See also ■ Arguing, with parent ■ Back talk ■ Disrespect ■ Fighting ■ Hate, expressions of ■ Meanness ■ Respect, teaching ■ Self-esteem, low ■ Siblings, fighting

SITUATION

My child can't control his angry emotions. He tends to lash out at others, verbally and physically.

THINK ABOUT IT

As a parent educator, one of my most popular lectures is entitled "Understanding and Managing Your Anger." Ask yourself, "If hundreds of adults attend a class about anger management, how can I expect my child to learn how to control his anger on his own?"

SOLUTIONS

1 Avoid responding to your child's anger with anger of your own. Your anger will tend to escalate your child's sour mood. Instead, control your own anger first. (*See also* Anger, parent's.) Reply to your child in a calm, even-tempered voice. You will be better able to direct your child's actions, and you'll be modeling the behavior you wish to see in your child.

2 Your child needs to learn that although angry emotions are normal, there are acceptable and unacceptable ways of dealing with them. You can help your child learn this by acknowledging the reason he's angry. Often, just knowing that you understand his feelings can calm him down. For example, what if your child is angry because his brother took his bike without asking, and he's shouting and swearing? Calmly acknowledge the reason for his anger by saying something like, "I know it's frustrating when Alex takes your things without asking." This will often cause a pause in your child's behavior as he ponders this new response from you. Next, ask a question that directs your child's thinking in a more productive way: "How do you think you can get him to remember to ask?" If he responds in an angry way, prompt him in a more positive direction: "Getting angry won't get your point across. What do you think will?" Stay with him and guide him through the resolution process.

3 If a child's angry behavior is out of line, immediately stop him and send him to his room to cool off. Don't try to deal with the behavior at the peak of his anger. Later, when he's calmed down, take the time to let him know, specifically, what he did that you disapprove of. Engage him in a conversation to develop a plan for avoiding the behavior in the future.

4 Talk to your child about his anger. Tell him that it's important for him to learn how to control his temper. Suggest that the first thing he should do is learn to get control of himself before he does or says things that are inappropriate. Let your child know, in advance, that the next time he explodes in anger, you'll help him by asking him to go to his room to cool off. Advise him that if he doesn't immediately do as asked, he will lose a privilege for the rest of the day, such as using the telephone, watching TV, or playing with friends.

5 Help your child develop an "anger control plan." At a quiet time, have a discussion about anger. Brainstorm to come up with a list of things he can do when he feels himself losing control. For example, he could put on his headphones and listen to music, go outside and throw a few basketballs, or take a shower. Have him write down the ideas on an index card and put them in a handy place. Encourage and support him when he uses some of the ideas. You might choose a code word that you can use to let him know his anger is getting out of control and he needs a cooling-off period. Either he or you can use the word to signal a pause in the conversation and allow him time to get himself together.

ANGER, parent's

See also ■ Arguing, with parent ■ Cooperate, won't
■ Disrespect ■ Introduction ■ Listening, not
■ Respect, teaching

SITUATION

I find myself getting angry with my kids much too often. I can't seem to help myself—they really know how to push my buttons. When they purposely disobey me, or are outright disrespectful, I fly off the handle. How can I control my own anger when it's the kids' misbehavior that makes me so mad?

THINK ABOUT IT

Is it your children's *misbehavior* that makes you angry? Or is it your view of their behavior that creates angry feelings? There's a big difference. The first question suggests that you have no control over your emotions or actions. The second implies that by changing your view, you can change your reaction.

SOLUTIONS

1 Put some space between you and the child who's pushing your buttons. When you feel your anger rising, either put your child in time-out or put yourself there! A few minutes away from the source of your angry feelings can help you calm down enough to address the situation rationally. Nothing can be solved in a fit of anger. You'll be better off if you take the time to calm down and then approach your child from a position of strength.

2 Learn more about child development by reading a book or taking a class. If you learn that your child's current behavior is age-appropriate and normal, you'll be less likely to overreact to the behavior. It's amazing how alike children are, and just knowing that your kid is responding in a typical way can help you handle the issue with a level head.

3 If your anger causes you to strike out at your child, you'll need to learn ways to control your outbursts. A creative solution is to channel your physical reaction into a burst of applause! Seriously, when you feel yourself about to strike, simply clap your hands, good and hard and fast, while you express your feelings of anger. Try it now! Pretend you're angry, clap your hands, and tell your imaginary child how you feel. You'll find that in addition to releasing your pent-up anger, it sends a very clear message to your child.

4 Act—don't react. Take the time to think about the things that make you angry. Put together a list of family rules. Enumerate the consequences for breaking the rules. Communicate clear expectations to your children. Decide in advance what methods of discipline you will use. If you have a plan up front, you'll be less likely to lose control when your children misbehave.

5 When you find yourself ready to put your hands around your kid and shake him, do put your hands around him—and love him. Embrace him. If possible, do this in front of a mirror or reflective window. A few minutes of quiet, while you embrace your child, will often temper your angry feelings with the strong feeling of love between you.

HELPFUL READING

Kid Cooperation, by Elizabeth Pantley
  Chapter 7, "Why Do I Get So Angry? How Can I Stop?"

When Anger Hurts Your Kids, by Matthew McKay et al.

APOLOGIES

See also ■ Manners, at home ■ Manners, in public ■ Respect, teaching

SITUATION

My child won't apologize when she hurts someone or when she does something wrong.

THINK ABOUT IT

Children aren't born knowing how to apologize—it's a learned skill. Most children will feel guilt or remorse over their actions, but some find it embarrassing or difficult to say they're sorry.

SOLUTIONS

1 It helps to teach a child how to apologize. For example, if your child throws a baseball that hits another child, quietly say, "I know that was an accident, but it's polite to say, 'I'm sorry the ball hit you. Are you OK?'"

2 Teach your child that actions speak as loudly as words. If your child shrugs out an insincere "Sorry," gently correct this behavior by saying, "Your brother is crying. It would be nice if you put your arm around him and say, 'I'm sorry I hurt you.'"

3 Teach your child how to make amends after saying "I'm sorry." For example, if your child throws a toy that hits another child, encourage her to run in to the house and get an ice pack. If your child breaks a sibling's toy, help your child mend the broken toy.

4 If your child stubbornly refuses to say "I'm sorry," you can give her ownership of the problem by directing her activities. "Katya, when you have made Tasha feel better you are welcome to play. Until then, please take a time-out in your bedroom."

5 Model the behavior you want to instill in your child. Children learn most by our example!

! If your child continually misbehaves and shows no guilt or remorse over negative or hurtful behaviors, it's a good idea to discuss this issue with a family therapist or counselor.

ARGUING, with parent

See also ■ Back talk ■ Disrespect ■ Introduction
■ Respect, teaching

SITUATION
I know my kid's going to grow up to be a lawyer! He argues whenever he's asked to do something. He debates his rights when he's asked to stop doing something. He pleads his case when I tell him he can't do something. He disputes every rule we create. How can I put an end to this?

THINK ABOUT IT
It takes two to argue. Your child cannot "argue" by himself. That's called "mumbling."

SOLUTIONS

1 Practice stating your case, then being quiet. Ignore your child's argumentative comments, and walk away if you must. Let your child get used to your word being "final."

2 As long as it's respectful, sometimes let your child have the last word. Often, a statement such as "Why do I have to do it?" doesn't require an answer, nor deserve one. Often, a child's mutterings really mean, "I'll do it 'cause I have to, but I don't like it."

3 Some children really do enjoy debating an issue. If your child is like this, set ground rules for when and how issues can be debated, for instance, no raising of voices, no name-calling, quiet listening to the other person's point of view. This behavior provides excellent practice for learning how to negotiate in life. In addition, your child must understand that some things *cannot* be argued, that there are some things the parents must decide. Have a standard reply for when an issue cannot be debated, such as, "This is not open for discussion."

4 Get in the habit of offering your child choices instead of issuing commands. Children who are argumentative will have less opportunity to practice the skill if you offer a choice. For example, instead of saying "Do your homework, right now," offer a choice, such as, "What would you like to do first, your homework or the dishes?" (If the response is "Neither," you can smile sweetly and say, "That wasn't one of the choices. Homework or dishes?")

ATHLETIC LESSONS/PRACTICE,
not wanting to continue

See also ■ Sports, reluctance to play

SITUATION

My child signs up for athletic lessons and then doesn't like it and doesn't want to practice. After a few sessions, she wants to quit.

THINK ABOUT IT

The first step is to determine the child's reason for wanting to quit. You can figure this out by talking to the child, talking to the coach, and watching a practice session and a game. There may be more than one reason. Review the solutions below for each reason.

SOLUTIONS

1 **Child isn't skilled in the sport.** Often children want to join a team because they enjoy watching the big league games on TV and playing with friends at the park. Once they join a team, however, they find that the game is harder than they thought, and they don't have the skills to play well. Practice—just what the child wants to avoid—is the key to an attitude adjustment. Explain to your child that it takes time and practice to play well, and because the session has just started, she must give it a fair chance. Make an agreement that she must do her best for the session (or a specific amount of time). After that point, she can either continue or stop and try something else. Put your agreement in writing and post it. Often, a child can handle an activity for a short, specific amount of time and at the end of the time period has adequate skills to enjoy the sport and can then make a better decision about continuing.

2 **Child is not having fun.** Sometimes, the actual involvement isn't as fun as the child imagined. First, make sure the coach or teacher is compatible with your child. If there is a major personality clash, it may be worth it to change coaches. If your child is not correctly matched to the skill level of the team, her inability to keep up could prevent her from having fun. If all seems to be OK in these areas, you can build your child's interest by taking her to a professional-level game and to a game involving kids a few years older than she is. Another way to increase your child's commitment to the game is to have enough equipment at home for casual practice and to take the time to enjoy the game with your child, without the pressure of the formal game.

3 **Sport takes up too much time.** Most sports activities do require a time commitment from both child and parent. A child who is committed to more than one activity can easily feel overwhelmed. It's usually best to focus on one extracurricular activity at a time so that the child still has some time left over after sports and school for free, unstructured play.

4 **Child feels too much pressure.** First experiences with team competition can be difficult for children. It's especially hard if a child is not a great player. One way to remove some of the pressure is to cheer for the whole team, as opposed to the individual in the spotlight: "Go Redwings!" Another method is to focus on effort, skills, and technique: "Good swing! Nice try!" If a child doesn't ask for advice about how to play better, don't give any! Leave it to the coaches. Watch how you, other parents, the kids, and the coaches respond after a lost game. Look for something positive to say: "What a great effort!" Focus on a few positive details from the game. Find some time to play a casual version of the game at home or at the park so your child can enjoy the process without worrying about who wins.

ATHLETICS, poor sport

See also ■ Competitiveness ■ Losing

SITUATION
My child gets extremely upset after losing a game. He stomps, complains, and blames everyone and everything for the loss.

THINK ABOUT IT
There will be many times in your child's life when he won't win or when things won't turn out the way he would want them to. You're doing your child a big favor by teaching him how to handle loss now, when the issues are relatively small and easy to overcome.

SOLUTIONS
1 Watch the messages your child is getting at home about winning and losing. Innocent comments such as "Last one in is a rotten egg" or "I bet I can finish before you can!" send the wrong message about losing.

2 Don't overprotect your child by always letting him win when playing with you. Losing in the safety of the family environment lets a child understand he can still be loved and valuable when he's not the winner.

3 Validate your child's sad feelings about losing—no one *likes* to lose! But the key is to help your child move past the feelings and look for what he did right or make his plans for the next game. You can refocus his energy with helpful comments, such as, "I noticed you were a team player today—you tossed some great balls to first base."

4 Make sure no adult in the family is comparing the child to a sibling or friend who is a better player. The child probably notices that the other child is more skilled, and even subtle comments can make a child feel inferior.

5 Check your own attitude about losing. Do you act energized and excited when your favorite team wins but angry and grumpy when it loses? Do you cheer louder and with more enthusiasm when your child's team is winning? Do you show your disappointment when your child misses the ball or makes a mistake? What messages are you sending about winning or losing?

BABY-SITTERS, grandparents as

See also ■ Grandparents, and spoiling

SITUATION

My children's grandparents are going to baby-sit for us. I'm already starting to worry that things won't go smoothly.

THINK ABOUT IT

If this is a rare occasion, don't fret over it. Your parents got you (or your spouse) to adulthood, so it's conceivable that they can get through a short period of time with your kids. If this is going to be an ongoing event, it's a different story. It's important that you set the pace for this new facet of your relationship right from the start.

SOLUTIONS

1 Decide ahead of time what the important rules in your household are. Take the time to create written instructions. Direct the rules and instructions at *the kids*, and review them with the kids prior to the grandparents' arrival. Point out the rules to the grandparents, and ask if they would make sure the kids adhere to them. This way, you're letting the grandparents know exactly what is expected but doing it in a way that won't offend them.

2 Take the time to have a conversation with the grandparents to review all your expectations. Don't think that a casual chat will suffice. Arrange for a quiet time, without the kids around, when you can talk. Find out how the grandparents view the situation. Let them know what your expectations are. Determine what rules are important and how you'll communicate with each other. Doing this up front will prevent many misunderstandings and problems in the future.

3 Relax. Don't worry about the small issues. Focus on the benefits of having a grandparent baby-sit for you, because there are many. Choose your battles wisely.

BABY-SITTERS, not listening to

SITUATION
My children don't listen to the baby-sitter.

THINK ABOUT IT
Kids are good at testing the rules. When a sitter is in charge, your children will test to see if this new person is privy to the standard rules and to determine just how far they can push the boundaries.

SOLUTIONS
1 Write down a set of rules to be followed when the baby-sitter is in charge. Having written rules will prevent the sitter from having to make arbitrary decisions and will give the children guidelines for expected behavior. Have specific consequences for not following a rule. For example, if the rule is "Homework done before watching TV," the consequence for breaking the rule may be losing all TV privileges for the next day. The sitter doesn't have to fight with your child to follow the rule; she simply needs to let you know the rule was broken so that you can impose the consequence.

2 Prior to the sitter's arrival, take a few minutes to let the kids know your specific expectations for the time that they will be with the sitter. The more clearly you define the behavior you expect, the more likely they will follow through. If you have a specific daily routine, let the sitter know what that is and encourage her to follow it.

3 Often children act out of line when they have a long period of unstructured time with an unfamiliar caregiver. Prepare ahead for the time by renting a video and arranging a snack or gathering all the supplies for a craft activity they can do with the sitter.

4 Many children don't listen to a baby-sitter because the sitter doesn't have good child-rearing skills. Children will pick up on this and learn that they can get away with things when this person is in charge. If the sitter has an ongoing job with you, it can be helpful to encourage the sitter to learn a few skills. An easy way to do this is to purchase a good parenting book and wrap it up as a gift. An alternative is to find a local parenting class through your hospital, school, or church and offer to pay for the sitter to attend the classes. Be sensitive to how you make the offer; you don't want to make the sitter feel defensive. You might say something like, "I just found out about this great class. Because you spend so much time with the kids, I thought you might enjoy it. Because my kids would benefit from what you learn, I'd be happy to pay the cost."

BABY-SITTERS, not wanting one

See also ■ Clinging ■ Separation anxiety ■ Shyness, around adults
■ Work, doesn't want parent to

SITUATION

Whenever I leave my child with a baby-sitter, he totally falls apart. You'd think I was leaving him *forever* by the pitiful theatrics he goes through! How can I convince him that everything will be OK?

THINK ABOUT IT

You need to reconcile your own feelings about leaving your child with a sitter. If you are feeling ambivalent, your emotions will be clear to your child. Whether you're leaving your child out of necessity or just for a break, you need to convince *yourself* that everything will be OK before you can convince your child of this.

SOLUTIONS

1 Keep your good-byes short and sweet. On one hand, prolonging the leaving with promises that everything will be OK will just heighten your child's anxiety, as he'll wonder why you're so worried about leaving him. On the other hand, avoid the temptation to sneak out so you don't have to deal with the tears. This behavior will breed confusion and worry. Instead, give a quick kiss and hug and a lighthearted "See ya later, alligator!"

2 Choose a person familiar to your child to baby-sit. A family member or close friend will make the adjustment easier for your child than a stranger would. Try to use one or two people consistently so that your child can become familiar with the arrangement. Make sure the sitter is familiar with your child's daily routine and important rituals. The more your child's typical routine is adhered to, the easier the time with the sitter will be.

3 If possible, arrange for your child to be with a sitter for a short amount of time at first. Gradually increase the time as your child becomes more comfortable with the situation. For some children, it's best to have the sitter come to your home at first, so that your child will be in his own comfortable environment. For others, an exciting new environment of toys and friends will help distract him from his worries about leaving you.

4 Spend time with the sitter and your child during a non-baby-sitting time. Because you will be there the entire time, the other person won't be so threatening to your child, and it will give them time to get to know each other.

5 Put together a "baby-sitter toy box," with toys and activities to be used only when the baby-sitter is over. If the box is interesting enough, it will create a fun focus for your child's time away from you. Another idea is to let your child plan some of the things that will be done with the sitter. Your child can select the meal, choose the video to watch, or decide what games to play.

BABY-SITTERS, siblings as

SITUATION
I'm wondering if I should have my older child baby-sit the younger one. If I do, how can I make sure things go smoothly?

THINK ABOUT IT

The decision to have one sibling baby-sit for another should never be based purely on the age of the children or what is convenient for the parents. Rather, the decision should be based on how responsible the older child is and on the relationship between the children. If the older child displays trustworthiness for homework, chores, and personal responsibilities, and if the two children have a *usually* peaceful relationship, it's safe to try out a baby-sitting situation.

SOLUTIONS

1 Have a few practice sessions when the older child baby-sits while you are still at home, in another room. Take advantage of the time to catch up on paperwork, write a letter, or read a good book. This practice session will give the kids a chance to feel things out, and you can keep an ear open to what's going on.

2 It's best to pay a child to baby-sit, even if it's a token payment. When a child sees this responsibility as a "job," he will take it more seriously. A child who is "hired" to baby-sit a sibling will often turn into a responsible "person in charge." (What's even more interesting is how quickly your child passes the responsibility back to you when you return home!) Another benefit of paying the sibling-sitter is that it will prevent the child from resenting the time he must spend baby-sitting.

3 Plan in advance for a successful baby-sitting situation. Rather than putting an older child arbitrarily "in charge," take the time to develop specific rules. Decide, in advance, the rules about telephone use; TV watching; snacks; homework; use of the microwave, oven, or toaster; visits from friends; how to answer the door and telephone; and other issues. Also include a method for handling disputes.

4 If the baby-sitting is to be a regular event, such as every day after school, approach the arrangement as you would hiring any baby-sitter for the job. Meet with the older child and get her feedback and input.

Help her understand that although the job is not optional, you are flexible. For example, if she has a special event, you would be willing to hire a sitter to cover that afternoon. If possible, break up the routine, with the younger child having a weekly play date or other extracurricular activity so that your older child has a chance to do something other than baby-sit after school. Evaluate the situation from time to time to make sure everything is working out well.

5 Have a standard check-in time, when the children call you at work. If you can't receive calls at work, have them check in with another adult. Keep a list of important phone numbers next to the telephone. Print the local emergency number (911) right on the face of each telephone in the house. Faced with a real emergency, many *adults* find it hard to remember this simple number. Give both the sitter and the other child emergency training. Many hospitals and schools offer a baby-sitters' emergency training class. The kids learn CPR and standard emergency procedures. I'd suggest having any of the kids old enough to understand the class attend, if possible. (Keep in mind that something could happen to the baby-sitter and a younger child would need to know how to get help.)

BABY TALK

See also ■ Whining

SITUATION
My child finds talking in a baby voice amusing. When she was a baby, that kind of talk was adorable. Now that she's not, it's extremely annoying. How do I get her to stop?

THINK ABOUT IT
This is a normal, temporary stage of behavior. It's one of those phases that will pass on its own but can drive you crazy in the meantime. You can give nature a nudge and move your child past this stage more quickly by using some of the following suggestions.

SOLUTIONS

1 Pretend you can't understand her when she uses baby talk. When she says, "Me wanna gas of mik," look at her with a very confused expression on your face and say, "I can't understand you. What do you want?" Don't respond until she uses her normal voice.

2 Sometimes, children use baby talk as a way of holding on to childhood as they take a developmental step forward. Acknowledge this as a real need, and give your child a bit more loving attention. A few extra hugs or a chance to sit on your lap may give her the courage she needs to grow forward.

3 Have a discussion with your child. Let her know how much the baby talk bothers you. Ask for her help in changing the behavior. If the baby talk continues, and pushes your "angry" button, pointedly turn your back to her and leave the room. (Leaving is better than lashing out in anger.)

4 Make an honest request: "The baby talk really annoys me, Sarah. You may use it with your friends, but please use your regular voice with me."

5 Give your child a few chores or responsibilities that signify she is growing up. Choose fun tasks, such as helping to prepare the salad for dinner or sweeping the floor. Often, when a child begins to see herself as a mature, responsible person, the baby talk will disappear.

BACK TALK

See also ■ Arguing, with parent ■ Cooperate, won't ■ Disrespect
■ Introduction ■ Respect, teaching

SITUATION

My child talks back to me in such a disrespectful way it leaves me speechless. How do I put a stop to this?

THINK ABOUT IT

Back talk is addictive so it must be handled as a serious offense. A child who talks rudely to a parent once or twice and gets away with it will continue the behavior, and it will progressively get worse. Most children will attempt back talk at some point. When a parent responds calmly and with authority, the behavior will stop.

SOLUTIONS

1 If a child has developed a habit of back talk, it will take firm action to stop the behavior. Have a meeting with your child to announce that back talk will no longer be tolerated. Decide on a series of consequences that will occur each time back talk occurs. Consequences may involve losing a privilege, such as telephone use, television watching, or visits with friends. There may be an additional chore or an earlier bedtime. Then announce the sequence in which the consequences will occur. "When you talk back in a disrespectful way, you will lose your telephone privileges for the day. The second offense will cause you to lose your TV show for the night. The third will . . . Each day will start with a clean slate." After the meeting, calmly and firmly follow through.

2 Whenever a child talks back, immediately stop the conversation and walk out of the room or walk away from the child. If the child follows you, calmly and firmly announce that you will not tolerate disrespect; then, pointedly ignore the child. Later, when you have calmed down, decide on an appropriate consequence for the back talk.

3 Tape your child's allowance, in quarters, to a piece of cardboard. Tell your child that each time he talks back to you, he will lose a quarter from his allowance as a "fine." He'll get what's left at the end of the week. If your child uses up all the quarters, add a chore or eliminate a privilege for each offense. Start fresh with each new week. This series of events is meant to be a temporary "training" situation. When the problem seems under control, let your child know that you appreciate his efforts to control the back talk and that you'll no longer be charging the fine. However, make it clear that if the behavior ever becomes a problem again, you'd be happy to head to the bank for a roll of quarters.

If a normally respectful child makes a disrespectful comment, look him in the eye and make a serious, firm comment, such as, "That is back talk and is not allowed." Continue the conversation as if the back talk did not occur, expecting the child to comply with your request. Do not empower the back talk by arguing about the issue that triggered it.

BATH, not behaving in

See also ■ Cooperate, won't ■ Introduction
■ Listening, not

SITUATION
My child has a grand time taking a bath. She splashes, throws toys, and sprays the entire bathroom with water. How do I get her to settle down in the tub?

THINK ABOUT IT
Imagine a bathtub the size of a double bed, filled with a mountain of bubbles. Add a glass of champagne and a stack of books and magazines by its side. Would you get in, wash, and get out without taking the time to enjoy the pleasure of a nice long soak? For lots of kids, the tub is a grand private swimming pool, and washing up is last on their list of priorities.

SOLUTIONS
1 Have a clear, specific list of bathtub rules. State your rules in a way that lets your child know exactly what you *want*, rather than what you *don't want*. As an example, instead of saying "No splashing," a better rule is "Keep all water in the tub. Keep the carpet dry."

2 Put only a few inches of water in the tub. Tell your child that when she has behaved herself twice in the bathtub, you'll increase the amount of water you put in the tub next time.

3 Do not put any toys in the tub. Get the child into the tub, washed, and out of the tub quickly.

Have the child take a shower instead of a bath.

 If you have a younger child, get in the tub with her and have a good time splashing together.

6 Relax—it's just water and can be wiped up! It may help if you put up a clear shower curtain and close it while your child splashes and plays. That way, you can still see in the tub, but the water stays contained.

BATH, not wanting one

See also ■ Cooperate, won't ■ Listening, not

SITUATION
My child fusses and whines when I announce bath time. She doesn't cooperate at all, and I usually end up yelling while I drag her to the bathroom.

THINK ABOUT IT
Take a minute to stop and think about why your child doesn't want to take a bath. Is it because she's having too much fun doing other things and doesn't want to stop? Is it because bath time usually includes a battle of wills? Is it because she always gets soap in her eyes? Once you figure out the real reason, you can take steps to move past the problem.

SOLUTIONS
1 Allow your child to use bubble bath or kid's bath foam to make it more fun. Buy a few exciting bath toys, and use plastic kitchen products for play in the bathtub. Allow your child to play for a while before washing up.

2 If your child fears getting soap in her eyes when you wash her hair, let her wear swimming goggles or a plastic sun visor while you wash her hair.

3 Be very consistent. Have a bath every other day at exactly the same time. Specific routines can overcome resistance after they've become regular occurrences. Let your child know ahead of time that bath time is nearing. If you give a few warnings—"Bath time in ten minutes" or "Bath time in five more minutes"—your child will respond better than if you just drop the bomb in the middle of a fun activity.

4 Bath time is often done at bedtime, when a child and the parent are tired and grumpy. Change your routine and let your child shower or bathe first thing in the morning, when everyone is fresh and energetic.

5 Use the "When/Then" technique to promise something fun after the bath is done: "When your bath is done, then we can read your new library books."

6 If your child is age six or older, tell her that you think she's grown up enough to handle her own bath. Take her through the steps the first time; the next time, let her run the water, gather her supplies, and handle the bathing herself, with your supervision. When you're confident she knows what to do, let her do it while you sit in the next room close enough to monitor her by peeking in and listening. Many children love to "surprise" you when they walk out freshly cleaned and in their pajamas.

(Do not leave a child younger than age six, or one with health problems or behavior disorders, alone in the bathtub, even for a minute.)

BATH, won't get out

See also ■ Bath, not wanting one ■ Cooperate, won't

SITUATION
My child fusses and whines when it's time to get out of the tub.

THINK ABOUT IT
This same kid probably doesn't want to get *in* the tub either! This is usually a child who doesn't adjust quickly to changes. The problem occurs when

he's doing something fun (splashing in the tub) and has to stop and do something not so fun (get dressed and ready for bed). A little motivation goes a long way in helping this child adjust to changes.

SOLUTIONS

 Use a timer or alarm clock. Set it for a predetermined bath time. Give a three-minute warning before the timer goes off. Announce that when the timer rings, your child will have ten minutes to get out of the tub and get dressed to be able to enjoy his evening privileges (such as watching TV or having a book read to him). Explain that if he's not ready when the ten minutes are up, you will help him finish and he'll go right to bed. Do as you promise! You'll only need to follow through *once* to teach him that you're serious about this new routine.

 When it's time to get out, stand by the edge of the tub, hold out a towel, and offer a choice, such as, "Do you want to dry your hair by yourself, or do you want me to help you?"

 Use the "When/Then" technique to promise something fun after the bath is done: "When you are out of the bathtub, then I'll turn the space heater on for you and you can warm up. When you're dressed, then we'll have some hot cocoa."

 Get silly! Hold the towel like a puppet and make it talk. Use your imagination: "I'm gonna close my eyes and see if a little leprechaun will appear in my magic towel!" Make a game out of the process: "I wonder if you can get out and get dressed before I count to one hundred!"

 Don't tell your child it's time to get out of the tub until you *really* mean it's time to get out of the tub. Repeating yourself six or seven times until you mean business is only setting yourself up for a struggle the next time and the next time and the next . . .

BATHROOM JOKES

See also ■ Humor, inappropriate ■ Rude comments, intentional
■ Swearing

SITUATION
My child thinks it's hysterical to talk about (and mimic!) bodily functions and waste products in a grossly funny way.

THINK ABOUT IT
Many children go through this phase. While normal, it's quite annoying, and the sooner you take action, the sooner it will stop.

SOLUTIONS
1 Teach your child what is socially appropriate. When a bathroom joke is made, stay calm, look your child in the eye, and say in a serious voice, "That's inappropriate" or "That's not something we joke about in this house." Keep in mind that your child will probably still use bathroom humor with his friends, because they are all at similar developmental stages.

2 If bathroom humor is used at the dinner table, give your child one warning to stop. If there is a second occurrence, simply stand up, remove your child's plate from the table, and say, "We're not enjoying your company, Beavis, so your dinner time is over. Please go to your room." As an alternative, invite him to finish his dinner by himself in another room, such as the laundry room or the garage (*not* in front of the TV!).

3 Pay attention to the television shows and movies your child is watching. He may be picking up the behavior from these sources. If so, let your child know that you see the connection and that if the jokes continue, the program will be off-limits.

BEDROOMS, cleaning

See also ■ Chores ■ Laziness ■ Mess

SITUATION

My child's bedroom looks like it's been put through a blender! I can't see the carpet, and to walk through the room I have to dodge clothes, toys, and last week's snack wrappers. My child doesn't care, but I do. When I yell and threaten, we sometimes end up with one day of cleanliness, but in no time at all, the disaster magically reappears.

THINK ABOUT IT

Every time you walk by the bedroom, the mess annoys you. You grumble and mumble until finally you reach the boiling point and explode in anger. When you finally put your foot down, you discover that you and your child have vastly different definitions of *clean*. While you envision an immaculate and orderly room, your child may be perfectly happy as long as she can find her way to the bed without a road map. You obviously have conflicting goals. Try to find a long-term solution that works for both of you.

SOLUTIONS

1 When the bedroom has reached the point of a national disaster, the mess is overwhelming for your child. At this point, you may have to grit your teeth and help with the initial cleanup. Use plenty of boxes, baskets, or tubs to sort your child's clothes and belongings. Label each container clearly (socks, books, schoolwork, and so forth). What happens next is most important. Initiate a *daily* cleanup time to prevent the buildup of another mess. Inspect every day after cleanup time. At that point use "Grandma's Rule," which is "work before play." "As soon as your room is clean, you may go outside." This rule is also known as the "When/Then" approach: "When you have cleaned your bedroom, then you may turn on the computer."

 2 Sit down with your child and develop a bedroom-cleaning contract. Work together to define what constitutes a "clean room" in very specific terms: clothes in dresser and closet (either hanging or folded), books in bookcase, stuffed animals on top bunk, and so forth. You might even consider allowing a "messy corner," where she can toss things temporarily. Just make sure the corner is clearly sectioned off, such as a section of the closet. Once you've agreed on the terms for a "clean room," choose a specific day of the week for cleaning. One schedule that works well for many families is to require a clean room Saturday prior to any activities or playtime. Include a specific plan for what will happen if the room is not clean by the scheduled time. Write up the contract and have everyone sign the agreement. Post it and follow though.

3 If you've reached the end of your rope, and you're really brave, pick a time when your child is away from home to do a more-than-thorough cleaning. Using baskets and shelves, neatly arrange the necessities and most favorite toys. Pack 90 percent of the stuff that litters the floor into small boxes. Store the boxes in the garage or attic. Display your child's beautifully clean room, and let her know she can earn back one box at a time at the end of each week that the room is kept clean. You can expect an outburst of hysterics, but stick to your guns. (If a school supply or a favorite toy is boxed by mistake, it would be OK to rescue it.)

4 Invest a weekend to clean and rearrange the bedroom. If possible, hang new curtains or cover the bed with a new bedspread. Pull a dresser out of the attic, or search a secondhand store for a new piece of furniture for her room. Let your child paint it however she'd like. Allow her to customize the walls with pictures or posters. Often, a fresh, new outlook like this will encourage a child to keep her "new" room neat and clean.

5 If your child is age ten or older, and a basically responsible kid, it's OK to turn her bedroom over to her as practice for her first apartment experience. (Take a security deposit if you feel you must.) Outline the basic rules, such as how often the bed linens must be changed, how often the floor must be vacuumed, and what type of food is allowed in the room. Once the basic rules are agreed to, give your child the responsibility to care for her room, her way. You can pile any of her laundry or stray belongings by her door each day. Let her know that as long as the basic rules are followed, she'll be in charge of her own room. (And if *you* can't stand looking at the clutter, shut the door.)

BEDROOMS, privacy between siblings (separate rooms)

See also ■ Sharing ■ Siblings, borrowing things without permission

SITUATION
My children are always going into each other's bedrooms without permission, borrowing toys, or making a mess. The ensuing fights are driving me crazy.

THINK ABOUT IT
It sometimes seems that siblings thrive in a love/hate relationship. "I love you and I want to be near you, but when I am, I'll make your life miserable." Kids are taught to share, but the line is fuzzy when it comes to "private property," such as each child's bedroom and personal belongings. The more specific and clear the rules, the less likely you'll have to deal with this ongoing irritation.

SOLUTIONS
1 Sit down with the children and create a list of rules pertaining to bedrooms. Include consequences for breaking the rules. Because these rules have more to do with issues between the kids than between you and them, allow them to come up with the consequences (you, of course, have veto power!). For example, one pair of siblings came up with the consequence for borrowing without asking: you get to pick one of the sibling's things to "borrow" back for a day. Once the rules are established, have the kids make attractive posters of the rules and post them on their doors.

2 Play "behavior baseball" with the kids—"three strikes and you're out." Tell them that if they have more than three fights in a week over bedroom issues, they will lose the privilege of having their own rooms. They will have to share a room, and you will take over the other bedroom as an office, a sewing room, or an exercise room. (No fair encouraging a fight!) Instead of hearing another fight, I guarantee you'll hear a whispered "Stop it, or Mom will use your room as her new office!"

(If you would like a more detailed explanation of "behavior baseball" read *Kid Cooperation*, Chapter 4, page 76.)

BEDROOMS, privacy between siblings (shared room)

See also ■ Sharing ■ Siblings, borrowing things without permission

SITUATION
My children share a bedroom, and they're constantly fighting. Both complain about not having their privacy, and I'm pestered by both of them until I solve their problems.

THINK ABOUT IT
Most children interact better as siblings if they have a private place to retreat to when they need to be alone. Be creative in finding a way to give each child some private space, and you'll find that they do better when they're together.

SOLUTIONS
1 Hang a schedule on the door. Allow children to "reserve" one hour a day for privacy. They will learn to respect each other's private time when no one disturbs them during their time. A child who badgers another during private time can lose half of his own time (or *all* of it if the badgering is persistent!). If the persistent child continues to be aggressive about disturbing his sibling's time, his lost time can be added to his sibling's private hour!

2 Even the smallest bedroom can be converted into several smaller private spaces. You can rearrange dressers in a row down the middle of the room as a "wall" or hang a bedsheet or two from the ceiling. (A few nail holes are easier to contend with than constant bickering!) Remember to section off a "neutral zone" from the doorway to each space! Initiate a simple rule: "You must ask permission before entering another's space."

3 Allow each child to create a private space somewhere in the house. Typically, the space doesn't need to be very large to be satisfying to a child. A few suggested places are a corner alcove, a section of the attic or basement, or a portion of a closet. Another area that works well is the cubby that's created behind a sofa when it's set at an angle in the corner of the room. A small child's tent set up in the corner of a room with a "please do not disturb" sign hanging on the flap makes a lovely private place.

BEDTIME, getting to bed peacefully

See also ■ Cooperate, won't ■ Listening, not

SITUATION
Bedtime around our house is a disaster. I beg, I plead, I threaten, and I yell. By the time I finally get the kids settled for the night, I'm too tired to enjoy the rest of my evening.

THINK ABOUT IT
Welcome to the club! This is one of the most common parental concerns. Kids seem to have never-ending energy, which only goes into overdrive at the end of the day. At the same time, the parent's battery is draining fast, and getting the kids to bed becomes an obsessive, urgent (and sometimes desperate) need.

SOLUTIONS
1 Create a "Bedtime Chart." Use a large piece of poster board. Number and illustrate each step. An example: (1) Put on pj's, (2) Have snack, (3) Brush teeth, (4) Read five books, (5) Go potty, (6) Turn on night-light,

(7) Kisses and hugs, (8) Go to sleep. Post the chart at child-eye level on the bedroom door. Allow your child to lead you through the step-by-step process. After a week or two the routine will be set, and bedtime will flow smoothly.

2 If your child is an independent reader, buy her a reading light. Allow her to read in bed with her special light for as long as she would like before turning out the light and going to sleep. Remind her of her awakening time, and suggest she get enough sleep to be well rested in the morning. At first, she may abuse this privilege and stay up too late. The next day she'll be tired. Show a bit of sympathy, attribute her tiredness to staying up late, but give her no slack. Make her follow her normal daily routine. Don't lecture. Simply repeat the routine at bedtime, and allow her to learn to monitor her own bedtime through experience. (As any parent knows, a few nights of sleep deprivation act as a great motivator to crave an earlier bedtime!)

3 Enjoy the special quiet, cuddly time that bedtime provides. Read in bed to your child; then, turn out the light and snuggle until your child, and perhaps even you, is asleep. Don't feel guilty. In a flash your child will be older and more mature, and you'll be longing for those extra cuddles.

BEDTIME, staying in bed

See also ■ Cooperate, won't ■ Listening, not

SITUATION

My child pops in and out of bed like a yo-yo and won't stay settled. I usually end up yelling at him and then feeling guilty as he cries himself to sleep.

THINK ABOUT IT

It's usually a parent's ambivalence about bedtime routines that allows a child to try to negotiate a new privilege every night. Be clear and concise about your bedtime rules, and you'll find bedtime will be much more enjoyable.

SOLUTIONS

1 When you put your child to bed, give him three "Get-Out-of-Bed-Free" cards. These are simply tickets that you make out of cardboard. Let your child know that each time he gets out of bed, for whatever reason, he must give you one card. So, if he gets up for a drink of water, to go potty, or to ask how many days 'til his birthday party, he needs to give you a card each time. When the cards are gone, he has to stay in bed. Let him know that if he gets up after all his cards are gone, he won't get *any* cards tomorrow night.

2 Create a very specific bedtime ritual that is loving and enjoyable. After you put your child to bed, take the time to read to him. After that, sing a song or rub his back. When a child is in a sleepy, comfortable state, he'll be less likely to want to get out of bed. Let him know that he can enjoy this special time, provided he stays in bed when the routine is completed. If he fusses and gets out of bed afterward, tell him he'll lose the privilege the following night. You may have to follow through with this. If you do, expect a major tantrum, but hold your ground. You'll only have to go through this once or twice for the message to get through loud and clear.

3 Consider the *reason* your child won't stay put in bed, and solve the problem based on this reason. For instance, maybe your child isn't tired and is ready for a later bedtime, or maybe he hasn't had enough time with you and is longing for some "cuddle time" before he settles down for the night.

BED-WETTING

See also ■ Toilet training

SITUATION
My child is out of diapers but continues to wet the bed.

THINK ABOUT IT
Bed-wetting has come out of the closet and is now recognized as a common childhood problem. Twenty percent of five-year-olds and 10 percent

of six-year-olds routinely wet their beds. This behavior is purely a symptom of an immature bladder system, and for most children, the problem will disappear when they get a little older. The following ideas may help speed the process along.

SOLUTIONS

1 If your child is age five or younger, the easy solution is to allow your child to wear disposable training pants to bed. These disposable pants are readily available and can be purchased where diapers are sold. Let your child pull them on and off by himself, and tell him that when he's ready to wear underwear to bed to just let you know. The more low-key you are about these pants, the easier it will be for your child to make the step to underwear. Many young children sleep very deeply and simply don't wake up to use the toilet.

2 If your child is over age five, the first step is to arrange for him to have a complete physical. Let the doctor know in advance what your concern is so that your child isn't embarrassed at the doctor's office. If there are any health problems, your doctor can identify them and help solve the problem. Ask your doctor about PNE (Primary Nocturnal Enuresis), which is caused by a hormone deficiency that causes bed-wetting and can be treated with a prescription nasal spray.

3 Your child is most likely embarrassed by this situation and really wants to control it. Empathize with his feelings, and offer to put together a plan to solve the problem. Some ideas are limiting fluids after dinner, using the toilet twice immediately prior to going to bed, keeping a night-light on to light a clear pathway to the bathroom, using a plastic mattress cover, and keeping clean pajamas and a sleeping bag near the bed for accidents. Allow the child to take responsibility for the problem by showing him how to change the bedding and launder the wet sheets. During this time, you may want to "double make" the bed. Put on a clean sheet, cover it with a plastic mattress cover, and then put another clean sheet on top. If an accident occurs, your child can simply peel off the wet sheet and mattress cover and have a fresh sheet ready to sleep on.

4 If your child is older than age five, has no health-related issues causing the bed-wetting, and clearly wants to eliminate the problem, talk to your doctor or hospital about purchasing a bed-wetting device. This is a pad that is connected to a buzzer that wakes your child up at the start of an accident so that he can use the bathroom. Typically, after a few weeks of use, a child becomes used to waking up to a full bladder and will do so without the pad.

5 Don't make bed-wetting a primary issue of the family. Take steps to control it and eliminate it, but don't focus too much energy on it. Try to be patient. It will take time and maturity for your child to get this part of growing up under control.

BICYCLE, care of

See also ■ Carelessness

SITUATION
My child is irresponsible with her bicycle. Her bike is always dirty or left outside in the rain. She's just unconcerned about its upkeep.

THINK ABOUT IT
Most kids aren't purposely irresponsible with their belongings. They simply don't have the experience to understand the value of conscientious maintenance.

SOLUTIONS
1 Decide on a set of very specific rules about bicycle care. Write down these rules. Decide on an appropriate consequence for not following the rules, such as locking up the bicycle for one day if rules are not adhered to. Each day check to see if the rules have been followed. Be consistent. When necessary, impose consequences, without anger.

2 Create a bicycle checklist and put it on a clipboard. Hang the clipboard from the bike's handlebars. Teach your child to do a "preflight" and "postflight" checklist—similar to what pilots do before flying a plane. Include several (perhaps unnecessary but fun) maintenance steps, such as checking the tightness of the tire bolts with a wrench.

3 Often, children with no proprietary interest in a possession show little concern for its care. In other words, if you bought her the bike, she knows you'll buy her another if this one gets ruined. For the next bicycle, or other major purchase, allow your child to contribute about half the cost of the item. Money can come from savings, extra chores, or odd jobs. A child who pays for a bike tends to take better care of it. At this point, let her know that she will contribute half the cost of her next bike, and give her a ballpark figure in terms she'll understand: "Your share of the cost of a new bike would be about $80. That's equal to fifteen weeks of your allowance." This information may encourage her to think about the value of a bike and the possibility of parting with that much allowance money. She may then take better care of her current bicycle.

! If a child continues to abuse a good bicycle, you can put the bicycle in storage. If your child needs a bike for transportation, purchase a used bike through the newspaper or a pawnshop. Let your child know that she can earn the right to the better bicycle by taking care of the used bike for a specified period of time.

BICYCLE, doesn't ride safely

SITUATION
My child continually rides his bicycle in an unsafe manner. He darts across the street without watching for cars, hops curbs, and attempts stunts that are downright dangerous.

THINK ABOUT IT
I'm glad you're searching for an answer to this question. This is too important a problem to leave unsolved. If your child and his bike do battle with a car, it's unlikely that he'd win. Don't risk it. Put your foot down and solve the problem today.

SOLUTIONS

1 Many children don't really understand the rules of the road or the reasons for following them. It can be very helpful for a child to take a bicycle-safety class. Often these classes are available through schools, hospitals, police stations, or youth groups.

2 Once a child learns he can get away with riding recklessly, he'll continue to do it. The key is to have an immediate, related consequence for riding unsafely. First, explain the reasons it's important to follow the rules. (Your police department or library will have information you can use as a reference. For example, bicycles are associated with more childhood injuries than any other consumer product, except cars.) Explain your concerns for his safety and the new requirement to follow the rules of the road. The first time you see your child ride recklessly, hop in the car and catch up with him. Tell him to put the bike in the car, and take him home (if it's a pleasure ride) or drive him to his destination. Tell him he can have the bike tomorrow with another chance. If someone else reports his reckless riding, he can lose his bike-riding privileges for the next day.

3 Require your child to do a written report about bicycle safety. The research will prove convincing to your child. If it's too difficult for you to make this assignment, enlist your child's teacher to help you.

! If your child persists in riding recklessly, and finds your attempts to change his behavior funny or annoying, you can take drastic measures. Lock the bike up for a specified period of time or even sell it. Don't wait for a tragedy. Take action today.

BICYCLE, won't wear helmet

SITUATION
My child continually rides her bicycle without wearing a helmet.

THINK ABOUT IT

Many kids see their parents' efforts to get them to wear a helmet as "just one more thing you make me do." It's helpful if your child learns the reasons a helmet will protect her and then chooses to wear it *for her own safety*, not just because you told her to.

SOLUTIONS

 Make sure your child's helmet fits properly. An uncomfortable helmet is difficult to wear. Also make sure the helmet is stylish. A child's self-esteem is easily affected by what peers think of her. If your child's helmet embarrasses her, she'll avoid wearing it.

2 If your child has frequently ridden without a helmet, she'll be reluctant to change this habit. It may get her attention if you apologize for being remiss in teaching her to wear a helmet. Explain that you've learned that in an accident a helmet has been shown to reduce the risk of head and brain injury by almost 90 percent. Tell her that because you love her, a helmet will now be required whenever she rides her bike. If you catch her riding without a helmet, impose an immediate, related consequence, such as taking away her bike-riding privileges for the next day.

3 Make it easy for your child to remember her helmet by having her strap it to her bicycle's handlebars when it's parked in the garage.

BIRTHDAY, bad behavior as birthday child

See also ■ Cooperate, won't ■ Listening, not ■ Manners

SITUATION

I dread my child's upcoming birthday party. My little guest of honor has a history of misbehaving at his own party.

THINK ABOUT IT

It's typical for a child to get so excited and wrapped up in the glamour of being the star and the thrill of the event that his behavior isn't his best.

SOLUTIONS

1 Avoid correcting your child in front of his guests; this is embarrassing to a child and will put a real damper on the rest of the party. It's best to remove him from the festivities to a quiet room and have a talk about what behavior is expected. Acknowledge the excitement of the event, and tell your child specifically what it is that you're unhappy with and what you would like to see instead. So, don't say "I want you to behave," which is vague and unhelpful. Be specific: "I know you're excited today, Harley. You have been jumping on the sofa and running in the house. That's against our rules, even at your birthday party. Please go out to the trampoline if you want to jump, and walk when you're in the house. Let's go have fun!"

2 It's likely that if your child is misbehaving, his guests are, too. Change the tone of the activity to a quieter event. A structured game, an activity where the children are spectators, or eating the cake and ice cream will calm things down.

3 Sometimes, a child's elaborate expectations of his birthday party don't match up to the real event. Or sometimes the event is happening so fast, or is so kaleidoscopic, your child is lost in the scramble. The child may be disappointed or overwhelmed and covering these feelings with misbehavior. It may be helpful to remove him from the activity for a few minutes of quiet to help him regroup. Help him focus on the good things that are happening. Give him a glass of water and a hug and a kiss, and hold his hand as you lead him back to the party.

BIRTHDAY, bad behavior, other children as guests

See also ■ Other people's children

SITUATION

During my child's birthday party, one of the guests keeps misbehaving. I'm trying to manage all the details of the event. What do I do about this kid?

THINK ABOUT IT

It's easy to lose your patience at a time like this, but the more calm control you demonstrate to this child, the sooner he'll settle down.

SOLUTIONS

1 Don't correct the child in front of others; it's embarrassing to the child who is misbehaving and to your child as well. Instead, walk over to the guest, put your hand on his shoulder, and talk quietly in his ear. Make a specific comment about what it is you don't like and what he should do instead: "Horace, I see that you like our chandelier, but please don't hang from it. You may look at it from here on the floor."

2 Distract the misbehaving child by giving him a task to do. He can assemble the parts of a game, carry the gifts to the table, or undertake any other activity that keeps him busy for a short period of time. This interruption in the negative behavior is often enough to settle him down.

3 If the behavior is really out of line—for example, the child is hitting other kids—it's okay to ask him to sit in a chair for a time-out. Don't call it *time-out* though; just say, "I think you need a minute of quiet time. Please sit here in this chair."

4 An older child who is misbehaving will tend to stop acting up if you're close at hand. Simply move close to the child and wait until he settles down. If you see him start up again, walk over near him, and see if your presence is enough to calm him down.

BIRTHDAY, bad behavior, your child as guest

See also ■ Cooperate, won't ■ Listening, not ■ Manners, in public
■ Parties, bad behavior at

SITUATION
My child is a terrible guest at birthday parties. She gets unusually hyper and misbehaves in ways she never would at home.

THINK ABOUT IT
Children typically misbehave at parties for three reasons. First, they simply get caught up in the excitement of the event; second, they feel jealous of the attention the birthday child is receiving; or third, the parents of the birthday child don't have control of the party, and all the kids are acting up. Examine your child to determine the reason for the behavior, and base your response on what you discover.

SOLUTIONS

1 If your child is caught up in the excitement of the event, remove her from the activity to a quiet room, such as a bathroom. Take a minute to allow her to separate herself emotionally from the frenzy of the party. Discuss specifically what behaviors you don't like, and explain what you would like her to do instead.

2 Your child may be jealous of the attention the birthday child is receiving and is trying to steal the limelight with her behavior. If so, give your child a little loving attention, let her sit on your lap, or give her something to drink. You can assign her a job that helps her feel important, such as handing gifts to the birthday child, gathering the ribbons and bows from the packages, or passing out pieces of cake. Remind her of her previous or upcoming party, when she will be the guest of honor.

3 If the parents of the birthday child don't have control of the event, your child won't be the only one misbehaving. It can be perceived as rude if you try to step in to fix things. Instead, focus on getting your own child under control or involving a group of the children in an activity or game. If things aren't being done in the way you would do them, sometimes it's best if you just walk out of the room, take a brief walk, or take your time in the bathroom. Say to yourself, "It's not my house and it's not my party."

BIRTHDAY, party planning

See also ■ Birthday, bad behavior, as birthday child
■ Birthday, bad behavior, other children as guests
■ Birthday, bad behavior, your child as guest

SITUATION
I'm about to plan my child's upcoming birthday party. Any suggestions?

THINK ABOUT IT
No matter what the age, a simple party tends to be more successful than an elaborate one. Ironically, many parents plan a complicated event, thinking it's necessary to please their child, when the kids would have had more fun at a simple, less-structured event.

SOLUTIONS
1 The maximum number of guests should be one to one-and-a-half times your child's age; hence, a four-year-old's party would involve four to six friends, an eight-year-old's party, eight to twelve friends. For a sleep-over party, divide that number in half. (Multiply the number of guests times three to determine the number of vacation days you'll need to recover from the event.)

2 Before discussing the party with your child, take time to think about how much time and money you are willing to spend on the event. Decide in advance what you're willing to do or not do. This preparation will prevent you from being pressured by your child into doing something you'll regret later. After you have your thoughts in order, have a talk with your child and find out what kind of party she would like to have. It's her party and you should consider her requests, but you are the one who should make the final decisions.

3 Keep in mind that a "package" birthday-party event at a local business will cost more money but will be much easier on you. You don't have to clean up before and after, you don't have to feed the kids or bake a cake, and you don't have to obsess about a swarm of boisterous children destroying your home.

4 Involve your child in the planning and setup. For example, a five-year-old can decorate and help fill the party favor bags, a nine-year-old can create her own invitations, and an eleven-year-old can call the skating rink to find out what dates are available and what's included in the package and, later, to schedule the party. A child who participates in the staging of the party will tend to be happier with the end results.

5 Discuss the specifics of the event with your child the day of, or the day before, the event. Review what manners are expected as guests arrive and during the activities. Talk about what manners are appropriate during the opening of gifts. Make sure your child knows to remember to look at each person after opening the gift, call the guest by name, and say thank you. Talk about what responses are appropriate if she opens a gift that is something she already has. "Just say thank you, and make a positive comment about the gift, and we'll handle exchanging it later." Review the proper response to a gift that the child doesn't like at all. Make a few funny comments and your child will remember to do this correctly; for example, "Oh Auntie Agatha, thank you for the remote-control monster truck! My new Barbie will look great in the driver's seat!"

6 Create a specific schedule of events. You can modify this slightly during the party, but having the plan will ensure that things run much more smoothly. You won't be in the middle of opening gifts when all the parents arrive to retrieve their children and have to endure their annoyed glares as you hurry your child through the unwrapping process. A sample plan might look like this:

> 2:00 to 4:00—Set up for party, decorate, and order pizza
> 4:00 to 5:00—Arrival, craft activity, party game
> 5:00 to 5:30—Pizza and pop
> 5:30 to 6:00—Cake and ice cream
> 6:00 to 6:30—Open gifts
> > 6:30—Collapse

BITING, child to adult

See also ■ Cooperate, won't ■ Disrespect ■ Introduction
■ Respect, teaching

SITUATION
My child bites me when she doesn't get her way.

THINK ABOUT IT
A child's mouth is a handy and useful device. Often, the first incident of biting is purely an accidental reaction. Once a child sees just how powerful this tool can be, she may make a conscious decision to use it again.

SOLUTIONS

1 Make certain you aren't responding in the tone of the pleading, distressed victim: "Now, Draculetta, sweetie, you know you're not supposed to bite Mommy. It's not a nice thing to do. Now, you say you're sorry to Mommy." Instead, use a low, serious voice and express your disapproval clearly, using brief, firm words: "Stop it. No biting."

2 Make sure you are not "play biting" or nibbling the child at any time. Children will do as they see done, even though they may do it at inappropriate times.

3 Respond to a bite in a firm, surprised voice, "Oww! That hurts. No biting." Avoid using a whining or pleading voice or lecturing the child, as these can be misconstrued as an interesting form of attention and actually increase the biting incidents. After your firm statement, stop playing with your child for five to ten minutes. This gives your child the message that the behavior does not gain attention, quite the opposite, it causes you to stop playing.

4 Every time the child bites, announce in a firm voice, "No biting." Then, end the interaction with the child and walk away for a few minutes. The child will learn that biting causes you to "go away" and thus does not suit the purpose of the bite—to get you to give in or give attention.

BITING, child to child

See also ■ Fighting, with friends, physical
            ■ Siblings, fighting, physical

SITUATION
My child has been biting other children in his play group.

THINK ABOUT IT
A child sometimes learns, through a chance blending of instinct and accident, that his teeth are a practical weapon. He needs to be taught that this is inappropriate and won't be tolerated.

SOLUTIONS
1 Watch the child closely during playtime. When you see him becoming frustrated or angry, intervene and redirect his attention until he has calmed down.

2 Teach the child how to express anger or frustration safely. This lesson can be taught by giving step-by-step instruction, role-playing, reading books about feelings and anger, and discussing the various choices that we have when we're angry.

3 Every time the child bites, you can immediately and gently cup your hand over the child's mouth and say in a firm voice, "No biting; time-out." Guide the child to a chair or other time-out place and require the child to sit for several minutes to calm down. (A good rule of thumb to determine the length of time-out is about one minute per year of age.) Or you can announce, "You may get up when you can play without biting," and give your child a chance to learn how to control his own behavior.

4 Make sure that you're not allowing "play biting" and that you're not nibbling your child at playtime. Children can't always determine the difference between times when this behavior is acceptable and when it's not.

5 Give more attention to the victim than the biter. After a brief statement such as "No biting," turn your back to the biter and give attention to the victim. Often the biter gets so much attention that biting becomes a way of gaining the spotlight.

! A child over the age of four who persistently bites is displaying atypical behavior, and you should talk with a professional family counselor.

BLAMING

See also ■ Self-esteem, low

SITUATION
My child doesn't accept responsibility for her mistakes. Instead, she blames other people and other things whenever something goes wrong.

THINK ABOUT IT
Children often place blame to cover their embarrassment over a mistake. Help your child understand that everyone makes mistakes. Encourage her to see that it is a valuable way of learning something new.

SOLUTIONS

1 Respond to your child by saying, "We don't need a reason—we need a solution. How can we solve this problem?"

2 Teach your child that life is brimming with choices and that most everything we do involves choice. Teach her that every action or lack of action involves a choice we make. Give your child more choices in her daily life, and point out that the decisions she makes are choices made of her own free will.

3 Make sure you are not modeling blaming behavior in subtle ways, such as saying things like, "I'm late because traffic was so heavy," "I forgot because I'm so tired," or "I burned the dinner because Grandma kept me on the phone so long."

BOREDOM

See also ■ Cabin fever

SITUATION

My child mopes around the house and complains that "there's nothing to do." Of course, his bedroom looks like a miniversion of a toy store, we have a multitude of art supplies and a big backyard, and our garage contains every version of entertainment on wheels. *How* can he be bored?

THINK ABOUT IT

When we were kids, we were never "bored" because we learned to use our creative energy to fill our time. Our parents weren't expected to entertain us. They were more likely to usher us outside with the ever-popular parting phrase, "Go find something to do."

SOLUTIONS

1 Avoid answering your child's complaint with a list of ideas. Typically, *your* creative inspirations won't sound interesting to your child.

Instead, in a very pleasant voice, offer to let the child do a few chores for you to fill the time. This is often the only encouragement they need to come up with a whole list of other possibilities!

 Take note of how much time the child spends watching TV or playing electronic games. Although these activities have certain benefits, they also stifle creativity. When these activities are limited, children will become more creative with their time. (*See also* Television, watches too much; Video games, excessive use of.)

Get the child involved in a hobby or sports activity that can create an ongoing source of things to do.

Determine if you have been a constant source of entertainment for your child. If so, it's tough to change the way things are. Begin to wean your child by starting him out in an activity and then leaving for increasing amounts of time to attend to something else.

Listen to your child's complaints with "half an ear" and interject a few noncommittal grunts, such as "oh," "uh huh," or "ummmm." When your child figures out that you're no help at all, he'll wander off and find something to do.

Encourage your child to create a "What to do when I'm bored" list and post it for future reference. Then, whenever the topic comes up, suggest that the child consult the list.

BOSSINESS

See also ■ Bully, your child is acting like a ■ Meanness

SITUATION
My child is always telling other kids what to do and how to do it. She decides what games to play and then makes the rules for the game.

Most of the time the other kids just go along with her, but I'm concerned about her bossiness.

THINK ABOUT IT

Lucky you! A strong-willed kid who leads the group is less likely than most to grow into an adolescent who follows the pack. Try to focus on the positive aspects of your child's behavior. You have a kid who's assertive, knows what she wants, and isn't afraid to ask for it. Another thought to consider—a bossy child often develops into a strong leader as an adult!

SOLUTIONS

1 If the other children don't seem bothered by the behavior, or if they seem to be protecting their own interests just fine, stay out of it and let them work things out on their own.

2 Avoid embarrassing your child in front of other kids. Instead, wait until later and take advantage of a private moment to discuss what you feel. Stay calm and don't accuse, but simply state what you saw: "Sandra, I noticed that you . . ." Then, ask what your child thinks of the situation. Direct the conversation with helpful questions: "How do you think your friend felt? Do you think you could have done something different?" Encourage your child to be a positive leader. Teach the difference between a bossy statement and one that is assertive but respectful.

3 Enroll your child in a team activity, such as baseball, basketball, Scouting, a YMCA program, or a church youth group. Being part of a team or special group may give your child a sense of belonging and respect from peers that will help reduce her bossy behavior. Take the time to select a group with an able, experienced leader. Look for a coach or director who is comfortable leading the group and who appears to enjoy spending time with children.

4 Watch to see if someone else is bossing your child around, such as an older sibling, a baby-sitter, or even a parent. (You?) If you can modify this person's behavior to be more polite when requesting things of your child, that person can become a positive role model. Instead of demanding that the child obey, offer choices or use the "When/Then" approach. "When your pajamas are on, then you may watch TV" is a better alternative than, "Shut the TV off now and get your pajamas on."

5 Give the child specific responsibilities that she can be in charge of, such as care of a family pet or responsibility for watering the garden. Chores that encourage independence and give a child control can fulfill the need your child has to be in charge of something.

6 If you have a younger or only child, make sure you aren't encouraging bossy behavior by giving in continually to your child's requests. Another behavior that promotes bossiness is when you play with your child according to her rules, even when you don't want to play that way. Instead, encourage your child to learn how to respect other's wishes and to compromise.

BRAGGING/BOASTING

SITUATION
My child brags to other kids about everything. "I'm the fastest, smartest, funniest, greatest kid in town." It really makes me uncomfortable, and I'm afraid it will damage his friendships.

THINK ABOUT IT
The insecurities of childhood can cause children to brag as they try to win the approval of others and find their place in the world. It's their way of saying, "This is me! I'm good at something! I'm important."

SOLUTIONS
1 Through your words and actions, you can help your child understand that he is loved for who he is, not for what he does. Avoid labeling your child a "*great athlete,*" "*excellent singer,*" "*good boy or girl,*" or other specific trait labels. Instead, point out what the child has done well,

using specific examples: "You must feel proud to have been chosen for the solo; all your diligent practice paid off"; "You were a very good listener today." Make regular comments of love without connecting them to any behavior, such as, "I love having you as my kid"; "You're fun to be with"; and "You're very important to me."

2 Don't correct your child in front of other people; it's embarrassing and will bring everyone's attention to the bragging. Later, during a private moment together, review what was said, and teach your child how to rephrase the comment so that it doesn't come out like bragging. For example, "Einstein, earlier you told Rebecca that you were the smartest kid in your math class. I know you're proud of your ability in math, and that's good. But it's bragging when you say 'I'm the best.' Can you think of something else that you can say that's not bragging? How about, 'I've worked hard at learning my times tables and now I can do it.'"

3 Be careful about how many competitive situations your child is involved in. Too much emphasis on competitive games and a strong desire to win can motivate a child to cover up his inadequacies with bragging.

4 Help your child create a memory scrapbook. Include certificates, awards, and photographs. Also include noncompetitive memorabilia, such as notes or cards received from others or stories, poems, or jokes your child likes or has written. Provide a variety of supplies to make this book an ongoing attractive art project, so that it becomes a hobby of sorts and gives your child a way of boosting his self-esteem and feelings of value.

5 Teach your child how to accept his mistakes as part of being human. Sure, it's great to hit a home run, but he can't do that every time he's up at bat! Help him appreciate his commitment to the team, his ability to cheer other players, and his other good traits. Point out that when his favorite major team player strikes out, it doesn't make him a loser.

BREAKFAST, won't eat

See also ■ Eating, disorders ■ Eating, picky eater

SITUATION
My child doesn't want to eat breakfast in the morning.

THINK ABOUT IT
Breakfast is critically important to your child having a successful morning, both physically and mentally. You need to be creative and encourage your child to eat something for breakfast.

SOLUTIONS

1 Some children aren't hungry until after they have been awake for a few hours. Allow a child like this to awaken slowly. Let her dress, make her lunch, and pack her backpack first. After some time has passed, she may be more interested in eating.

2 Purchase a variety of breakfast drinks. These are similar to milk shakes but are enriched with vitamins. Put the drink in a cup with a lid and let your child sip it as she goes about her morning routine.

3 Expand the choices for breakfast foods. Some children don't care for typical breakfast foods but can be persuaded to eat something else. Leftover chicken, soup, or even pizza can make a fine breakfast.

4 Pack a muffin or bagel, a yogurt, and a piece of fruit "to go," and let your child eat on the bus or during the car ride to school.

BREAKING THINGS

See also ■ Carelessness ■ Clumsiness

SITUATION

My child just broke one of the lamps in our living room. How should I handle this situation?

THINK ABOUT IT

Look for the real reason the accident happened. Kids don't break things on purpose. Was it carelessness, angry actions, or distraction? Was the child trying to do something he doesn't have the skills to do? Once you determine the actual reason, you will be more able to deal with the situation.

SOLUTIONS

1 Acknowledge the fact that what happened was an accident and not intentional. Teach that even though we make mistakes, we must take responsibility for them. (Compare this to an adult who has a car accident and must pay for the damages.) Allow your child to take responsibility. Have him call several stores to find out the value of the broken object. Help him figure out which shop to call for repairs. Have him decide how he will pay for a replacement or repair. If the object is quite expensive, he may be able to pay a portion out of his savings and work off the balance via extra chores around the house.

2 If the child was trying to do something that he doesn't have the skills to do, take this as a sign that he's ready to accept more responsibility. Training and experience will help him learn how to handle the task on his own.

3 If the object was broken because of angry actions, you may decide to impose a consequence over and above repair or replacement of the item. A child needs to learn that his angry feelings are OK, but angry actions must be controlled. Old-fashioned grounding or losing privileges may be appropriate in this case. (*See also* Anger, child's.)

BULLY, your child is acting like a

See also ■ Anger, child's ■ Bossiness ■ Fighting, with friends, physical
■ Hate, expressions of ■ Meanness ■ Respect, teaching
■ Self-esteem, low

SITUATION

**It has been brought to my attention that my child has been bullying
other kids at school.**

THINK ABOUT IT

At first, you may want to blame the other kids or the adult who brought the
information to your attention. You need to be honest with yourself to determine the truth in the situation. If your child has been acting in aggressive
ways, you'll want to help your child have more positive interactions with
other children. Your child needs you on his side right now to help him learn
how to control his own behavior.

SOLUTIONS

1 Do not accuse your child or label your child a "bully." Instead talk
about specific incidents. Ask helpful questions to determine the reasons for your child's behavior. Brainstorm with him a variety of options he
would have as an alternative to being rough. Help him learn new ways to
handle the conflicts that arise with other children. Use role-playing to help
your child practice new ways of responding to other children.

2 If possible, arrange to have your child spend some time with an
older, responsible child. If you don't have any close family members
or friends that fit the bill, look into a Big Brother or Big Sister program. It
may help to find a mentor for your child who can teach good social skills by
example.

3 If you must discipline a child for a specific act, such as punching
another child at school, use discretion when deciding on a consequence. Yelling, hitting, or harsh punishment will only encourage your child

to continue his own aggressive behavior. Instead, look for constructive consequences, such as assigning chores at home or writing a note of apology to
the child who was hurt.

4 Discourage your child from spending time with friends who behave
in aggressive ways. (*See also* Friends, inappropriate choice of.) Encourage your child to become involved in an organized youth activity. Participation in a team or group often gives a child the social experience he may be
lacking. Another option is to enroll him in one of the social-skills classes
that are now appearing in schools, churches, and hospitals.

5 Enroll your child in a quality martial arts school. Visit the school
first, and watch a few classes in action *before* you mention the idea to
your child. Choose a program with smaller class sizes. An authentic program
will teach restraint, respect, and self-control. A good martial arts teacher will
convey a quiet, reserved confidence. Talk with the teacher in advance of
classes to let him know your concerns about your child's behavior and what
you hope to achieve with the class. An experienced teacher should make you
feel confident that you are making the right choice for your child. This may
be just what your child needs to learn to control his physical power and to
develop self-discipline. (And it's heartwarming to see your child bow to the
master and hear him end every sentence with a hearty "sir" or "ma'am"!)

! If your child displays a continuing pattern of aggression, he may
display other negative behaviors as well. He may display signs of
low self-esteem, have problems in school, spend excessive time alone, and
have a hard time controlling his anger. If so, it would
be wise to seek professional counseling for your
child so that the reason for the behavior can be
discovered, and the child can learn to control his
emotions and to succeed socially.

BULLY, your child is victim of a

See also ■ Friends, doesn't have any ■ Fighting, with friends, physical
■ Self-esteem, low ■ Shyness, around children ■ Teasing

SITUATION
A bully is picking on my child.

THINK ABOUT IT
As much as you'd like to step in and solve this problem yourself, it's probably in your child's best interest to teach him how to solve the problem. Once he's learned the skills to stand up for himself, he can use them in other life situations.

SOLUTIONS

1 Teach your child how to respond to a bully in a bold, assertive way. Practice with him at home in a role-play situation. Demonstrate the difference between cowering and whispering, "Oh, go away—please leave me alone" versus standing tall; using a deep, loud, voice; and saying with authority, "*Leave me alone!*"

2 Suggest that your child stick with two or more other children when at the playground, the bus stop, or wherever he comes face-to-face with the bully. Most aggressive children will leave yours alone if he's in the middle of a group.

3 If the bully problem is at school, tell your child that if he's not successful in fending the bully off on his own, it's OK to ask for help from a teacher or playground attendant. Rehearse with him what to say when he approaches an adult for help so he doesn't sound like he's whining or tattling. "Excuse me, Mr. Watanabe, but Jason keeps chasing me and throwing stones at me. I've asked him to stop, but he won't." If your child practices saying this at home, he will come across sounding confident and will more likely get assistance from the teacher.

4 Teach your child to turn and walk away from a child who is being a verbal bully, without so much as a word. Being ignored may cause the bully to give up.

5 Determine if your child has healthy friendships with other children. If your child is a regular victim and doesn't have many friends, he can benefit by developing better social skills. Encourage your child to invite friends over to your home or to invite them to accompany you on an outing. (*See also* Friends, doesn't have any.)

! If your child tries many different approaches but is continually harassed by a bully, or if the bully is physically aggressive, you may need to step in. It is rarely, if ever, effective to approach the bully or his parents directly. Instead, approach the school principal or another person in a position of authority. If you lose your temper and yell, it is unlikely you'll get the help you need. Instead, take the time to think about what you will cover in the meeting, and call ahead for an appointment. Outline the specific behaviors that concern you, review the tactics you have used to try to stop the behavior, and have several solutions to suggest. Approach the principal with a calm, matter-of-fact attitude, and you should be able to put together a plan to control the situation.

CABIN FEVER

See also ■ Boredom ■ Siblings, bickering

SITUATION
The weather's kept us in the house for weeks! The kids are bored and antsy, and their bickering is driving me crazy.

THINK ABOUT IT
Look at the bright side. There *is* beauty in being trapped in the house with no escape. Honest! This can be a wonderful time to strengthen your family relationships. In other words, make lemonade out of lemons!

SOLUTIONS

1 Have a dance contest. Move the furniture aside, turn up the music, and dance 'til you drop. Give awards for funniest, most athletic, and so forth. If you're feeling creative, dress up in costumes, and create a stage with spotlights.

2 Make a movie or create a play. Allow the kids to write a script, create costumes and a set, and videotape a movie or enact a play. The kids can make tickets and sell snacks to the audience.

3 Enjoy an indoor picnic. Pack a lunch and spread a blanket in a rarely used corner of the house. The more unusual the location, the more fun the picnic.

4 Let the kids build a megafort using tables, chairs, and blankets. Keep the fort up for days and let them play in it, eat in it, and sleep in it, too!

5 Have a treasure hunt. Leave notes throughout the house, each one leading to the next (for example, "Look in the dishwasher"). Do as many as you can, and be creative, perhaps using clues, such as "Look in a place that would keep a penguin happy." Have a prize waiting at the end. An alternative is to let the *kids* create hunts for each other or for you.

6 Have an "Easter egg"–style hunt. Hide small toys or pennies all through the house, and let the kids hunt for them. (Be prepared to rehide them many times, as kids really enjoy the hunting process.)

7 Have a game-a-thon. Bring out the board games. Order pizza for dinner and relax. You might even pull out the sleeping bags and camp out in the family room.

8 Bake cookies! Make your favorites. (Who says you can't make cut-out Christmas cookies in the middle of March?)

CAR, fighting in the backseat

See also ■ Fighting, with friends, physical ■ Fighting, with friends, verbal ■ Siblings, bickering ■ Siblings, fighting, physical ■ Siblings, fighting, verbal

SITUATION
It never fails. The minute I pull out of the driveway, it starts. "She took my pen!" "She pinched me!" "He's looking out *my* window on purpose!" If there were a car with two soundproof boxes instead of a backseat, I'd be the first in line to buy one.

THINK ABOUT IT
You strap two energetic children into a space the size of a toy box with no escape route. The fact that they happen to be siblings complicates the mat-

ter, because they have a hard time coexisting in an entire *house*, let alone this little space. It will take a specific plan of action to change the way things are.

SOLUTIONS

1 When the bickering starts, calmly pull to the side of the road. Get out, pull out your checkbook, and pretend to read it (or take this opportunity to balance it!). Within a minute or two, your children will call out to ask what you're doing. Announce, "I can't drive with the fighting going on. Let me know when it's over."

2 Plan a "training session." Head for the toy store or some equally exciting place. As soon as the ruckus breaks out, announce that you refuse to drive with the fighting going on, and turn around and go home. Let the kids be mad at you. The impact will last, because for future trips you can announce, "If the fighting continues, we will go home." And they know that you've done it before and could do it again.

3 Create "car rules." Write them down and keep them in the car. Review the rules each time you get in the car. Plan a consequence for breaking the rules. For example, kids who break the rules get to clean the car when you get home.

4 Boredom can encourage fights. Keep books, travel games, car bingo cards, or radio headsets in the car. It's also helpful to keep a few healthy snacks, such as dry cereal or pretzels, on hand. Kids who are occupied or snacking are content and less likely to fight.

5 Ward off fights by using the time to talk to your kids. Ask thought-provoking questions, recount the events of the week, or play guessing games.

 Turn on your favorite radio station, crank up the volume, and sing.

CAR, seat belt or car seat refusal

See also ■ Cooperate, won't ■ Introduction ■ Listening, not

SITUATION

My kids put up a fuss about wearing a seat belt and getting in the car seat. We argue about it every time we get ready to go somewhere.

SOLUTIONS

1 Habits are a powerful thing, and after a few weeks of wearing the belt or riding in the seat, arguing about it will no longer be an issue. So, fight the battle by staying firm and in control. Live by this rule: "We do not drive until everyone has a seat belt on." You can refuse to even get in the car until everyone else is buckled. If you look like you have all the time in the world (look through your wallet or put on your lipstick), the kids will respond. (Letting them know you are in a hurry and their lack of compliance is holding you up can cause kids to dawdle and complain, hoping you'll let them ride without a belt just so you can get going.)

2 Let the child play in the car seat at home, sit in it to watch a movie, or decorate it with stickers. If it becomes more of a personal possession, then it will be more inviting in the car.

3 Keep a box or bag of "car toys" that can be played with "as soon as your seat belt is buckled."

4 Have a contest: "I bet I can get in the car and buckle my seat belt before you can!" Make a big show of "hurrying"; fumble a bit so your child can win. Make a big production of her winning. Say, "Next time, I'm going to win for sure!"

CAR, who gets to sit in front

See also ■ Siblings, bickering

SITUATION
Every time we get in the car, the kids fight over who gets to sit in the front seat. I'm really tired of it.

THINK ABOUT IT
After the third car trip of the day, you finally screech, "*Nobody* gets to sit in front! Just get in the car!" Why do we do it? Why do we get angry about the same issue over and over again without finding a solution? Do we honestly think that one day our kids will approach us and say, "Guess what, Mom? We've decided that because the fighting bothers you so much, we'll never fight over the front seat again. Isn't that good-hearted of us?"

SOLUTIONS

 If you have two children, assign one child the even days of the month; assign the other the odd days. Use this as a standing arrangement. All you have to know is what day of the month it is. Of course, some days you'll not travel at all, and some days you'll travel quite a bit, but over the long haul it evens out. Calmly explain this rule of averages each time a complaint arises. For three children, assign each child two days of the week. On Sunday, either the front seat stays empty or they can alternate. (Keep a notepad in the glove box to keep track.)

Assign permanent seats. At first, the kids will express outrage at the injustice of such a preposterous idea. But after a week or two of hearing you say, "Everyone get in your assigned seat," they will accept it, maybe grudgingly, but who said your kids always have to be happy with your decisions? You can change assigned seats on the first of every month, if you desire.

Keep dice in the car and roll for seat choices (highest number picks first and so on). Or use a deck of cards to draw for first choice.

Enlist the cooperation of your children. Express your distress at the situation and ask them to come up with a solution. Often, if you ask kids for their help, and treat their ideas with respect, they will come up with the best solution for them.

5 Use accident statistics to solve this problem for you. Children are 30 percent more likely to survive a car crash when they're sitting in the backseat rather than the front. The National Transportation Safety Board has asked states to consider legislation to make it illegal for children under age twelve to ride in the front seat. Australia and some European countries already have front-seat restrictions. Also, cars with air bags carry warnings recommending that children not sit in the front seat because of dangers caused by deployed air bags. In light of this information, you can post a rule in your car: "No children under age twelve in the front seat."

CARELESSNESS

See also ■ Breaking things ■ Clumsiness ■ Forgetfulness

SITUATION
My child doesn't seem to think about his actions, forgets things, breaks things, and makes too many mistakes. He's just *careless.*

THINK ABOUT IT
No child *chooses* to be careless. There are usually hidden reasons for the child's behavior. If you can get beyond your emotions for a few minutes and really think about your child, you may be able to identify the actual problems.

SOLUTIONS

1 Sometimes, a child who appears to be careless is actually just clumsy. Some children develop coordination at a slower pace than others do. These kids can benefit from help with their physical maturation through lessons in gymnastics, ballet, martial arts, or other physical activities.

2 Some children who appear careless are simply disorganized. Help this child by purchasing a large wall calendar and a notebook. Help him write down all his activities and responsibilities. Have him create a daily "to do" list in his notebook. Post a chart for him; include chores, homework, or other responsibilities on the chart.

3 The child may be rushing to get things done with a misguided goal that timeliness is most important. This child needs to learn that the quality of a job is equally important. Teach him how to do tasks one step at a time, and encourage and compliment him when he does a good job. Try to get him interested in an activity that takes slow, specific effort to complete, such as a paint-by-number set, model building, sewing, or embroidery. When the child can learn to enjoy the process as much as the outcome, you may see the carelessness disappear.

4 The child may be overwhelmed with too many things to do: school, lessons, friendships, chores, sports. In his struggle to keep up, he acts in ways that make him appear careless. If this is the case, simplify his life until he can master his world, and gradually add more facets to his day.

CAR POOL, bad behavior

See also ■ Car, fighting in the backseat ■ Other people's children
■ Trips, car, short

SITUATION
I drive in a car pool, and the other kids misbehave in the car. I'm not sure how to handle this, because I can't exactly discipline other people's children.

THINK ABOUT IT
Car pools are a terrific answer for any parent who begins to feel like a private taxi service. Of course, the challenge is to find ways to make a carful of rambunctious kids act like civilized citizens. It can be done! It takes a good plan, consistency, and a level head.

SOLUTIONS
1 Create a list of car rules. Write them down. Review them each morning before you leave. Let the kids know that whoever breaks a rule will have to sit up front with you for the rest of the trip. (Although *your* kids want to sit there with you, other people's kids usually don't!) From then on,

when a rule is broken, simply pull over and ask the child to move up front with you.

2 When misbehavior occurs, pull to the side of the road and stop the car. This action is as much for impact as it is for safety. Look the child in the eye and respectfully request that the behavior stop. "Marvin, I would appreciate if you stop kicking the back of my seat. Thank you."

3 Put a few simple activities in the car, such as a car bingo game, a deck of playing cards, kid's magazines, or books. Kids who are occupied are less likely to misbehave. (Keep the games noncompetitive, and don't put in one really great thing, like a radio headset, that all the kids will fight over.)

CHEATING, at games

See also ■ Losing ■ Self-esteem, low

SITUATION
My child cheats when playing games.

THINK ABOUT IT
As adults, we see a child cheat and we assume that it's the first step on the low road leading to delinquency and a life of crime. Most children who dabble at cheating, though, eventually learn that it's an inappropriate way to play. It's all a matter of learning right from wrong.

SOLUTIONS
1 A child younger than six who doesn't follow the rules of the game is not really cheating in the adult sense of the word. Young children don't understand the logic of rules or why breaking them is wrong. Typically, they change the rules as they play so that they can win. (A neat idea, if you think about it!) Calmly tell your child that if she wants to play with you, or others, she'll have to play by the rules; and if she wants to make up her own way to play, she can play by herself. Teach that rules are a way we can all play together in the same way.

2 Your child may not clearly understand the rules. Stop the game and review the rules. Answer any questions, and then, narrate the steps as you begin, so that the rules become understood. This approach is also a respectful way to let a child who *knows* that she's cheating see that you're aware of what's going on and that it's wrong.

3 Some kids cheat because they hate to lose. A child who becomes very upset and throws a tantrum if she loses needs to learn that it's OK not to win every time. This child can benefit through practice losing at short, simple games, like ticktacktoe, or guessing games such as "I spy." She may also benefit from playing more noncompetitive games that don't have a winner or loser.

4 Model a pleasant attitude when you lose. Make it obvious that losing is not the end of the world: "Oh well, I lost. But the game was really fun."

CHEATING, at schoolwork

See also ■ School, behavior problems at ■ Self-esteem, low

SITUATION
My child was caught cheating on a test. When I asked her why she did it, she just shrugged and said, "Everybody does it."

THINK ABOUT IT
There are different reasons that children cheat at schoolwork. Perceived necessity, anxiety, and laziness are several examples. It helps to understand your child's motivation for cheating so that you know how to approach the transgression. However, the bottom line is that cheating is wrong, and this is the primary message you want to convey to your child.

SOLUTIONS
 A child who cheats on *one* test may have been unprepared and panicked when she realized she didn't know enough to pass the test. If she feels embarrassed and remorseful, she may have already learned a lesson from

the experience. Discuss the situation and make a plan—with a specific study schedule or the use of a tutor—to prevent it from happening in the future.

2 If you catch your child cheating on a test or homework, schedule a conference with the teacher and arrange for the work or test to be redone. Have your child attend the conference with you, because the discomfort of the meeting and the additional work assigned may prevent the situation from happening again.

3 A child may feel pressure from parents to perform well in a subject she's weak in. Take an honest look at your expectations for your child and make sure they're realistic. Let your child know that what's most important is that she put forth her best effort with a good attitude.

4 A child who has very high expectations for herself may focus so much on the grade that any method to achieve it becomes valid. She needs to learn to enjoy the learning process and to take pride in her other traits. Help her to see her strengths. (*See also* Homework, perfectionism; Perfectionism.)

5 Children who are in over their heads, or have undiagnosed learning disabilities, may cheat out of fear. Talk with your child's teacher or a counselor if you suspect this type of problem.

6 Be sure you're giving your child opportunities to try new things and complete tasks without an adult rescuing her. If a parent is finishing a child's science projects, cookie recipes, and household tasks, the message is that her work is not good enough and that it's OK to accept someone else's work as her own.

! If the cheating is not an isolated issue but is accompanied by lying, stealing, or other disturbing behaviors, it's a good idea to speak with a professional counselor or therapist. You may be able to get ideas and direction from the school guidance counselor or nurse.

CHORES, complains about

See also ■ Chores, how to get them done ■ Complaining

SITUATION

"How come *I* have to do *everything*?" "Riley's mom doesn't make *him* do chores!" "It's not faaaiiiiirrr!" That's what I hear from my kid whenever I ask her to do her chores. I'm tired of the complaints! How do I get my kid to just buckle down and do her chores without whining about them?

THINK ABOUT IT

This is one complaint that tends to bring out the beast in many parents for the simple reason that we have about five *billion* times the number of chores that our child has. Take a deep breath, and use a few of these solutions to cut down on your child's complaints.

SOLUTIONS

1 Let your child know that chores are not optional and that you are going to ignore complaining—and do just that.

2 Use the broken-record technique. An example: The parent states, "Please empty the trash." The child argues, "Why do I have to do everything around here? It's not fair." To which the parent calmly responds, "Please empty the trash." And the child responds, "How come my sisters never have to do any chores?" The parent echoes, "Please empty the trash." Eventually, Cinderella will figure out that it's useless to argue, and she'll empty the trash.

3 Maybe it's time to allow your child to trade her daily chores for something else. Often, children get bored with their chores because after doing them day after day, they become tedious and monotonous. A trade might be fun for you, too! Make a list of the family chores, and see if some trading can revitalize everyone's attitudes about household duties.

4 Invite your child to sit at the table for a talk. Bring a pad of paper with you to the table. Make a column on the pad for each family member. Announce that you're going to do a review of household chores. Write down the chore under the person's name who's responsible for it. Your opening comments might sound like this: "Okay. Let's see. Who does the grocery shopping? That's me. How about paying the bills? Me again. Cooking the meals? Me. Laundry. Me. Taking you to soccer games? Me. Handling maintenance of the car? Me. Taking out the trash? Hey! That's one of yours!" As your child views the never-ending list under your name, her three chores will suddenly seem pretty easy to handle.

5 At a time when you're both in a good mood, have a talk with your child. Let her know how important her contributions to the family are. Explain that it takes a family "team" to run a household. Ask, sincerely, for her help in coming up with a solution for the problem she's complaining about. Brainstorm with her to come up with a plan for curbing the complaining. After the chat, you're likely to see an effort from your child to comply. It's critically important at that point to compliment your child and praise her for her pleasant attitude.

6 Give your child a history lesson. Tell her that in the 1600s American Puritans expected children over the age of seven to learn a trade and become productive members of society. Of course, only about 70 percent of children lived to age seven. Point out that, in 1842, the state of Massachusetts created a law to limit the allowable workday hours for children under the age of twelve. It became illegal for them to work any more than (are you sitting down?) ten hours per day. Depending on your child, you can either tell her about these things you've learned or encourage her to research "child labor" on the Internet or at the library.

CHORES, how to get them done

See also ■ Bedrooms, cleaning ■ Mess, kid's constant

SITUATION

My child forgets to do her chores or won't do them unless I nag and complain. Eventually, I either get angry or do them myself.

THINK ABOUT IT

Assigning children household chores is one of the best ways to build self-esteem and a feeling of competence. Regular chores establish helpful habits and good attitudes about work. Having chores also teaches valuable lessons about life and creates an understanding that there are jobs that must be done to run a household. Children who grow up perceiving chores as a normal part of life will find the flow into adulthood much easier than those without responsibility will.

SOLUTIONS

1 Choose age-appropriate jobs for children based on their physical and mental abilities. Most parents underestimate their children's abilities in this area. Keep in mind that a child who has mastered a complicated computer game can easily run the dishwasher! Preschoolers can handle one or two simple daily jobs. Older children can manage two or three daily jobs along with one or two weekly jobs. (*See also* Chores, suggested list.)

2 Take time for training. Don't assume that because your child has seen you do the task that she can do it herself. Be very specific in your instruction, and demonstrate step-by-step as your child watches. The next step is to let your child help you, followed by your child doing the chore as you supervise. At the point you feel that your child has mastered the job, she can take over responsibility for it.

3 Children need a visual daily reminder to keep them on track doing chores. (This need compares to your need for a daily planner or "to do" list.) A chore chart on which a child can make daily check marks is one helpful technique. An alternative is to use a key rack as a holder for tags that list a daily chore on each one. A child can flip the tags over as she completes each daily chore. At the end of the day, a parent can check for any unturned tags and have the child finish up before getting ready for bed.

4 Use the "When/Then" technique. An example: "When the pets are fed, then you may have your dinner." As a quiet reminder, the child's dinner plate can be left upside down, which means "Run and feed the pets; then, you can eat!" Other "When/Then" routine suggestions are "When your homework is done, then you can play outside" and "When your pajamas are on and teeth brushed, then we will read a book." This idea works best when you follow the "When/Then" rule every day.

5 Be very specific in your instructions. For example, "Clean your room" is vague and can be interpreted in any number of ways. Instead, be explicit by saying, "Put your clothes in the closet, books on the shelf, dishes in the kitchen, and toys in the toy box."

6 Once in a while, just for fun, have a "Coin Collection Day." Prior to having your child complete her chores, hide pennies, nickels, or dimes around the house under the items that need to be cleaned. When all the chores are done to your satisfaction, the child gets to keep the bonus!

CHORES, money and

See also ■ Allowances ■ Money

SITUATION
I have several friends who pay their children to do their chores. I'm wondering whether I should pay mine to do their daily chores.

THINK ABOUT IT
When's the last time *you* got paid to make dinner, do the laundry, or clean the house?

SOLUTIONS
1 Pay children to do chores only if they can choose to forgo the chore if they don't want the money. "Ya know what, Dad? I don't need any money this week, so you can take out the trash and do the dishes yourself."

Because I'm sure this isn't your intention, I think it demonstrates a valid reason not to pay kids to do chores. Also, you don't want to suggest to your kids that, in life, there will always be a monetary reward for handling usual basic tasks. There's another reason I don't think you should pay a child to handle regular daily chores. Children should contribute to the daily maintenance of the home because they're productive members of the family, not because they want to earn a few dollars.

2 Offer a list of special chores for pay for the motivated child. These should be tasks that are over and above regular daily chores. A few ideas are cleaning the garage, basement, or attic; organizing a closet or drawer; washing the car; clipping coupons; waxing floors; polishing silver; fixing broken things; washing windows; mending clothes; polishing shoes; cleaning silk plants; or cleaning out the refrigerator. If you own a business, there may be tasks your child can do for pay, such as photocopying, labeling, folding or sorting, filing, or cleaning.

3 Encourage your child to look around the neighborhood for jobs. If a child is motivated to earn money, there are plenty of opportunities. Think about pet care, yard care, baby-sitting, car washing, newspaper routes, and other odd jobs.

CHORES, sloppy or slow work

See also ■ Carelessness ■ Laziness, at home ■ Procrastination

SITUATION
My child procrastinates when it's time to do chores. When he *does* get around to them, he's usually slow and sloppy when getting them done.

THINK ABOUT IT
"Play my new computer game, sort my rock collection or take out the trash? Gee. How will I *ever* decide what to do first?" Putting chores last on the list is a natural inclination, not just for kids, but—admit it—for you, too. It's

just that, as an adult, you've learned that putting off doing something that needs to be done just gives you more to do later. As your child matures, he'll learn that lesson too. In the meantime, you need to help him along.

SOLUTIONS

1 A child who procrastinates can be nudged to begin if you work with him to get him started. Some children have a hard time when you expect them to get started on their own, because they don't know where to begin or what exactly they should do.

2 Acknowledge the contribution instead of criticizing the quality of the work or complaining about the length of time it took to get the work done. Children tend to blossom under your compliments and wither under your criticism.

3 Your child may be bored with his current chores. Increase the challenges, and your expectations, as your child masters his responsibilities. New and different jobs may spark more interest and commitment.

4 Refrain from redoing a chore or correcting a child's mistakes. Doing so will discourage your child from trying next time and will often result in sloppy, careless work, because the child knows that you'll finish up for him.

5 Chores that must be done day-after-day can become tedious. Allow one day a week (typically Saturday or Sunday) as a chore-free day, except for those things that must be done, such as pet care or dish washing.

CHORES, suggested list

See also ■ Chores, how to get them done

SITUATION
I'm trying to decide what chores are appropriate for my children.

THINK ABOUT IT

What follows is a list of ideas from which you can choose a few chores for your child. The idea is not to turn your child into Cinderella! Simply review the list; consider your child's age, ability, and personality; and select chores appropriate for your child. Preschoolers can handle one or two simple jobs. As children get older and more capable, they can handle a larger quantity of jobs, as well as those that are more complex.

Ages two to three: Put toys away, fill pet's food dish, put clothes in hamper, wipe up spills, dust, pile books or magazines, choose clothes, or dress self.

Ages four to five: Above, plus make own bed, empty wastebaskets, bring in mail or newspaper, clear table, pull weeds, use handheld vacuum to pick up crumbs, water flowers, unload utensils from dishwasher, wash plastic dishes at sink, or fix bowl of cereal.

Ages six to seven: Above, plus sort laundry, sweep floors, handle personal hygiene, set and clear table, help make and pack lunch, weed, rake leaves, keep bedroom tidy, pour own drinks, or answer telephone.

Ages eight to nine: Above, plus load dishwasher, put away groceries, vacuum, help make dinner, make own snacks, wash table after meals, put away own laundry, sew buttons, run own bath, make own breakfast, peel vegetables, cook simple food (such as toast), mop floor, take pet for a walk, or pack own suitcase.

Ages ten and older: Above, plus unload dishwasher, fold laundry, clean bathroom, wash windows, wash car, cook simple meal with supervision, iron clothes, do laundry, baby-sit younger siblings (with adult in the home), mow lawn, clean kitchen, clean oven, change bed, make cookies or cake from box mix, plan birthday party, or have a neighborhood job, such as pet care, yard work, or a paper route.

CLINGING

See also ■ Separation anxiety ■ Shyness
■ Work, doesn't want parent to

SITUATION
My child doesn't want to be separated from me at all. She attaches herself to my arm or leg, and I can't peel her off! She refuses to play with other kids or by herself.

THINK ABOUT IT
Children go through clingy phases. Typically, these are short-term and something the child will "grow out of." As annoying as clingy behavior is to a parent, it's best that you avoid pushing the child away with actions or such words as, "Don't act like a baby; go play." Instead, use some of the following ideas to encourage your child to be more independent.

SOLUTIONS

1 Give your child permission to stay with you. Say, "You can stay here as long as you want to, or you can play and come back for a hug whenever you want one." Ironically, giving your child *permission* to cling is often enough to encourage her to move away from you.

2 Children often become clingy during times of change or stress, such as the birth of a sibling, parents' divorce, or moving to a new home or starting a new school. If this is the case, allow the clingyness to run its course. As your child becomes accustomed to the new situation, the need to cling will abate.

3 Go with your child to the place you'd like her to be, such as a play area at the park. Play with your child for a few minutes; then, step a few steps back and watch. Gradually move farther away. If your child starts to look panicky, take a few steps forward and make a positive comment: "Wow! That looks like a really fun slide! Can you go down it on your tummy?" Eventually, you'll be able to move farther away for longer periods of time. Announce where you'll be—"I'll be right here on this bench"—so your child doesn't worry when she looks up to find you gone.

4 Give your child something of yours to keep close, such as a small scarf, an old wallet, or a picture she can hold on to that reminds her of you.

5 Give your child a "magic nickel" and tell her that it will help her feel safe and happy. (I suggest using a nickel, as opposed to any other token item, because a nickel's easily replaced if it gets lost!)

6 Watch your words and actions. You can inadvertently encourage your child's clingy behavior via your body language, facial expressions, and worried words: "Oh, honey, it's OK, really. Don't worry; I'll be right back." Reassure her by showing that you have confidence that she can be away from your side and still be happy and secure.

! **If clinging continues for more than six months, is excessive, or combines with other fearful behaviors, it may be helpful to discuss your child's behavior with a professional.**

CLOTHING, carelessness about

See also ■ Bedrooms, cleaning ■ Carelessness ■ Mess, kid's constant
■ Sloppiness

SITUATION
My kid leaves his clothes laying about in great heaps. He wears his good clothes at play and tears or stains his clothes excessively. I used to spend money on clothes for myself; now, my entire budget goes toward *his* wardrobe!

THINK ABOUT IT
As parents, we sometimes fall into a pattern of behavior that actually *encourages* our children to continue their careless actions. Carelessness with

clothes is a perfect example. We clothe our children from the time they are babies, and we take full responsibility for their belongings. In turn, they accept this situation as their "due" and don't even realize that they're being irresponsible. When you make a conscious decision to turn over more responsibility to your child for his personal belongings, he'll learn to take better care of them.

SOLUTIONS

1 A child often abuses his clothing when the parents buy all the clothes and he knows that more will show up when he needs them. You can change this pattern by increasing the child's allowance to include a "clothing allowance." The child must use this portion for school and play clothes, including underclothes and socks. Allow the child more choice when purchasing. Budget an amount that covers the minimum requirements, and don't provide extra to cover for poor choices or ruined or lost clothing. A child who is given this responsibility will quickly learn the value of clothes and the importance of taking care of what he has.

2 Create a new rule: Clothing belongs folded in your drawers or hanging in your closet. Any clothes found laying around will be put in a box in the garage until the first of next month. *Be firm* and follow through. For some children, you may have to hide the box to prevent them from sneaking their favorite things out of it. When your child is down to the stuff he hates at the end of the month, it will virtually guarantee that next month more clothes will find their way into his closet and drawers!

3 Teach your child how to run the washing machine and dryer (an easy task, because it's much simpler than the computer games he frequently plays!). When you're confident he can handle the task, turn over the maintenance of his own wardrobe to him. Create a few rules regarding size of load, number of loads per day, and so forth. When he complains he has nothing clean to wear, tell him to talk to the person in charge of his laundry!

CLOTHING, chewing of

See also ■ Habits, bad

SITUATION

My child has a habit of chewing on the sleeves and collar of her shirts. It frays the edges and leaves a big wet spot on the shirt. She ends up looking like her only missing accessory is an empty gin bottle!

THINK ABOUT IT

This is a surprisingly common habit. As children's molars start to come in, they have a real desire to chew. It's the big kid's version of teething.

SOLUTIONS

1 Don't belittle or embarrass a child over this habit; just help to control it. It usually passes quickly. One option is to give a child a small piece of cloth to chew on or designate an old sweatshirt for the purpose.

2 Allow your child to chew sugarless chewing gum at home, or encourage her to chew an apple when she has the urge to chew.

3 Talk with your child about this habit and get her to commit to trying to stop. It will be easier for her to stop if she sees you trying to help her, rather than nagging her about something you don't like. Create a subtle sign you can give her to point out that she's chewing and should stop, such as a tap on her arm or a code word or phrase.

CLOTHING, choice of

SITUATION

My child has an entire closet full of nice clothes. Yet she chooses to wear the same old stuff and the oddest combinations.

THINK ABOUT IT

This is one way that children of all ages display their independence and difference from their parents. Actually, it's a tradition for each generation to choose clothing that is distinct from their parents' style. (Remember your own parents' opinions of *your* choices?)

SOLUTIONS

1 Pick your battles. If the clothing is weather appropriate and meets your standards for cleanliness and modesty, then let it go. If your child's outfit is odd, chances are good people will know *you* didn't pick it out!

2 Organize your child's closet and dresser to make choices easier. It may help to put school clothes and play clothes in two different places. You can place large rubber bands around matching outfits, and use a variety of baskets or tubs to sort and separate clothes.

3 Have specific rules about clothes. Give your child freedom to choose within the set boundaries. For example, T-shirts with bizarre pictures or phrases can be worn in the home or as a nightshirt; new clothes can be worn only to school.

4 Include your child in shopping trips on days when you have the time to make careful selections. Most children will wear a few favorites over and over. If they have more choice when purchasing, and you OK the purchase, you'll have fewer daily battles.

CLOTHING, dawdling while dressing

See also ■ Dawdling

SITUATION

When I send my kid upstairs to get dressed, every little thing distracts him. I usually end up nagging and yelling, and we're still late getting out the door.

THINK ABOUT IT

Oh, to be a child. To live without constantly glancing at your watch, checking your planner, and rushing off to yet another appointment. To enjoy the simple pleasures of smelling a freshly washed T-shirt, comparing stripes on a new pair of socks, or watching a dust bunny float gently to the floor. Alas, there are things to do, and schedules to be met, and it's the job of a parent to keep things moving along.

SOLUTIONS

1 Some younger kids appear to dawdle because getting dressed, believe it or not, can be very complicated with all those zippers, buttons, and ties. To make things easier, stick to simple clothes—elastic waists, Velcro, and snaps.

2 Use "Grandma's Rule," otherwise known as the "When/Then" technique: "When you have finished dressing, then you may have your breakfast."

3 Develop a specific morning routine. Write down the routine and post it on your child's bedroom door. (If your child can't read yet, use stick pictures.) Help your child adhere to the routine for a few weeks until it becomes habit; then, simply keep your child on track by asking, "How are you doing with your morning routine?"

4 Organize your child's closet and dresser so that they're conducive to a smooth process. If your child has to sort through stacks of clothing, it can slow down the process. Keep things neat and in labeled drawers or baskets. It may be helpful to fold entire outfits together: the shirt, pants, underclothes, and socks rolled into one easy bundle.

5 Create a routine of choosing and laying out all clothes at night when your child is changing into pajamas.

6 Have a standing rule that when your child has eaten, dressed, and completed morning chores, he can do what he wants with the extra time before leaving, such as play a game or read.

7 Decide on a specific time that dressing must be completed, for example, 7:30. If your child is not dressed by that time, then she will suffer a previously announced consequence (such as going to bed fifteen minutes earlier that night, folding the laundry for you after school, or getting up fifteen minutes earlier the next morning). Do give a five-minute warning to allow her the chance to be successful.

CLOTHING, frequent changing of

SITUATION
Every time I see my daughter, she's wearing a different outfit. To make matters worse, she leaves each discarded choice in a pile on her bedroom floor. When the pile gets too big, she simply deposits the whole stack in the hamper and expects the family "laundress" to handle it. Well, the laundress is ready to go on strike!

THINK ABOUT IT
As children become more conscious of their appearance, they begin to judge their wardrobe more harshly. Nothing seems to look right, and every mood is reflected by a change of attire. It helps to understand that this behavior is normal and to make a few adjustments that allow your child some freedom while meeting your needs for a clean room and less laundry.

SOLUTIONS
1 Rearrange a part of your child's bedroom to become a "dressing room" with a variety of shelves, lots of clothes hooks, and a few boxes for clothes. Or clean out a closet that's full of rarely used junk and create a neatly organized wardrobe room.

2 Give your child full responsibility for her clothes. Teach her how to use the iron and the washer and dryer. If she abuses this privilege by washing one item at a time, start charging a fee "per load" that is deducted from her allowance or have her use cold water to wash in and let her purchase her own laundry soap.

3 Have a problem-solving discussion with your child. Calmly explain why you perceive the clothing issue as a problem. Sincerely ask for your child's help in coming up with a solution. Brainstorm together until you come up with a workable plan. Make an agreement to follow through. Communicate daily. Compliment and praise your child when progress is made.

CLOTHING, won't dress self

See also ■ Cooperate, won't ■ Listening, not ■ Stubbornness

SITUATION
My child is capable of dressing himself but refuses to do it.

THINK ABOUT IT
Lots of young kids would be happy to wear their pj's all day. Dressing is simply a task that takes time away from other fun things they'd rather be doing. Because they feel no pressing need to dress, it takes some creative parenting to get them motivated to cooperate.

SOLUTIONS
1 Make a standing deal: "When you dress yourself, you can wear whatever you want from your school clothes. If I dress you, then I get to choose." At first your child will let you choose, so it's important to make choices that you *know* your child doesn't like. (Sneaky, but effective!) When he fusses, just calmly say, "If I dress you, I get to pick. If you dress yourself, you can wear what you want." Be flexible with your child's choices—if they are weather appropriate and event appropriate, then ignore the odd color combinations or strange layers. He won't have to wear a sign that says "I dressed myself"—trust me. It will be obvious to other adults that you're the kind of parent who's encouraging a child's independence and personal responsibility.

2 Pick your battles. Dress your child when you're in a hurry and require that he do it himself when you have time to encourage and remind. By the time children are five or six, most will outgrow the desire for your help.

3 Set specific terms and use the "When/Then" approach, which gives your child the priority sequence of events. "I'll set the timer for ten minutes. If you're dressed before it rings, then I'll have time to read you a book before we leave." Or "As soon as you're dressed, you can have breakfast."

4 Get silly or play a game. You can relieve the tension of the morning by playing a dressing game, having a race, or being silly. Younger kids, for example, respond very well to clothing that talks: "Hi there! I'm Salvador, the magic shirt. If you put me on, you'll have magic powers, too!"

5 Praise success! Positive encouragement helps to keep a child on the right track.

CLOWNING

See also ■ Bathroom jokes ■ Humor, inappropriate

SITUATION
My kid's never serious! He can find the joke in a plate of dry toast! Sure, at times he's funny. But, most often I find his clowning quite annoying.

THINK ABOUT IT
I know it's aggravating. But it's sure a lot easier to deal with than whining, fussing, or screaming would be!

SOLUTIONS
 Don't laugh at the funny actions or words when they're inappropriate. Keep a straight face and ignore the antics.

2 Allow your child an outlet for his humorous tendencies. Sign him up for an acting class, or let him join a club or activity that focuses on lighthearted fun.

3 Teach your child how to determine if it's an appropriate time to be funny. Do this with love and patience. If your child is acting silly and shouldn't be, take him quietly aside and say, "I need you to be serious right now."

4 Give your child positive attention during times when he's behaving properly. Sometimes clowning is a method of getting attention, and if the attention can be had without the clowning, it may go away.

5 Enjoy it! You may be raising the next Robin Williams!

CLUMSINESS

See also ■ Breaking things ■ Carelessness

SITUATION
My child seems to be always spilling, knocking things over, and breaking things. I must say "Be careful" a hundred times a day.

THINK ABOUT IT
Many children between age two and six are clumsy. This is a time when coordination is developing. In some children, it's more noticeable. Clumsiness rears its ugly head again during growth spurts or adolescence. Be patient. No child chooses to be clumsy. Find ways to be helpful, and you can help your child move through a clumsy stage.

SOLUTIONS
1 Provide safeguards. Use cups with lids and plastic dishes, and put breakable objects out of reach.

2 Help your child develop more grace by enrolling her in a gymnastic, martial arts, or ballet class. Other sports, such as baseball, soccer, and swimming, are also helpful in developing motor skills. Just be sure to pick a less-competitive league for your child so she isn't embarrassed by her lack of skills.

 Provide puzzles, color-by-number posters, and other activities that involve the use of small motor skills. The development of small motor skills will also help your child's large motor skills.

 Encourage your child to try new things and practice them until she can master the activity. Often, clumsiness disappears with practice.

Sometimes, excessive clumsiness is a sign of poor vision or motor development problems. If you suspect that either of these problems may be an issue for your child, make an appointment with a pediatrician or a health professional.

COMPETITIVENESS

See also ■ Athletics, poor sport ■ Losing

SITUATION
My child feels everything's a contest, and he must be the winner every time.

THINK ABOUT IT
Some competitiveness is healthy for a child. It will help motivate him to be his best and test his limits. An overly developed sense of competition, however, may rob your child of many of life's pleasures because he's so focused on the "win" that he doesn't enjoy the process. In addition, a child with an

intense sense of competition will find it hard to lose, and no one can win all the time. The goal is to temper your child's competitive nature to a more balanced level.

SOLUTIONS

1 Play games with your child without keeping score: a backyard baseball game without specific teams, with everyone taking turns batting; or time on the tennis court, just hitting the ball back and forth; or tossing a basketball and counting how many turns you take, not how many baskets you make. Help your child enjoy the process without thinking about the score.

2 Introduce the idea of "personal best," with the focus on doing a good job purely for the feeling it gives you, not for what others see.

3 Spend more time praising effort, attitude, and the development of skills than you do praising the results. Make positive comments when your child tries hard, when his skills have improved, or when he's a good cheerleader for someone else's efforts. When your child talks about his score, guide the conversation toward talking about other aspects of the game.

4 Examine your own behavior. Are you subtly sending the message that your love or approval is greater when he wins? Do you go overboard with jubilation when he gets first place? Do you celebrate the winning games but display disappointment when his team loses? Are you framing and posting what you judge to be the best artwork and sticking the rest in a drawer? Are you giving a sibling a great amount of attention for a skill or ability that the sibling excels at, without encouraging your other child to discover her own special skills? Take an honest look at the messages that you and other adults are sending your child about winning.

5 Discourage the constant need your child has to make everything a competition. When he says, "Last one in is a rotten egg!" respond, "I think last one in has the good sense to let you test the water first!" If he says, "I have the biggest pancake!" respond by saying, "Great! Then when everyone else has seconds, we'll know that you're already full."

COMPLAINING

See also ■ Chores, complains about ■ Whining

SITUATION

My child gripes whenever he's asked to do something. He does what he's told, but he sure tells me how unhappy he is with the situation.

THINK ABOUT IT

Learning to do the things we must, even when we don't want to, is a process of maturity. (And even the most mature among us is heard to utter a complaint now and then!) Understanding how to voice our opinions in a proper and respectful way is a learned skill.

SOLUTIONS

1 Restate the complaint in the way you want to hear it. An example: A child says, "Yuck! I hate this green stuff!" You respond, "What I'd like to hear you say is, 'Dad, I don't care for spinach.'"

2 Let your child know you are going to ignore complaining—and do just that. When you ask your child to do something and he responds with a complaint, just repeat your request and walk out of the room.

3 Use the broken-record technique. Continue to repeat your request in a bland, unemotional way. Your child will tire of hearing it and get the message that you're not going to give up.

4 Tell your child what you want to hear. "Snidely, I'll be happy to listen to you when you use a normal voice and give more thought to your comments." Then end the discussion.

5 After the child has voiced his complaint, respond by saying, "Oκ, I've heard your problem. What do you think are some possible solutions?" Do not ask in an angry, sarcastic way but to encourage your child to think of ways to solve his own problem.

6 Make sure you're not modeling complaining behavior with such comments as, "Why can't you put your stuff away? I'm the only one who does anything around here. You kids never clean up after yourselves. I'm sick and tired of . . ." (Incidentally, all this is usually said as a monologue as the parent walks through the house picking up after the kids! This behavior clearly demonstrates complaining at its best.)

COOPERATE, won't

See also ■ Introduction ■ Listening, not

SITUATION

How can I get my kids to cooperate with me? I'm constantly nagging and complaining, not that it does any good! Help!

THINK ABOUT IT

This is the number one complaint of parents around the globe. It's a biggie—purely because there are so many things we must get our kids to do (or *not* do!). If you're waiting for your child to start cooperating of his own free will—you might want to pack a lunch. Things won't change on their own. It takes consistent, effective parenting skills to change your children's behavior and to encourage your children to cooperate, willingly, on a regular basis. It will take practice, patience, and persistence on your part. Once you've made a few changes in your approach, you'll find that you're no longer praying for bedtime but actually enjoying your children.

SOLUTIONS

1 Don't make general comments that hint at what you would like done, such as, "It would be nice if somebody helped me clean up." Don't make it sound as if compliance is optional by starting your sentence with "Will you? Could you? Would you?" or ending your sentence with "Ok?" Make your request clear, short, and specific: "Please put your dishes in the sink and wash the table" or "It's six o'clock. Gather your homework and come to the table."

Use the "When/Then" technique, also known as "Grandma's Rule." It simply lets your child know the sequence of his priorities: work first; play second. "When you have finished your homework, then you may play your new computer game." "As soon as your pajamas are on, we'll read a book." "The minute the dishes are washed, you can go out and ride your bike."

Offer your child a choice: "Would you like to sweep the floor or dry the dishes?" You can also use a sequence choice, such as, "What would you like to do first—put on your pajamas or brush your teeth?" Another way to use choice is the time-focused choice: "Would you like to start at 8:00 or 8:15?" If a child creates a third option, simply say, "That wasn't one of the choices," and restate your original statement. If a child refuses to choose, you choose for him.

Use humor to gain cooperation. A bit of silliness can often diffuse the tension and get your child to cooperate willingly.

Avoid letting your emotions take control. Don't yell, threaten, criticize, or belittle. Instead, out loud, ask yourself a question: "What is the problem?" Then, make a statement of fact, such as, "There are dirty dishes and snack wrappers in the TV room." Pause. Be silent. And stare at your children. It's amazing that kids will know exactly what you're thinking. Most often, they'll respond by cleaning up. If not, back up your approach with one of the other solutions.

Read my book, *Kid Cooperation*, for many more suggestions and practical ideas.

CRYING

See also ■ Whining

SITUATION

My child cries easily, often, and usually for unimportant reasons. The result around our house has been a "Boy Who Cried Wolf" story. When he's crying about a valid injury, nobody listens.

THINK ABOUT IT

When your son was a baby, his cries brought love and attention. He's just never learned how to replace the crying with more mature ways of calling for help.

SOLUTIONS

1 Don't say, "Stop crying," because that never works and only makes *you* angry when your child cries harder! Instead, tell your child what you *do* want: "I need to hear your words. Tell me what's wrong. Use your big-boy voice." Sometimes it helps to get him started: "Georgie, talk to me. Say, 'Mommy, I want . . .'"

2 Acknowledge the reason your child is crying to validate his feelings. "You're so frustrated because you want a cookie" or "I know you really wanted to go with Daddy." Often, crying is a call for understanding. Acknowledgment can offer what your child needs to hear and may help him stop crying and move past his sad or angry emotions.

3 If the crying is manipulative (for example, you said no more ice cream and your child is crying), simply ignore it and leave the room.

4 Determine if the crying is related to insufficient sleep or poor eating habits. If so, move bedtime earlier or have a daily nap or rest time for recharging. Also, watch your child's eating habits and make sure he's getting three meals plus healthy snacks and not going more than three hours without food.

5 Increase the amount of one-on-one time your child gets from the important adults in his life. Sometimes crying is a plea for attention. Just remember to give the attention prior to the start of the crying, not as a reward for crying.

6 Recognize that your child is a sensitive person by nature. Use lighter discipline. Often, with this type of child, a firm tone is enough to get your point across. Also, try to use alternate discipline methods such as distraction or the use of humor to keep him on track. Avoid being too harsh, as this behavior will just prolong the incidents of crying.

7 Using index cards (or small pieces of paper), make ten cards that show happy faces, colored bright yellow on the front. Draw sad faces, colored blue, on the back. Poke holes in the cards and put a small loop of yarn through the hole. Hang the cards on a piece of cardboard or a key holder, with the smiling face up. Show them to your child in the morning. Explain that each time your child cries, you will turn a happy face over into a sad face. Say that if there are more happy faces than sad at the end of the day when you are putting pajamas on, you will read an extra book (or substitute some other pleasant treat your child can look forward to). Often, the faces alone are enough to motivate a child. (Expect a strong reaction the first time you turn a happy face over! Because this is so visual, children are often angry when you turn the face to a sad one.)

DARK, fear of

See also ■ Bedtime ■ Fears

SITUATION
My child is afraid of the dark and doesn't want to be alone when the lights are off.

THINK ABOUT IT
Fear of the dark is one of the most common childhood fears. If you think back to your own childhood, you can probably remember running up the stairs, heart pounding, as you imagined some unknown creature nipping at your heels. As a matter of fact, have you noticed that in horror movies, the scary scenes almost always take place in the dark?

SOLUTIONS

1 Acknowledge your child's feelings: "I know you don't like to be alone in the dark. Maybe it's because you can't see everything in the room." Admit if you used to be afraid of the dark when you were a child, and explain that the more you knew about the world, the less afraid you became. Let her see that the room is the same one even when the lights are off. You can experiment by looking at, and walking around in, a room during different levels of light, from having all the lights on to only the light of a tiny flashlight. Select spooky-looking shadows in the dark; then, illuminate them with a strong flashlight or overhead light to identify what the object really is.

2 Allow your child to sleep with a bright night-light or even a regular lamp on. Most kids love Christmas lights, and a string of green or blue bulbs gives a very soothing glow. Most kids sleep normally with even the brightest light burning. This need for a light will eventually disappear.

3 Try to make the dark less mysterious. Plan a family candlelight dinner, take a walk at dusk, or build a bedspread fort and play games by flashlight. Buy or borrow a book about constellations, and spread out blankets in the yard on a clear night to enjoy watching the stars.

4 Don't overreact to your child's fear of the dark or you may actually make it worse. Treat it as what it is—a normal childhood fear that goes away over time. If you keep looking under the bed or checking the closet to reassure your child that everything is OK, she may begin to wonder why you have to keep looking if you know that nothing's there!

5 Avoid having your child watch scary TV shows or movies or read books that scare her. This rule applies to any time of the day, as children have good memories and can remember at bedtime something they saw that morning. (Watch your child carefully; what he may view as "scary" may not be scary to you!)

DAWDLING

See also ▪ Clothing, dawdling while dressing

SITUATION
My child moves at an agonizingly slow pace when I need her to hurry.

THINK ABOUT IT
Children live according to a much slower clock than we adults do. They don't give a moment's thought to what they might be doing next. They prefer to enjoy each moment. They pause as they watch the cat sleep, examine the color patterns in the carpet, and ponder the reasons for having toes. It's a shame that we can't all live according to "kid time." But our daily schedules don't permit that luxury. Try a few of these solutions to avoid sounding like a cranky prison guard or an exasperated parrot with a vocabulary of two words: "Hurry up!"

SOLUTIONS

1 Avoid letting your differences in perception of time become a problem by making clear, specific statements that don't leave room for misunderstanding. For example, instead of the vague statement, "Get ready to go," clarify by saying, "Right now, please put on your shoes and your coat and get in the car."

2 Children often dawdle out of habit. A parent will announce, "Time to go to bed," and then be distracted by a phone call or a household task. Children come to expect that you'll repeat yourself numerous times before you mean it. Practice this: think before you speak, make a very specific request, and then follow through.

3 Some children dawdle because they become distracted and forget what they're supposed to be doing. To fix this, give your child one clear task at a time, and when it's complete, assign the next. Another idea is to write down the sequence of tasks and give the list to your child with a pencil to cross things off as they're done.

4 Avoid rushing your child with the words, "Hurry up!" This request tends to frustrate your child, and she'll rush to the point of taking extra time to make up for the mistakes that happen when she hurries. Instead, make a specific request that she can follow: "Please put your puzzle in the box and go upstairs to the bathroom."

5 Encourage your child to finish the task with a "When/Then" statement, such as, "When your pajamas are on, then I will read you a story."

6 Check your own daily schedule and honestly determine if you are trying to do too much. If so, start focusing on the priorities in your life and slow *yourself* down a little bit.

DAY CARE, cries when left at

See also ■ Crying

SITUATION
My child cries every morning when I drop him off at day care.

THINK ABOUT IT
As frustrating as this is, when you stop to think of the real reason your child is crying, it may give you a different perspective and a bit more patience. Your little one is crying because he loves you so very much that he can't bear to be parted from you. That kind of love isn't easy to come by.

SOLUTIONS

1 Don't rush in the morning. Wake your child early enough so that he can adjust to the day before being whisked off into the car. Give your child something from home to keep in his pocket, such as a picture of the family, a "lovey" toy, or a T-shirt that smells like Mommy.

2 Schedule five minutes to settle your child at the day-care center. Ask, "Is there something you'd like to show me before I leave in five minutes?" Show interest in something and try to get your child started in an activity. This brief amount of time can help your child make the adjustment to day care. (Avoid letting the time extend to longer and longer amounts. Your good-bye should be short and sweet.)

3 Have a special good-bye routine. This routine can include a silly sequence of a certain number of hugs and kisses or a funny way to say good-bye. Make your routine quick and simple, and immediately leave afterward, with a wave and a smile. If you look distressed at leaving, your child will absorb those emotions. Act as though he's going to have a great day. Communicate this message through your words, body language, and actions.

4 Let your child know exactly when you'll return in relation to his day. An example: "I'll be back right after your snack time." Let your child know what you'll be doing while you're gone and make it sound boring. "I'm going to the office, where I'll sit at my desk and talk on the phone."

5 Most children stop crying within five minutes of your departure. Ask your day-care provider if this is true for your child. If you feel uncomfortable leaving a crying child, call the center when you get to work, or arrive at home, so they can reassure you that your child has finished crying and is playing. Talk to other parents who drop their children off later, and ask them to let you know how your child seems to be doing. It may also help if you drop in unannounced once or twice to peek in on your child yourself.

! If you've tried all these solutions, and given them thirty days to work, and your child still cries for extended periods of time (more than fifteen minutes or periodically throughout the entire day), maybe it's time to make a change. Perhaps your child is not emotionally ready to leave you for such a long period of time. If so, see if you can shorten the day-care stay or keep your child at home for a few months and try again. Take a look at the environment at the day care. Perhaps there are too many other children or some other reason your child is uncomfortable. If so, consider changing to a center, or to a smaller home day care, that better suits your child's personality.

DAY CARE,
dropping off and picking up

SITUATION
My child dawdles and complains when I drop her off at day care. You'd think she doesn't want to be there. But what's really weird is that she repeats the behavior when I pick her up in the afternoon!

THINK ABOUT IT
Some children have a difficult time adjusting to changes, even daily ones. They like things to flow in a predictable way. Anything that upsets their

current state of affairs is cause for alarm. These kids require a bit more thought to help them maneuver the changes they encounter in their day.

SOLUTIONS

1 Very specific routines can help your child be more comfortable. *Very specific* means that you do and say the exact same things every time you drop her off and pick her up. For example, park in the same area, enter through the same door, hang the coat, check the job chart and comment on the day's assignment, give two hugs and two kisses, and say, "See ya later, little alligator!"

2 Arrive at exactly the same time to pick up your child every day. It's comforting for a child to know you will be there every day following a specific activity, such as afternoon snack time.

3 When you drop off your child, and again when you pick her up, allow a five-minute adjustment period. (The time is worth it, as you'll save at least fifteen minutes of fussing!) When you arrive at the center, catch your child's attention, blow a kiss, and hold up five fingers, meaning "We leave in five minutes." Allow your child to play or show you something for five minutes. When it's time to leave, use a fun indicator, such as a tickle on the neck; or hold up a toy or your key ring and have *it* tell your child (in a funny voice) that the car is waiting and ready to go.

4 Have a fun routine for the drive home. Leave a snack bag on your child's seat with different contents every day, such as graham crackers, dry cereal, pretzels, fruit, or other snacks. Play a specific game in the parking lot as you walk to the car, such as counting all the red cars you see or counting your steps. Mention something that your child can look forward to at home, such as reading the new library books or Grandpa coming over for dinner.

DAY CARE, misbehavior at

See also ■ Cooperate, won't ■ Listening, not

SITUATION

My day-care provider called to advise me that my child is misbehaving during the day.

THINK ABOUT IT

As annoyed as you may get with your own child, it's distressing to have someone else tell you that your child is "bad." Your first response is likely to be anger or defensiveness. Try to work through those emotions so that you can get to the bottom of the problem, be helpful to your child, and find a solution to the problem.

SOLUTIONS

1 Immediately set an appointment with the day-care provider. Try your best not to get defensive but to keep an open mind. Ask for details about the exact behaviors, when they occur, and how often. Ask the provider for specific suggestions.

2 Make several unannounced visits to the center. Without letting your child see you, watch his behavior and interaction with the other children and teachers. You know your child better than anyone else and can more easily determine the reasons for the behavior.

3 Analyze your child's days, including time spent at home and at the center. Are there major changes that may be affecting your child's behavior? Or are there changes you would consider minor, but they have affected your child? Often there is an overlooked reason for a change in behavior, such as a friend who leaves the day care or the reassignment of a favorite teacher. Sometimes, it's an odd, simple thing that is causing your child to react in negative ways, such as the rearrangement of his favorite painting easel or the disappearance of his favorite fish in the fish tank. Take a close look, and you may find the reason for this change in behavior.

4 Does your child clearly understand the rules and routines at day care? Often, they are different than those at home, and your child's confusion may be the cause of the problems. If so, see if you can repeat some of the rules used at day care in your home. For instance, if the teacher blinks the overhead lights to mean "Everyone be quiet and listen," use this same technique at home. If your child has been displaying the same misbehavior at home, coordinate with your day-care provider so that both of you are using the same methods to control the behavior.

5 Talk to other parents of children at the center. How are their children adjusting? Are they happy with the discipline used by the teachers? Have they experienced any problems? This information will give you insight into the center as a whole beyond the isolated situation with your child. If you find that some other parents are having problems, perhaps the issue is more complex than your own child's behavior.

6 Is your child overwhelmed because of the number of children at day care? Or is there a personality conflict with one or two other children or a teacher? If so, your child may be acting out as a way of struggling with his feelings. If you can pinpoint any specific, unrelated problems and solve them, the misbehavior may disappear or it may lead you to investigate a new day-care situation for your child.

7 Talk to your child about what's going on at day care. Ask opening questions that will encourage your child to talk without giving too much information, since little ones will often pick up on your ideas and expand them. Ask specific questions that require more than a simple yes or no answer. Be patient and give your child plenty of time to think and answer. Young children may not be able to verbalize their problems accurately, but if you listen carefully you may discover what's going on with your child.

DIAPER, doesn't want changed

See also ■ Cooperate, won't ■ Toilet training

SITUATION
My child is a bundle of energy. He hates to lie still to have his diaper changed. He cries, fusses, or runs away. Such a simple issue turns into a major tug-of-war between us.

THINK ABOUT IT
Many active toddlers could not care less if their diapers are clean or not. They're too busy to concern themselves with such trivial issues. It may be important to you, but it isn't a priority for your child.

SOLUTIONS

1 Give the diaper a name and a silly voice and use it as a puppet. Let the diaper call your child and talk to him as you change it. (For many children, this technique is all you need to solve the problem! If you get tired of making "Dweezle Diaper" talk, just remember what it was like before you heard of this idea.)

2 Keep a flashlight with the diapers, and let your child play with it while you change him. There are some cool kid's flashlights that have a button to change the color of the light or shape of the ray. Call this his "diaper flashlight" and put it away when the change is complete. At first, he will cry and complain, but be firm and soon he'll be looking forward to being changed.

3 If your child is old enough, consider potty training. Announce that because he doesn't like his diaper changed, he must be old enough to use the potty. Keep him in disposable training pants during the training period.

DISRESPECT

See also ■ Arguing, with parent ■ Back talk ■ Introduction ■ Meanness
■ Respect, teaching

SITUATION

**There are many behaviors I can deal with, but flagrant disrespect is one
thing that drives me to the brink of hysteria. When the same child that
used to adore me lets loose with insolent comments that I wouldn't use
with my worst enemies, I'm at a total loss about what to do.**

THINK ABOUT IT

Disrespect is often a sign that your child doesn't have a clear understanding
that you are in charge. Therefore, the disrespect cannot be handled as an individual problem but should be viewed as a symptom of a bigger problem. Take
an honest look at your parenting style, and start to make some changes that
will improve your entire relationship with your child. It will take some time,
so be patient. But the end result, a more respectful child, is definitely worth it.

SOLUTIONS

1 Starting *yesterday*, take these five steps: first, allow yourself to take the
position of authority and expect your child to obey you. Second, take
a quiet moment to create a list of appropriate consequences for misbehavior
so that when you're in the heat of the battle, you'll have a plan. Third, talk
less, act more, and when you say it, mean it! Fourth, follow through. And
fifth, learn and use good parenting skills.

2 Pay attention to how you talk to your child when you're unhappy
with him. Children learn from example more than any other way. If
you yell, call him names, or are rude and disrespectful to your child when
you're angry, you'll often see the same behavior mirrored back to you. (An
example: "What is the matter with you? Why can't you ever do it right?
You're acting like a wild animal! I'm sick and tired of this %@*.")

3 If a normally respectful child makes an out-of-character comment,
make a brief, firm, and calm statement, such as, "You are being disre-

spectful. I'll be happy to listen to you when you are respectful." Then, leave the room. If your child follows, go into a bathroom or bedroom and close the door, repeating your previous statement.

4 During a peaceful time, have a conversation with your child about his behavior, why it upsets you, and what behavior you expect instead. Create a written contract between you that covers what behavior you expect, what is unacceptable, and what the consequences will be for failure to uphold the contract. When each of you has signed the contract, post it in a conspicuous place. Follow through when necessary.

5 Let your child know in advance that any time he is disrespectful, he must immediately go to his room when you ask. If he does not, he'll lose a privilege (such as using the telephone, watching TV, playing outside, or staying up late). Then follow through in a calm manner, incorporating Solution 3.

6 When your child expresses angry feelings to you in a *respectful* manner, be willing to discuss and compromise. This response will demonstrate that you are open to discussion when approached in a proper way.

DOESN'T COME WHEN CALLED

See also ■ Arguing, with parent ■ Cooperate, won't ■ Dawdling
■ Listening, not ■ Respect, teaching

SITUATION
I always have to call my child repeatedly before he'll respond. It's like he has cotton in his ears! I can't stand being ignored.

THINK ABOUT IT
If your child knows that the worse consequence for not coming when called is that he has to listen to your repeated yodels, he may decide that you're easy to ignore. He may have learned that he doesn't have to take your calls

seriously until your face is bright red, the veins are sticking out on your neck, and you bellow his middle name.

SOLUTIONS

1 Children learn through experience. When you repeatedly call but he doesn't show up until *he's* ready, you're actually teaching him to ignore you. Follow this procedure: visually locate your child. Call once. Wait three minutes. Go to your child, take him by the hand, and say, "When I call, I expect you to come." Then lead him to the desired location. If you do this once or twice in front of his friends, I guarantee he'll change his ways.

2 Watch how the adults in your family call to each other and respond when someone calls them. Does the caller yell from two rooms away? Does the called one mumble, "In a minute," and then have to be reminded several times before responding? These are the models for your child's behavior. Change the ways you respond to each other, and you'll see your children change, too. Children learn what they live!

3 Making a transition from one activity to another can be difficult for many children. Instead of calling, "Come here now!" try giving two warnings first: "Willard, you'll need to come in five minutes." A few minutes later, "Willard, two minutes." Then, "Willard, please come in now." At this point, wait a minute, and if he doesn't respond, go to him and take him by the hand, saying, "When I call, I expect you to come."

4 Acknowledge your child's desire to continue playing, followed by a firm statement and an action that promotes compliance: "I bet you wish you could stay in the pool forever, but it's time to go now. Here's your towel."

5 Use a dinner bell or timer to call your child. Tell him that when he hears the bell, he needs to come before you count to fifty. After a few practice runs, you can create a consequence for not coming in response to the bell, such as skipping dessert—just let your child know the specifics in advance as fair warning!

EATING, disorders

See also ■ Self-esteem, low

SITUATION

My daughter seems obsessed with food. She's extremely picky about what she'll eat. She counts calories and fat grams. Even though her weight and height are normal, she complains about being "fat."

THINK ABOUT IT

Eating disorders are becoming more prevalent, even in children as young as ten or eleven years old. Unrealistic media ideals give children the wrong message about what's "normal." It's a parent's job to counteract these negative messages with more appropriate information.

SOLUTIONS

1 Point out that TV stars and magazine models don't represent what's typical and that even models look better in photographs than they do in real life because of computer enhancements and touch-ups. Encourage your child to look at the people she sees during the day at the grocery store, the mall, and at school. Have her cut out a picture of a model from a fashion magazine and a picture of a "normal-looking" woman from an advertisement. (Sad to say, *this* task may be somewhat of a challenge!) Have her paste them on two separate sheets of paper. Take her to the mall, the library, or a grocery store. Find a bench to sit on. For about an hour, watch people walk by. Make a mark representing each woman you see on the page with the picture that is closest to the way she looks. I guarantee that you'll end up with a colossal number of "normal" women versus a miniscule number of models. Have a discussion about what this means.

2 Educate your child about nutrition and fitness as opposed to skinniness. Teach her that skinny does not mean healthy. Subscribe to magazines or purchase books that focus on health and fitness. Avoid labeling foods as "good" or "bad" and instead focus on nutritional value. Also, help your child understand that eating the occasional hot fudge sundae is not a mortal sin.

3 Be careful about comments and actions pertaining to your own body. A daughter who sees her mother weighing herself every morning, hears her grumbling about her fat thighs, and sees her refusing to wear shorts in public, even when it's ninety degrees in the shade, will be getting some powerful messages about body image. This behavior is especially dangerous if your body type resembles hers. Avoid critical talk about body shapes, even in jest, and present the concept that all people are different and that "normal" comes in a very wide range of differences.

4 Don't let food issues become a major battleground in your family. Demanding that a child eat a certain food, or at a certain time, will often cause a child to assert her independence by refusing to eat. Instead, educate her. Buy her a good book about nutrition and fitness, or enroll her in a class on that topic specifically designed for young people.

5 Show your child that you value her for much more than her looks. Focus on her positive character traits, and downplay comments or compliments based on the way she looks. Help your child learn to appreciate herself for who she is. Encourage your child to become involved in music lessons, a club, or a sports team; this will help her focus on something productive and build her self-confidence in the process.

! **If your daughter is abnormally thin or if you discover that she has been making herself vomit or is using laxatives, there is a problem that requires professional help. Make an immediate appointment with a physician.**

EATING, out with children

See also ■ Manners, at mealtime ■ Manners, in public
■ Public behavior

SITUATION
We'd like to take our children to a *real* restaurant—one that serves food on a plate, with silverware—and actually enjoy it for once! But every time we try this kind of adventure, we end up wishing we'd stayed home and ordered pizza.

THINK ABOUT IT
Ironically, this problem is one that gets better with practice, but the experience is so painful, the sessions end up being too far apart to be of value. With a specific game plan, you can increase the odds that your children will behave appropriately in a restaurant.

SOLUTIONS

1 If you are very casual about mealtime manners at home, don't expect your kids to develop table manners just because you happen to be sitting in a restaurant. Practice appropriate restaurant manners at home. On a daily basis, require good manners. Next, on a regular schedule, maybe once a month, have a "formal family dinner." Actually *use* the good china that warms the shelf in your cabinet; cover the table with a tablecloth, and light some candles. Allow your children to help plan the menu, and let them make a centerpiece for the table. Formal meals are likely to become a wonderful family tradition.

2 Don't choose a restaurant based on its menu but rather on its level of child friendliness. What's important? The availability of a children's menu that includes food your kids will actually eat. The absence of a long wait for a table. Booster seats or high chairs. Private booths or eating nooks as opposed to one large open room.

3 Review your expectations for behavior before you enter the restaurant. Be very specific and leave no stone unturned. A sample list of "restaurant rules" follows: Sit in your seat. Use a quiet "inside" voice. Use your silverware, not your fingers. Have nice conversation; no bickering. If you don't like something, keep your comments to yourself and fill up on something else. If you have to use the restroom, ask me privately, and I'll take you.

4 If your kids are starving, they will get quite anxious waiting for their meals to arrive. Consider an appetizer that can be served quickly so that the kids can settle in.

5 If a child's behavior gets out of hand, take her to the restroom or out to the car for a time-out. If she continues to misbehave, don't be afraid to leave the restaurant. Don't stay and suffer. If possible, hire a baby-sitter for that night, or another night soon afterward, and go to dinner without her. Leaving her behind with a sitter will speak volumes about expected behavior.

EATING, overeating

See also ■ Junk food excesses ■ Self-esteem, low

SITUATION
My child seems to be constantly eating and has a voracious appetite.

THINK ABOUT IT
Children go through growth spurts, and they seem to be eating from sunup to sundown. If your child is of healthy height and weight, then don't be concerned about this phase. What is important, though, is to have a variety of healthy choices of food available and a limited amount of junk.

SOLUTIONS
1 If your child's overeating has caused him to be overweight, it's important that you take steps to modify his behavior now to prevent a future lifetime of bad health habits and a continual struggle with weight. Focus on healthy choices, not "dieting." If the weight problem is minimal,

it's best not to make an issue of it with your child. Instead, make subtle changes in the food available to your child. Reduce the amount of junk food in the house, and have a variety of healthy food and snacks available. Do allow your child a few treats now and then, or your child may be driven to sneaking a candy bar behind your back.

2 A child should not diet but, rather, learn to make better food choices and to eat when he's hungry and stop when he's full. Prohibit eating in front of the TV or while reading, because your child will eat much more than necessary without being aware of it. You may need to alter the entire family's eating habits so that high-fat, high-sugar junk food is not handy. A child can eat often, and eat lots, if the foods he's snacking on are the right choices.

3 Find ways to encourage your child to be more active. Enroll him in an athletic program, get him a bicycle or roller blades, and encourage more playtime and movement throughout the day. In addition, limit TV watching to no more than one hour per day, preferably less, as research has proven the more TV that kids watch, the more excess weight they will carry. As your child begins to make healthier food choices and becomes more physically active, he will become more fit and healthy.

4 As a family, avoid using food as a reward or as a means of comfort. Instead of offering an ice cream cone as a reward for a job well done, try to find a nonfood alternative, such as a trip to a favorite park, a few dollars to spend at the toy store, or a special privilege, such as staying up thirty minutes later. Limit food surprises during holidays. For example, fill his Easter basket with a stuffed toy, Silly Putty, marking pens, and a few coins, instead of the usual piles of chocolates and candy. (Do include a few goodies, though!)

5 Model healthy eating habits. Learn more about nutrition. Set a good example for your child, and improve your own life in the process.

6 Some children are predisposed to a larger "normal" weight. Help your child learn to accept himself for who he is and to value himself, and others, for character and personality. Thinness does not equal happiness. Contrary to what advertisers lead you to believe, being thin is not the ticket to becoming rich, happy, and popular.

> **!** If your child is notably overweight, his health and self-esteem can be affected, so please take this situation seriously. In this case, it is best if you search for a specialist to help your child learn how to take control of this area of his life. Check with your local hospital, your pediatrician, a dietitian, or a successful weight-loss clinic that has a special program for children. Look for a program that focuses on health and fitness, as opposed to losing weight. A good program will not only help your child regulate his weight and develop healthy lifestyle habits, it will provide him with a support system for the emotional sides of this issue and teach him how to modify his behavior for lifelong success. (Do not put your child on an adult diet or sign him up for an adult weight-loss program.)

EATING, picky eater

See also ■ Breakfast, won't eat ■ Eating, disorders
■ Junk food excesses ■ Vegetables, won't eat them

SITUATION
My child wants to eat only her two favorite foods: cereal and peanut butter and jelly sandwiches. She eats tiny amounts of any other food and complains about what's put in front of her.

THINK ABOUT IT
As long as your child is healthy and is of normal height and weight, relax your attitude about food. The more you worry and scold, the bigger battleground food will become. In addition, if you also have specific rules about food, and enforce them with a calm demeanor, you'll have fewer battles.

SOLUTIONS
1 Limit the high-fat and high-sugar foods that are available to your child. Offer healthy choices, and don't worry so much about the

occasional food jags. Evaluate your child's diet on a weekly, not daily, basis. Most kids, when given nutritious options, will eat a balanced diet when viewed over a weekly time period.

2 Have a specific schedule for mealtime and snack time, and don't allow eating at other times. If your child is hungry when a meal is served, she'll more likely eat what's put in front of her. Modify mealtimes, if possible, to take advantage of your child's hungry parts of the day. For example, most kids are truly hungry when they walk in the door after school. Take advantage of this by serving dinner at that time and a light snack later. This way, the kids will eat a healthy meal instead of filling up on snacks while they wait for dinner.

3 Serve smaller portions. Your child's stomach is about the size of her clenched fist—smaller than you thought! If you serve meals on smaller plates and include just a small amount of each food, the meal won't appear so intimidating to your child.

4 Serve your child's favorite food as a small side dish to meals. A half of a peanut butter and jelly sandwich makes a fine side dish to roasted chicken!

5 Do you remember eating the dinner your parents set in front of you without a fuss? Most of us do. The reason is that our parents did not feel the ambivalence about serving meals that we do. Try to modify your way of thinking to one simple thought: "This is dinner. If you're hungry, eat; if not, you're excused from the table." Save a plate of dinner for your child, and if she's hungry an hour later, offer the dinner and nothing else. Be consistent with this rule, and your child will begin to eat what's served, just like *you* did when you were a kid.

6 Allow your child the option to have toast or cereal for dinner *one* night a week, passing on a meal he doesn't like. When he knows he can skip *one meal,* he'll make a decision to eat things that aren't favorites and save his "cereal day" for the day you're having the food he likes least.

FEARS, of imaginary things

See also ■ Dark, fear of

SITUATION
My child is afraid of monsters, ghosts, aliens, and other imaginary beasts. She thinks they're lurking under her bed. She knows they live in her closet. She insists she's heard them making noise in the basement. Why has she created all these ghoulies? How can we make them go away?

THINK ABOUT IT
Children who enjoy the fun of Santa Claus, the tooth fairy, and Big Bird also fear the wild things hiding in their closets. Having an imagination is healthy, but the more vivid your child's imagination, the more likely she will create scary creatures in her mind.

SOLUTIONS
1 Begin teaching your child the difference between "real" and "imaginary." When you see something on TV or in a movie that's pretend, point it out. Talk about the differences between the bunny you see at the zoo, her favorite stuffed bunny, and Bugs Bunny. When you're driving in the car or waiting in a line, play a word game where one of you names something and the other tells if it's real or pretend, such as giraffe, mermaid, dolphin, unicorn, and so forth.

2 Children with active imaginations can use pretend devices to get rid of pretend monsters. Give your child a spray bottle with water and tell her it makes monsters disappear or that it makes them turn friendly. Or, believe it or not, one idea that works for many children is to create a large sign that says "No monsters allowed" and hang it on their bedroom doors.

3 Don't overreact. Your intense response to your child's imagined ghoulie will just give it validity. If you're trying to convince your child that there are no monsters in her closet, but every night you check in the closet and announce, "See? No monsters," she'll wonder why you keep looking. Maintain a light, positive attitude while still acknowledging your child's fears.

4 A few simple steps can often help a child feel more comfortable, such as leaving the bedroom door open, giving your child her own flashlight, or leaving the closet door closed (or open, depending on the child). For many kids, sleeping with a bedside light on can ease their fears. (A tiny night-light can cast spooky shadows!) Be flexible. Kids often handle their fears in unusual ways—wanting to sleep on the floor or in the bathtub or singing as they run up the stairs. If it makes them feel safer, why not?

5 Avoid forcing your child to face her fear head-on. For example, don't make her go down the basement stairs to get over her fear of the dark cellar. The poor kid just might have a heart attack!

FEARS, of natural disasters

SITUATION
My child is afraid that we'll have a tornado or an earthquake. She keeps asking questions about these and won't go to sleep until she is reassured that we'll know what to do if anything happens. Night after night, we run through the same sequence.

THINK ABOUT IT
Children hear of a natural disaster happening and assume that the random occurrence puts them in great danger. In addition, in our attempts to keep our children safe, we sometimes, unknowingly, perpetuate the fear. Without the wisdom to understand that events like these are unlikely to happen to them, children may become overly concerned for their own, and their families', safety. Time and maturity will temper your child's fears. In the meantime, try some of the following solutions.

SOLUTIONS

1 Children will pick up emotional cues from you about how to respond to these fears. It's important that you stay calm. Point out any facts that reduce the likelihood of your family being involved in the disaster: "We aren't at risk for a flood because the nearest ocean is more than eighty miles away." If you *are* in an area where the focus of a child's fear *is* a possibility (an earthquake in California, for example), calmly enumerate the steps you and your community have taken to protect yourselves from a disaster. Explain that by being prepared you can handle an emergency.

2 A child who is afraid of a disaster happening, such as a house fire, often needs to talk about it quite a bit before she can sort it all out in her mind and is able to let it go. Avoid superficial answers that are intended to end your child's worry but are not accurate, such as, "We won't have a fire." Instead, provide brief, specific answers to questions, tempering your information to reassure your child. Some of their concerns may seem silly to you but are very serious to them, so take the time to discuss and validate their feelings. Don't allow your child to dwell on the topic. When you feel the conversation should end, simply change the subject or distract your child with an activity.

3 Have a family safety drill. Your child may not want to do this, and may express fear of the drill itself, but once you've completed it, your child will be reassured that everyone knows what to do in an emergency.

4 If your child has experienced a natural disaster you may find that she has lingering fears. It's important that you don't ignore her fears or make her feel silly for having these feelings. Acknowledge her feelings and let her talk about them, but keep control of the conversation; don't let her scare herself. Teach her how to accept the past, but move forward with confidence. You can help by explaining all the precautions that have been taken, by your family and your community, to prevent or prepare for any future emergencies.

FEARS, of real things

SITUATION
I have one child who's afraid of animals and one who's afraid of the vacuum cleaner. I know that they will "grow out of it," but is there a way to speed up the process?

THINK ABOUT IT
Fears are your children's instinctive way of protecting themselves. As they get older and learn more about the world, the fears will fade away. In the meantime, don't tease your children about their fears, trivialize them, or force your children to confront the feared object on their own. Instead, use some of the following solutions to help your children move past their fears.

SOLUTIONS
1 Acknowledge your child's feelings: "I know you don't like big dogs." Admit if you used to be afraid of something when you were a child, and explain that the more you knew, the less afraid you became. Encourage him to talk about the reasons that he's afraid, and discuss the logical reasons that demonstrate that he's safe. Your child can learn that it's OK to be afraid, but he doesn't have to be immobilized by the fear.

2 Don't buy into the idea of a sink-or-swim showdown. Allow your child to overcome the fear one small step at a time. If your child is afraid of the water, start with a walk on the shore, progress to wading, and then pull your child around on a float. Be patient, and don't push him into swimming across the lake if it scares him. If your child is afraid of dogs, start by petting a puppy, visiting a pet store, or watching a dog show on television. Progress to a short visit with a bigger, friendly dog that is tightly controlled by the owner.

3 There is a fine line between empathy and overprotection. Don't rush to protect him from something that is not really harmful. Respond in a calm, unimpressed manner. Show that you have no fear that your child will be harmed, and your child will learn to trust you and become less fearful himself.

4 Read books that give your child information about the object of his fears. Knowledge can often conquer fear. For example, a child who is afraid of spiders will benefit from knowing that there are few spiders that pose any threat to human beings. In addition, if he learns about spiders, they will become familiar, and familiarity will reduce fear.

! Children who demonstrate intense fears and cannot seem to be reassured should see a professional to help them handle these anxieties.

FEARS, of violent situations

SITUATION
My child is afraid he, or someone he loves, will be hurt, murdered, kidnapped, or the victim of other situations of random violence.

THINK ABOUT IT
These fears are a result of children's exposure to the news in the papers, on television, and discussed during adult conversations. Children can be deeply affected by real-life news stories. Responding to these fears by saying "Nothing bad will happen" will not alleviate the fears, because a child who is aware enough of the world to have these fears also knows that you can't guarantee that nothing bad will happen to him or his family. Instead, allow your child to talk through his feelings. Answer his questions honestly but without graphic details.

SOLUTIONS
1 Point out the precautions you have taken to keep your family safe (burglar alarm, fenced yard, watchdog, car phone, and so forth). Talk about your city's police and fire department and how well equipped they are to handle an emergency.

2 Some children feel embarrassed about their fearful feelings. If you ask direct questions about their fears, they may feel silly. Broach the subject by saying, "A lot of kids feel scared about _____. How about you?" An alternative is to ask him how he thinks his friends feel about the situation. His response will usually be a description of his own feelings. Acknowledge the feelings as normal, and open the door for discussion. Let your child's questions lead the direction of the conversation. Don't give your child more information than he needs.

3 If your child is in the room when a frightening news story airs, take the time to talk about it right away. Begin by asking your child what he thinks of what he heard, and let him lead the conversation. He may have misunderstood it or been thinking of something else and missed it entirely. Your child will take his emotional cue from you, so demonstrate a calm, rational response.

4 Explain that the television news and the papers sensationalize events to make them more interesting. (Compare this situation to advertisers who tell you their product is the "best.") Let your child know that violent situations don't happen as often as they appear on TV. Explain that the disproportionate emphasis on violence in the news makes our world seem much more frightening than it really is. If you've had no violent occurrences in your circle of family and friends, you can point that out.

5 If a violent crime has happened to someone you know, or if you live in an area where there is an increased chance of something bad happening, you need to be more sensitive to your child's fears, because they have a valid source. Focus on letting your child know the specific steps you are taking to keep her safe. Teach her how to protect herself. It may be helpful to enroll yourself and your child in a class on personal safety. Look into joining a support group of people who have similar issues to face.

6 Some children are afraid of strangers and fear they may be hurt or kidnapped by someone they don't know. The irony here is that more often children are harmed by someone they know and trust. It's important to teach our children that a person's appearance is not an indication of whether they are good or bad. Teach children to judge *situations* instead of people. Your child will be less fearful if he has knowledge and a plan for self-protection. Teach your child the important ways of protecting himself, such as trusting his feelings, learning to say no, avoiding any adult asking him for directions or assistance, and other valuable safety rules. A great place to find information on what to teach your child is available through your public library or through the National Center for Missing and Exploited Children (NCMEC) at www.missingkids.org.

FIGHTING, with friends, physical

See also ■ Biting, child to child ■ Hair pulling, of others
  ■ Hitting, child to child ■ Meanness
  ■ Siblings, fighting, physical ■ Spitting

SITUATION
My son and his best friend play nicely most of the time. Sometimes, though, they get upset with each other, and I'll see them push or hit one another. How do I stop this behavior?

THINK ABOUT IT
Just like adults, children can get frustrated or angry with a friend. Unlike adults, however, they don't have the self-control or wisdom to handle their frustrations in a socially proper way. As a parent, you'll need to teach the kids how to negotiate and compromise when they have a problem.

SOLUTIONS
1 Ask both children to sit on a sofa at opposite ends or on two adjacent chairs. Tell them that they may get up when they have solved the problem. Don't ask, "What happened?" or "Who started it?" because they each have their own opinion. Unless *you* see one child hit another, hold them equally responsible. If the children are young or inexperienced in handling their own battles, you may need to guide the conversation between them. They may direct their comments to you, looking for you to solve the problem. Just be consistent in letting them know that you are there to help, but they must talk to each other.

2 If you see one child hit (push, scratch, or otherwise hurt) another child, take immediate action. First, make a firm statement; then, ask the aggressor to sit on a chair for a few minutes. Let him decide when he's ready to get up: "Arnold, we don't hit people in this house. Please sit here in the kitchen. You can get up when you can play without hitting."

3 Step between them and make a firm statement: "No pushing. Use words to tell each other what you want." Then, lead the conversation between them: "Arnold, what do you want from Sylvester?"

! If fighting continually happens with one particular friend, it's wise to stop having them play together. If this is unavoidable, plan for the time by organizing specific activities to keep them occupied. Plan a craft or nonphysical game, or rent a video to keep them quietly entertained.

FIGHTING, with friends, verbal

See also ■ Self-esteem, low ■ Siblings, fighting, verbal ■ Tattling
■ Teasing

SITUATION
When my child has a friend over, and disagreements arise, they say cruel and hurtful things to each other.

THINK ABOUT IT
Kids are sometimes honest to the extreme. If your son thinks his friend is acting like a jerk, he'll voice that opinion without a thought to the way that it sounds. If your daughter thinks her friend is purposefully cheating, she'll let the kid know in no uncertain terms what she thinks of that behavior. In addition, kids want what they want, when they want it, and are often quick to try to force a friend to "do it their way." Most children will learn how to be tactful, and how to compromise and negotiate, but it takes time, experience, and direction from an adult.

SOLUTIONS

1 Listen from afar. Often children will work through a verbal disagreement on their own. Step in only if the argument continues on a negative note with no sense of resolution in sight.

2 If the kids are good friends who usually get along well but are having a minor argument, use distraction to end it. Simply walk in the room, pretend you're unaware of what's going on, and ask who wants a snack or if they're ready to play outside. Sometimes a change of scenery is all that's needed to end the bickering.

3 Interrupt the argument, but don't take sides and don't ask what's happening. If they're both really angry, separate the kids for ten or fifteen minutes. Let them know that you think they need a few minutes apart. Depending on the children's personalities and the severity of the argument, you can then either talk to each child separately or bring them together to discuss the situation. Ask them to each state in one sentence what the problem is. Then ask for ideas for solve it.

4 Give the kids a choice. For example, tell them that they can work out the problem and play together nicely or they'll have to end the play date. They will typically choose to work it out. Ask if they would like your help to resolve the issue. If they would, don't place blame and don't focus on finding out "who's right." Instead, let each have a turn talking and direct the conversation toward finding a solution.

FORGETFULNESS

See also ■ Carelessness ■ Procrastination ■ Promises, doesn't keep

SITUATION

My child constantly forgets things: his chores, schoolwork, lunch box, where he leaves things, what time he has to leave for practice. This behavior really bothers me, and because of it, I'm turning into a nag.

THINK ABOUT IT

Is your child *really* forgetful? If so, he would also forget to watch his favorite TV show and he would forget that you promised he could have ice cream after dinner. Perhaps he just needs motivation to remember the less-exciting details in his life. Maybe he needs to learn to look past the current moment and start planning and organizing his life.

SOLUTIONS

1 Don't label your child as "forgetful," as this only reinforces his belief that it's part of his personality. Avoid repeating the phrase, "Don't forget . . . your homework, your coat, your violin, your head . . ." It implies that he will. If you must remind him, change your words to "Please remember!" Don't give too much attention to the forgetfulness; simply go about the business of improving your child's memory. Don't rescue your child when something is forgotten, but let him live with the consequences of his behavior.

2 Buy your child a large wall calendar and a spiral notebook. Help him write down his appointments and assignments. Help him get in the habit of making a "to do" list in his notebook every morning at breakfast. If you know he's neglecting to do something, don't do his remembering for him. Just ask him to check his "to do" list to see if there's anything he needs to take care of.

3 If the forgetfulness occurs with homework and schoolwork, take yourself out of the loop. Let your child's teacher know that you are handing responsibility over to your child in an attempt to get him to do a better job of remembering things. Give the teacher permission to be tough with your child when things are forgotten. One or two poor grades or reprimands from the teacher, and your child will make remembering schoolwork a priority.

4 Determine if your child is using "I forgot" as a way of saying "I don't want to." If so, tell your child that he has certain responsibilities, and "I forgot" will no longer be accepted as a reason for not getting them done. Tell him that "I forgot" now means "I don't want to," and you will impose the same consequence you would for defiance. For example, what if your child is supposed to feed the dog before he leaves for school, but he returns at the end of the day, saying, "I forgot"? Tell him that you did his job for him, and now he'll have to do one of yours, such as fold laundry or wash the kitchen floor.

5 Create more specific routines in your household. Kids thrive on routine and can learn to be more responsible when they follow a specific routine. If you have a morning routine, for example, your child is less likely to forget to make his lunch. Write down your routine activities on lists. For example, the after-school list says "Arrive home. Unpack lunch bag. Have a snack. Do homework. Set table. Have dinner." If you have a varied weekly schedule, it's OK to have a Monday-Wednesday-Friday list and a Tuesday-Thursday list and a weekend list.

FRIENDS, doesn't have any

See also ■ Self-esteem, low ■ Shyness, around children

SITUATION
My child doesn't have any real friends and spends a lot of time alone. How do I solve this problem?

THINK ABOUT IT
First of all, determine if *your child* perceives this as a problem. Many parents are disturbed by a child's lack of friends, but the child is perfectly content with things as they are. Some children are more introverted and comfortable spending time by themselves. If your child seems happy, has healthy self-esteem, and is doing well in school, don't worry about the number of friends she has. If, however, your child is bothered by her lack of friends, review the following solutions.

SOLUTIONS

1 Try to figure out why she says she doesn't have any friends. Sometimes, it may not be true. One or two children in the class may say something unkind, and your child suddenly feels that "nobody likes me." Maybe the mix of kids in the class this year is not suited to your child. If so, look for social interactions outside of the class, such as clubs, sports teams, or neighborhood children. Often, it takes only one comfortable friendship to help a child feel good about herself.

2 Avoid getting overinvolved. You want to help your child feel she can make friends on her own. Take the time to teach social skills and role-play or discuss possible scenarios. For example, if your child says that no one ever plays with her at recess, teach her how to approach other children. Tell her to look for a child playing alone or for several children playing a game that could use more players (such as soccer or baseball). Suggest she approach the kids with a positive attitude and a friendly, "Hi! Can I play?"

3 Encourage your child to invite a friend over to play or to accompany you on an outing. Often, when children have a chance to spend time one-on-one, they form a friendship. This contact will also give you an opportunity to watch your child with another child so that you can see if there is something specific that you can help her with. Perhaps she's reluctant to share her toys or bossy and unwilling to be flexible. If you spot something that may be preventing her from nurturing a friendship, take time after the friend has left to gently point out what you observed and suggest an alternative behavior.

4 Give your child an opportunity to meet kids with interests similar to hers. If she loves to sing, let her participate in the school choir. If she enjoys science, sign her up to participate in the science fair or after-school science program. If she loves horses, sign her up for riding lessons. Children with similar interests have a great foundation for forming a friendship.

FRIENDS, eating all your food

SITUATION
The kids and their friends love to eat. When they congregate at my home, they empty the refrigerator and the pantry.

THINK ABOUT IT
The good news is that the kids feel comfortable at your place. It's great when the kids play at your home. You can keep an eye on them, you know who your children are with, and you know what they're doing.

SOLUTIONS
1 You can limit the damage by designating one specific cabinet for snacks. Fill it with less-expensive options, such as popcorn, apples, pretzels, rice cakes, boxed macaroni and cheese, or noodles. You might also designate an area in the refrigerator, or post a list on the door that lets them know what they can have. Buy the large discount bags of Popsicles or frozen bagel pizzas or great big watermelons. The kids will then know they have one specific place to go for approved snacks, and you'll relax when you see them chewing.

2 Create a house rule that only *your* kids can get into a cabinet or refrigerator. Let them know when and what they can eat. Put them in charge, and give them privileges about making choices, within guidelines you have set.

3 Serve a snack at a preappointed time only. Make up a tray with finger foods, such as cheese and crackers and popcorn. At other times, hang a sign that says "Kitchen is closed," and keep the kids out of the kitchen.

FRIENDS, inappropriate choice of

SITUATION

My child has a friend who is a real negative influence. I don't want her to spend time with this kid, but I don't know the right way to handle it.

THINK ABOUT IT

As children grow, their friendships become very important in their lives. Although peers don't make children who they are, they can influence their decisions and lead them toward making different choices. As your children spend more time with their friends, you'll start to realize how important *your* guidance is in their lives. Make sure you are thoughtfully parenting your child and that you are teaching important values that will shine through, even when influenced by peers and society.

SOLUTIONS

1 Avoid making negative comments about the friend in front of your child or forbidding that they play together. This behavior usually causes your child to defend her friend and may even push them closer together. Instead, focus on your own child's specific behavior. Be firm and consistent in requiring that your child continue to follow family rules and adhere to family values.

2 Invite the friend to your home often so that you can have some control over the children's time together. You will then be able to minimize the negative impact this friend has on your child. Focus on the ways your child, and your family, can become a positive influence in this friend's life. Perhaps you can make an impact that will improve this child's behavior and her future.

3 Look for reasons, not related to the friendship, to decline when this child invites your child out. Conversely, find reasons to have your child spend time with other children that you find to be more suitable companions. Sign your child up for a club, sports team, or other activity so that she has an opportunity to make new friends.

4 Take the time to discuss your feelings with your child, without attacking the friendship. Describe the specific behavior that bothers you, and ask your child what she thinks of it. Use helpful questions to direct the conversation, and allow your child to come to her own conclusions. An example: "When Effie calls her mom on the phone, she sure talks rudely. I wonder why?"

FRIENDS, sleep overs

See also ■ Fighting, with friends

SITUATION

My child wants to have a friend sleep over. I know "sleep overs" are a popular event for kids, but I'm not particularly excited about the idea. Because I know I'll have to give in eventually, what can I do to ensure a relatively peaceful event?

THINK ABOUT IT

Allowing your child to have friends sleep over gives you a great opportunity to learn about your child's friendships. It's an opportunity to peek in on your child's development and learn more about her friends. Sleep overs also give kids a chance to bond with their friends in a deeper way than they can on the school playground. Good preparation can ensure a successful event.

SOLUTIONS

1 When your child asks if a friend can sleep over, it's best to say, "Give me ten minutes to think about it, and I'll let you know." This break gives you time to review your evening plans and analyze your frame of mind to determine if it's a good night for a sleep over. When you choose the right night for company, you and your child will enjoy the time more. If your child says she can't wait for an answer, say, "If you can't wait, then the answer is no."

2 Set the rules in advance. Decide what activities will be allowed, what food will be on the menu, where they will sleep, and what time they'll be expected to go to bed. Be flexible when you can. Review your expectations with your child prior to the friend's arrival. When your child, or the friend, is misbehaving, use simple, specific requests to get the behavior back on track.

3 The kids may get all wired up, and things may start to get too rowdy. If that happens, it's a good time to play a video, bring out the supplies for a craft activity, or move the gang outdoors.

4 Children as old as nine or ten may become uncomfortable at bedtime and miss their homes. Most kids will work through these feelings if you arrange to have them in pajamas and ready for bed at a reasonable hour. Overtired kids tend to be more emotional. If a child seems to be homesick, it often helps to get the kids into bed and read to them. Some kids do well to call home to say good night. If a child seems overly distressed at bedtime, it's OK to call the parent and ask that the child be picked up. Help the child understand that it's perfectly OK to change her mind about sleeping over and that you'll try again another time.

5 What about when your child is invited to another family's home to sleep over? First, make sure your child is ready for a sleep over. Is she excited and eager to pack? Has she stayed at a family member's home before? (Maybe a grandparent's?) Talk to her about what to expect. Answer any questions she may have. Decide on a pick-up time in advance, so she'll know when to expect you. Make sure you know the friend's parents and that you've visited their home. If the child is a classmate, and you don't know the parents, take a few minutes when you drop your child off to meet them. Let your child know in advance that if she's uncomfortable at any point, even if it's really late, it's perfectly OK for her to call you to ask to come home. The first few sleep overs should keep you close to a phone so that you'll be around to reassure her if she gets homesick.

GIFTS, rude response to

See also ■ Birthday, bad behavior as birthday child ■ Manners, at home ■ Manners, in public ■ Parties, bad behavior at

SITUATION

I just attended a friend's child's birthday party and was shocked by the responses the child gave as he opened his gifts. "I already have one of these" or "This isn't the one I wanted." After I was done judging this "nasty" child, I suddenly realized that my daughter's birthday is approaching fast and that she would be just as capable of making some of these comments! How can I prevent this rudeness from happening?

THINK ABOUT IT

Children are not born knowing how to politely respond to gifts, and in their childlike honesty, they can say some pretty rude things. The easiest way to prevent this is through teaching.

SOLUTIONS

1 Have a training session prior to the expected gift giving (before the birthday party or before Grandma arrives at your house). Review the possible situations. "What would you say if you get something you already have—like another Monopoly game?" "What should you say if you get something you don't like at all?" And even "What should you say if it's something you like?" It's amazing what wonderful results occur with a bit of practice.

2 Even though your child's comment appears rude and thoughtless, it never helps to embarrass your child in front of the gift giver. If an impolite comment is made, simply excuse yourself and your child, go to a private place, and point out the error. Suggest something nice to say and return to your guest, allowing your child to save face.

3 If your child isn't aware that his comments are inappropriate it's a sign that you could do a bit more training about manners. This situation may be an indication that there are other areas where your child could benefit from education about appropriate manners.

GIFTS, thank-you notes

See also ■ Birthday, party planning ■ Manners, in public

SITUATION
My child doesn't want to, or forgets to, write thank-you notes for gifts she receives.

THINK ABOUT IT
Doing the things that demonstrate good manners isn't always easy or fun. But good manners will help your child have better friendships, happier family relationships, and an easier time adjusting to the nuances of our society. No child is born with good manners. Manners are definitely something that need to be taught. Over time, and with practice, your child will naturally begin to repeat the things she has been taught from a young age.

SOLUTIONS
1 Soon after your child receives a gift, sit down with her and help her compose and write a thank-you note. Put the paper in front of her, hand her a pen or crayon, and suggest an opening line: "Let's write Grandma's thank-you note. Maybe you want to say . . ."

2 Have your child compose thank-you notes on the computer. Most kids enjoy working on the computer and are comfortable with it. Created with care, a computer-generated note, with an added personal comment, is an acceptable way for kids to show their appreciation.

3 Create a new family rule: You may only play with a gift after the thank-you note has been written.

GIMMEES

See also ■ Manners, in public ■ Materialism ■ Money

SITUATION

I've reached the point where I don't want to take my child into a store. It doesn't matter if we're in a toy store, the grocery store, or the gas station—my kid finds something he "must" have. He usually starts out with a gentle plea, moves to an annoying whine, and eventually works himself up to frantic begging and pleading. Help!

THINK ABOUT IT

It's a simple equation. Take lots of exciting TV commercials, and add a peek at a friend's prized possessions. Multiply the result by attractive store displays. Sprinkle liberally with a child's natural desires, and the result is *the gimmees*. It's a hard lesson, but kids *can* learn to enjoy viewing the finer things in life without demanding that they have a piece of every pie they see.

SOLUTIONS

1 Let your child know in advance what you will or will not be buying that day. An example: "We're going to the mall to buy shoes for school. We may get socks as well, but that's all we'll be purchasing today." When your child makes a request for a sweatshirt, simply remind him, "That's a great shirt, but remember, we're here to buy shoes today."

2 Acknowledge your child's desire for nice things: "Wow! That is an amazing game. It looks like fun." Follow this with a statement of why you'll not be buying it, without sounding reproving, such as, "We're only buying groceries today" or "We're here to buy a gift for your cousin Oishi today."

3 Create a wish list for your child and keep it in your wallet. Whenever your child says, "I want this," make a comment such as, "Do you prefer the blue one or the rainbow-colored one?" *Then*, pull out the list and add the item, saying, "I'll add this to your wish list, and that way I'll remember it when I'm shopping for your birthday next month."

4 Validate your child's wish for new things by using a fantasy statement: "Wouldn't it be great if the owner of this store told us we could fill up our cart with anything we wanted for free!" What typically ensues is a fun game of make-believe.

5 Don't ever say, "We can't afford it." The message is that if you could, you'd buy that $200 pair of shoes! Instead, make a comment that can teach your child something about making money decisions, such as, "Those are pretty, but we choose not to spend $200 on a pair of shoes when we can find ones we like for $30."

GLASSES

SITUATION
My child doesn't want to wear his glasses.

THINK ABOUT IT
For a child to learn to live with an expanse of metal and glass on his face takes some adjustment. It's not just the way it looks, but how it feels and how it affects his view of the world. It's also one more possession to have to keep clean, keep track of, and keep safe.

SOLUTIONS
1 Peer pressure can often influence a child's desire to not wear glasses. One rude comment can make a child self-conscious about glasses. Allow your child to choose frames that he likes and is comfortable wearing. If possible, spend the extra money to buy scratch-proof lenses and flexible, break-resistant frames. If he is comfortable with his choice, and the glasses are lightweight and unobtrusive, he's more likely to wear them.

2 Point out respected friends, sports figures, or movie stars who wear glasses, using casual comments, such as, "Wow, I like the glasses that Harrison Ford has on. They make him look so handsome and rugged. Hey, you know what? They kind of look like yours!"

3 Acknowledge your child's feelings about having to wear glasses. Let him know you understand that they're a nuisance and why he wishes he didn't have to wear them. Also, reinforce the fact that he must really enjoy seeing things so clearly. Let him experiment by looking at something both with and without his glasses, and talk about the difference. If you also wear glasses, you can make this a fun experience you can do together. "Take your glasses off and try to read that sign. Now, put them on. Wow! Cool! What a difference!"

4 Once a child becomes used to wearing glasses, it won't be an issue. When a child first gets glasses, he may honestly forget to put them on. Remind him gently and without anger.

5 Help your child clean his glasses every morning, after school, and after playtime. Dirty or smeared glasses are very unpleasant to wear.

6 Ask your child's eye doctor about contact lenses for kids.

GRANDPARENTS, and spoiling

See also ■ Baby-sitters, grandparents as

SITUATION
If you ask my kids "What's the magic word?", they'll tell you in a heartbeat: "Grandma." She allows them to eat a never-ending string of junk food, never enforces a rule, and she's always buying them the latest new toy. And, believe it or not, *she's* a tough cookie compared to Grandpa!

THINK ABOUT IT
All children benefit from being loved unconditionally and spoiled completely by someone important in their lives. And grandparents deserve a chance to enjoy their grandchildren without observing all the rules that

applied when they were raising you. If your children see their grandparents infrequently, for example, once a month or less, try not to obsess about the spoiling. But you can use some of the following ideas to make the relationship more peaceful for all of you. (If the grandparents are regular caregivers, the rules change.)

SOLUTIONS

 Let the kids know that when they're with their grandparents, they can enjoy the time as a vacation from the normal rules. However, once they return home, it's business as usual. If they seem wired up after a visit, calmly let them know that although things are different at Grandma's, at home they need to follow the rules, as always.

2 If a few rules are very important to you, let the grandparents know that. When you approach them, however, don't judge or condemn. Instead, in a polite, respectful way, state your wishes. An example: "Dad, the kids really enjoy when you take them to the beach for the day, and I enjoy the break. Please remember to put lots of sunscreen on them first thing in the morning. Without it, they get sunburned and the pain lasts for a week, and it's bad for their skin." As an extra encouragement to have the rule followed, offer to help out in some way: "Would you like me to put a bottle of sunscreen in their beach bag for you?" Follow up by discussing the issue with the kids and asking them to "help" Grandpa remember the sunscreen.

3 Remind *the kids* of the rules when the grandparents are within hearing distance, such as, "Remember! Only one treat after dinner."

GRANDPARENTS, buy the kids too much stuff

SITUATION
Every time the kids' grandparents come over, they come bearing gifts. It's always the type of toys and junk that the kids already have too much of. Is there a graceful way to put an end to this?

SOLUTIONS

1 Let the grandparents know that you appreciate their generosity with the children. Tell them that because they enjoy buying things for the kids, you've taken the liberty of making a list of things that you think would make good gifts. Include clothing sizes, school supply needs, advertisements about children's book clubs, and other helpful information.

2 Suggest that the grandparents buy the kids a few shares of stock in a company that interests the children, such as Pepsi, Disney, or Toys "R" Us. Teach the kids how to watch the changes in their stock. Grandparents can then add to the kids' portfolio with each gift. This strategy will be teaching the children something new and investing in their future.

3 In a gentle, loving way, tell the grandparents that the best gifts are the time they spend with the kids. If they want to, they can take them to a ball game, a play, or a day at the park.

GRANDPARENTS, disagreements with

SITUATION

Whenever we spend time with my parents, I usually end up getting upset over the way they handle my kids. They think they know more than I do about everything, even though lots of their ideas about child rearing are outdated. Is there any way I can get them to back off?

THINK ABOUT IT

Your parents think they did a pretty great job raising you, and they feel they have a lot of wisdom to share. Their approach may not always be the best, and their facts may, indeed, be outdated. Usually, though, their interference is presented with the best intentions—they love you and their grandchildren. Using a few subtle techniques, you can make your visits with them much more enjoyable.

SOLUTIONS

1 Avoid blaming or accusing, because this will cause the grandparent to become defensive. Instead, use "I" statements to explain your feelings, and include a specific request for a change. For example, don't say, "You always let the kids eat too much junk." A better choice would be, "I feel it's important to limit the kid's sugary treats. I'd really appreciate if you'd help me by offering them healthy foods as a snack. They like pretzels, bagels, and peaches quite a bit."

2 Ask helpful questions to find out what's motivating the grandparent to act in the way she is. Be empathic and a good listener, and you may learn a few important things. For example, you might ask, "Do you ever find it difficult to say 'no' to Satoshi?" You may be surprised to discover that she's frustrated and would welcome ideas about how to handle your child.

3 Show by your example how you would like things to happen. Address your comments to your child, instead of to the grandparent, knowing full well that you will be overheard. An example: "Rachel, you know that our rule is 'No jumping on furniture.' You may sit or lie on the sofa."

4 Give specific ideas to the grandparent under the guise of "sharing something exciting that I learned." Read a section from a parenting book or an article. Quote an expert that you saw on TV, or tell a story about a friend who handled an issue in a way you thought was admirable. Don't specifically say that this is something the grandparent needs to hear, just share the idea with enthusiasm.

5 Make peace with your differences. You can learn to accept the different ways that you each deal with your children. Don't sweat the small stuff, and save your energy for dealing with the bigger issues.

HABITS, bad

See also ■ Clothing, chewing of ■ Hair pulling, of self
■ Nail biting or picking ■ Nose picking

SITUATION

My daughter has started making a strange sniffing noise. She does it whenever she's bored or nervous. How can I get her to stop it?

THINK ABOUT IT

Bad habits such as sniffing, hair twisting, nail biting, ear pulling, scratching, making strange noises, or nose picking are often initially done to relieve anxiety and bring comfort. Repeated often enough, they become habits. With a specific plan, you can help your child stop her habit.

SOLUTIONS

1 Nagging or reprimanding the child won't stop the habit and may, in fact, make it worse. Talk with your child and bring her attention to the habit (she may not be aware of how often she does it). Explain the reasons you'd like her to stop. Try to find the underlying cause of the behavior. Talk to her about her feelings. Show her—via a mirror or a demonstration—what the habitual action looks like to others. Once your child becomes more aware of the habit, she'll be more willing to try to stop. Agree to a subtle, gentle reminder that you'll use to ask her to stop, such as a tap on her arm or a code word. Keep in mind that even if she is trying to stop the habit, it's difficult; and you'll need patience to see her through this.

2 Notice the times your child demonstrates the habit most, such as when she's sitting in the car, watching TV, or in social situations. During those times, give her something to funnel her nervous energy, such as a string of beads, Silly Putty, a cat's cradle string, or a smooth rock. You may even teach her how to knit, crochet, or do needlepoint or embroidery. Once your child has broken the pattern of behavior, it will no longer be automatic for her to engage in it as she participates in her usual activity.

3 Enlist your child's cooperation by talking gently with her about the habit. Don't just assume she would like to quit! Once she has agreed to make an effort, your encouragement and consistent, gentle reminders will do more good than nagging or embarrassing her.

4 Set up an incentive for abstaining. Agree to a specified time period and a specific behavior modification. One plan is to give your child ten nickels (or pennies or dimes, depending on your child's age) first thing in the morning. Tell her that any time you see her engaged in the behavior, you'll ask for a nickel. At the end of the day, she can keep any of the nickels that are left.

5 Teach your child relaxation skills. When your child realizes that she's doing the habitual behavior, teach her to stop, sit down, close her eyes, and breathe slowly for a few minutes.

! If your child makes noises, has uncontrolled verbal outbursts, or has unusual body tics, it may indicate a more serious problem known as Tourette's syndrome. If you have any suspicions that your child's problems are more than typical childhood habits, discuss your concerns with your physician.

HAIR BRUSHING

SITUATION
My daughter hates to have her hair brushed. She cries, complains, and fusses every time I even come near her with a brush.

THINK ABOUT IT
This situation usually starts with *one* bad hair day. It's the day your daughter has a big snarl in her hair. You tug and pull. She complains. You yell.

And from that point on, she's on the defensive every time you attempt to brush her hair. Her attitude is contagious, and soon you *both* hate the hair-brushing routine. Take a deep breath, try a few of these suggestions, and soon the problem will be history.

SOLUTIONS

1 Demonstrate a no-nonsense, matter-of-fact attitude. Having her hair brushed every day is not optional. Just do it, and ignore the fussing. Eventually, she'll learn to live with it. Of course, it helps if you're gentle and use a detangling conditioner or a detangling hair spray.

2 Allow your child to choose a variety of hair ribbons, barrettes, or other hair jewelry. Allow her to make the decision each day about what to wear in her hair and how to have it styled.

3 Style your child's hair while she's watching TV, reading a book, or playing a game. If she's otherwise occupied, she'll pay less attention to what's going on with her hair.

4 Teach your child how to brush her own hair. At about age six, a child can begin to learn this task. At first, you'll have to "finish up," but, with practice, she can take over her own hair care.

5 Once in a while, play "hairstylist" with your daughter. Let her style your hair, and you do hers, in unusual styles. Take pictures and make it a fun game.

6 If all else fails, and you're really tired of dealing with the hair issues, have her hair cut in a short, simple style. There are many cute short hairstyles. Her hair will grow again, and when she's a bit older, she'll be more ready to manage a longer style.

HAIRCUTS

SITUATION

My child hates to have his hair cut. He cries, fusses, and carries on each time I attempt to cut his hair.

THINK ABOUT IT

Is it *really* the haircut that your child objects to? Has he had a bad haircut experience? Or is it the fact he must sit perfectly still and bored while you hover, clip, and comb for far longer than he's willing to sit? Once you've figured out the reason for his aversion to haircuts, you can make a plan to overcome his objections.

SOLUTIONS

1 Plant your child in front of his favorite movie while you cut his hair. When he has something to watch and distract him, it will keep him happy while you tend to business.

2 If you are ambivalent or tentative about giving your child a haircut, he'll pick up on your wishy-washy emotions and be more than willing to give you a fight. Use a matter-of-fact, businesslike approach to haircuts. They need to be done; there are no options. It doesn't hurt, it doesn't take that long, and your child *will* live through a haircut (and so will you). Your attitude will affect your child's response.

3 When possible, give your child choices about the style to be cut, when to have it cut, or who to cut it. "Do you want Mom to cut your hair or the barber?"

4 Choose a hairstylist who is good with kids and a location that's kid friendly. Some shops even offer unusual seats, such as race cars or plastic ponies for children to sit on.

5 Try a longer hairstyle that requires fewer haircuts for a while until your child is better able to deal with haircuts.

HAIR PULLING, of others

See also ■ Fighting, with friends, physical ■ Siblings, fighting, physical

SITUATION

When my daughter gets angry with her friend, she sometimes grabs a fistful of hair and yanks. I've lectured and yelled at her, but it doesn't seem to help.

THINK ABOUT IT

Hair pulling, biting, and hitting are all typical behaviors of young children who have not learned how to control their emotions. It would be wonderful if children were born with refined social skills, but, of course, that's not the case. It's up to us to teach our kids how to handle their anger in appropriate ways.

SOLUTIONS

1 Watch your child closely during playtime. When you see her becoming frustrated or angry, take the time to intervene. Redirect her attention until her emotions level out.

2 It's one thing to tell a child what *not* to do. It's another thing entirely to teach her what *to do*. Take the time to teach your child how to express anger or frustration safely. You can do this via role-playing, reading books about feelings and anger, and discussing the various choices we have when we're angry. Make sure you discuss these ideas during a quiet, private time, not in the middle of a battle!

3 Every time you see the child pull another child's hair, immediately step in. Make a firm statement of displeasure: "No hair pulling; time-out." Guide the child to a chair or other time-out place and have her sit for a few minutes to calm down. Or you can announce, "You may get up when you can play without pulling anyone's hair." This break gives her an opportunity to "get herself together." By telling her that she can get up when she's ready, you let her know that *she* is responsible for controlling her own behavior.

Often the hair puller gets so much attention that the action becomes a way of gaining the spotlight. Instead, give more attention to the child who was hurt. After a brief statement—"Delilah. No hair pulling!"—turn your back to that child and give attention to the child whose hair was pulled: "Come here, Samson. Mommy will give you a hug and read you a book."

HAIR PULLING, of self

See also ■ Habits, bad

SITUATION
My daughter has developed a habit of pulling and twirling her own hair. She used to do it only when she was falling asleep. But, lately, I've noticed her doing it during the day as well. How do I get her to stop?

THINK ABOUT IT
A habit such as hair pulling is usually done to relieve tension and bring comfort, and it often becomes a subconscious action. Therefore, nagging or reprimanding the child won't stop the habit. Be sensitive and creative, and you can help your child stop the behavior.

SOLUTIONS
1 Style your child's hair so that it is up off her face and pulled back. Allow her to choose some pretty hair barrettes or ribbons. Buy her a doll with long, brushable hair and hair accessories.

2 Have a talk with your child and bring her attention to the habit, because she may not be aware of how often she does it. Explain the reasons you'd like her to stop. Let her express her feelings and thoughts. Agree to a subtle, gentle reminder that you'll use to ask her to stop, such as a tap on her arm.

3 Notice the times your child pulls her hair the most, such as when she's sitting in the car or watching TV. During those times, give her an alternative object to keep her hands busy, such as a string of beads, Silly Putty, or a smooth rock.

4 If the hair pulling occurs when she's falling asleep, create a comforting bedtime routine that includes a warm bath, story time, or soft music. Give her a stuffed animal to cuddle as she falls asleep. Enlist her help in stopping the habit.

5 Try to determine if the habit is related to stress in your child's life. It may be a temporary stress, such as the birth of a sibling, the beginning of a new school year, or a recent divorce. If so, be loving and supportive, and give your child a little more one-on-one time to help her through the tough time. It's possible the stress is related to a too-busy schedule, and your child isn't getting enough "down time" to just relax and regroup. If so, try to build some low-key relaxing time into her schedule.

! If nothing else works, take your child to a hair salon and get her a short, stylish cut. It's best if you don't even mention the habit as the reason for the cut. By the time her hair grows back, the habit should be forgotten. Compliment her on her pretty new do!

HATE, expressions of

See also ■ Disrespect ■ Meanness ■ Respect, teaching
■ Self-esteem, low ■ Siblings, hateful emotions

SITUATION
When my son gets angry with me, he yells, "I hate you! I wish you weren't my mother!" and other hurtful things.

THINK ABOUT IT
When children feel angry and powerless, they sometimes resort to hateful words to express their feelings. These outbursts should not be taken at face value. In other words, your child doesn't really mean he hates *you*—he

means he's extremely angry that he can't have his way, and you're the one imposing the rules! These reasons don't mean you should tolerate the behavior. But when you look at it this way, you can temper your own emotions so that you can take control of the situation.

SOLUTIONS

1 Children need to be taught that it is OK to have angry feelings but that there are acceptable and unacceptable ways to express their anger. It's usually best to walk away from a child who uses such strong language after making a short parting comment: "I won't stay and listen to you talk like that." Allow some time to pass so that both you and the child can calm down. Then, tell your child that his outburst was unacceptable. Instead of telling your child what you don't want, teach what alternatives you *will* allow, such as, "I'm really mad at you for saying no."

2 If this is an unusual behavior for your normally respectful child, you might want to respond in a calm manner: "That language is unacceptable. I know you're smart enough to come up with an acceptable alternative."

3 Determine if your child is hearing someone else talk this way, perhaps a friend. Talk about this person's behavior, and ask your child what he thinks of it. This is a good time to have a chat about the power and meaning of words, what you feel is acceptable, and what you will accept as alternatives to hurtful comments.

4 Let your child know in advance that if he uses those kinds of expressions with you, he'll be restricted to his room. The length of time would be determined by the intensity of the words; for example, "I hate you!" might warrant a one-hour solitary confinement. Swearing at you in a verbally aggressive way would warrant spending the remaining day in his room. Should he not follow orders and go to his room when asked, he'll lose a specific privilege (such as watching TV, talking on the phone, or going outside after school). Once you've set the limits, be calm and consistent when enforcing them.

HITTING, child to adult

See also ■ Anger, child's ■ Arguing, with parent ■ Cooperate, won't
■ Disrespect ■ Introduction ■ Respect, teaching

SITUATION

When my child is upset with me because I've said no to some earth-shattering request (such as having candy before dinner), she gets angry and hits me. I've tried to explain to her that hitting is wrong, but she keeps doing it.

THINK ABOUT IT

Hitting an adult is a serious offense and should be treated as such and nipped in the bud. I've heard many a parent respond in a timid voice, "Honey, sweetie pie, luv bunches, it's not nice to hit Mommy. So please don't hit me any more, OK snookems?" Avoid, at all costs, using this whining, pleading voice or lecturing the child, as these can be misconstrued as an interesting form of attention. It also will lessen the child's perception of the severity of the misbehavior and may actually increase the hitting incidents.

SOLUTIONS

1 Every time the child hits, immediately take the child by the shoulders, look her in the eye, and say in a firm, unpleasant voice, "No hitting; time-out." Guide the child to a chair or other time-out place and announce, "Stay here until I tell you to get up." After a few minutes, when both you and your child have calmed down, you can give the child permission to get up. It's OK to make a brief statement to recap the situation, but avoid a long follow-up lecture because it doesn't serve the intended purpose of "teaching a lesson." It's more important to respond appropriately each time the child hits.

2 If you suspect that your child is hitting to gain your attention, stop rewarding her with the attention she seeks. Every time the child hits you, announce in a firm, unpleasant voice, "No hitting." Then, end the interaction with her and walk away for a little while. The child will learn that hitting causes you to "go away" and thus does not suit the purpose of the hit—to get you to give in to her demand or to get you to give her attention.

3 Make sure you are not "play hitting" the child at any time. Children will do as they see done, even though they may do it at inappropriate times. If you are in the habit of playful roughhousing with your child and allowing her to "hit" you in fun, she may find it difficult to draw the line between the play behavior and the angry behavior.

! **A child who continues to hit may benefit from time with a family counselor or therapist. A trained professional can determine the reasons the child is hitting and help the family work out a plan to stop the behavior.**

HITTING, child to child

See also ■ Anger, child's ■ Fighting, with friends, physical ■ Friends ■ Meanness ■ Siblings, fighting, physical

SITUATION
My child hits other kids when he gets mad or frustrated.

THINK ABOUT IT
You aren't alone. Many children will resort to hitting a playmate during an angry moment. Kids exhibit this behavior because of a lack of knowledge, wisdom, and self-control. Kids *will* get angry—we can't prevent that. It's our job to teach them appropriate ways to deal with their anger.

SOLUTIONS
1 Watch the child closely during playtime. When you see him becoming frustrated or angry, intervene and redirect the child's attention to another activity until he calms down.

2 Teach the child how to express anger or frustration safely by role-playing or discussing options. It can also be helpful to read children's books about anger together, and then talk about what you've read.

3 Every time the child hits, immediately and gently take the child by the shoulders, look him in the eye, and say in a firm voice, "No hitting; time-out." Or "When you hit, you sit." Guide the child to a chair or other time-out place and have him sit quietly until you feel he has calmed down. (A good rule of thumb to determine the length of a time-out is one minute per year of age.) Another option is to announce, "You may get up when you can play without hitting." If the child gets up and hits again, say, "You are not ready to get up yet," and direct the child back to time-out.

4 Make sure you are not "play hitting" the child at any time. Children will do as they see done, even though they may do it at inappropriate times. Often young children who wrestle with a parent will then use these same actions during nonwrestling times. Also, pay attention to the television or movies the child is watching that involve hitting or other violence. Young children can become immune to the impact of the violence and also model what they see as an appropriate way of handling anger.

5 Give more attention to the victim than the hitter. After a brief statement—"No hitting"—turn your back to the hitter and give attention to the victim. Often, the hitter gets so much attention that hitting becomes a way of gaining the spotlight.

6 Teach the child how to use positive physical touches, such as back rubs or foot massages. One preschool engages the school "bullies" to become back rubbers for the toddler group at naptime. Under direct supervision, children who are more physical gain a positive outlet for their physical energy.

7 Teach the child to clap his hands together ten times whenever he feels an urge to hit another child. This action gives him an immediate physical outlet for his angry emotions and helps him learn to keep his hands to himself. Reward him with praise any time you see him doing this successfully.

! A child who continues to hit may benefit from time with a family counselor or therapist. A trained professional can determine the reasons the child is hitting and help the family work out a plan to stop the behavior.

HOME ALONE, child is

See also ■ Home alone, when is a child ready to be

SITUATION
I think my children are ready to be home alone for short periods of time. I'm wondering how to make this a successful endeavor.

THINK ABOUT IT
Letting children stay home alone is a big step for everyone in your family. It gives your children a new level of responsibility, and it gives parents a new-found, eagerly anticipated, exuberant feeling of freedom. I know it sounds liberating, but don't rush into this big change. Take your time to plan and prepare for success.

SOLUTIONS

1 With your children's help, create a list of rules that will apply when they're home alone. Include specific "dos"—such as homework, chores, and so forth—and "don'ts"—such as answer the door, use the stove, or tie up younger siblings. Include a list of acceptable activities, specify the amount of TV they can watch, and state what foods they can eat. The more you think ahead and cover possible issues up front, the less likely it is you'll have to deal with such problems later.

2 Provide your children with emergency training. Many hospitals, YMCAs, or schools offer classes for children who want to baby-sit. These are a good option, as they typically cover all standard emergency procedures. Have *all* your children take the training, not just the oldest one. Make certain there is a list of important telephone numbers near the phone in an easy-to-find location (not buried under a pile of old mail). Write the main emergency number on the telephone itself. (I've heard of *adults* who forget the sequence of 9-1-1 when faced with an emergency situation.) If your city does not have a 911 system that provides your address upon calling, make sure your address and directions to your home are also written on the emergency pad. Provide your children with the telephone number of an adult you know and trust who is close by, particularly if you're quite a distance away from home.

3 Discuss or role-play various situations that may come up. Ask "What would you do if . . ." questions to be certain your children are prepared. A few examples of those situations you would want to review follow: (1) What if you lose your house key? (2) What if someone comes to the door? (3) What if you're hungry? (4) What if you need help with your homework? (5) What if Dad's not home exactly at 5:00? (6) How will you answer the phone? (7) When would it be OK to call me at work?

4 If you have more than one child, decide in advance if one of them is "in charge" or if they hold equal responsibility. Clearly identify the rules that will apply. Decide how arguments will be resolved in your absence.

HOME ALONE, when is a child ready to be

See also ■ Home alone, child is

SITUATION
I'm trying to decide if my children are ready to be home alone for short periods of time. I'm thinking specifically of the time after school until I arrive home from work or in the evening when I attend a meeting or go out to dinner.

THINK ABOUT IT
As your children get older and require less one-on-one parental supervision, it's tempting to bypass the hassle of arranging for a sitter, not to mention paying for the service. Keep in mind, though, that this decision should not be based on a "best case" scenario, but, rather, it should be based on your child's ability to handle an unforeseen emergency in your absence.

SOLUTIONS

1 The first thing to consider as you determine if your child is ready to be home alone is your child's age. There are laws that dictate how old a child must be before spending time alone without an adult. Check the laws in your area. Typically, a child should be age twelve or older before you consider leaving her alone, even if the law permits a child of a younger age to go unchaperoned.

2 The second thing to consider prior to allowing a child to be home alone is the child's level of responsibility. Take a look at how the child handles homework, chores, and personal responsibilities. Does the child display trustworthiness and the ability to self-manage? Is your child emotionally mature and capable of good judgment? Some children show these traits as young as age ten; others, not until thirteen, fourteen, or older. In addition to considering these issues, check with your child to make certain *she* feels ready to stay home alone. Sometimes, children are responsible and capable but have fears about being alone in the house. These fears should be respected.

3 The third consideration, if you have more than one child, is whether the children have a usually peaceful relationship. Of course, all siblings bicker from time to time, but if the children fight constantly, physically or intensely, it is unwise to leave them alone.

4 The fourth area of consideration is the safety of your home and neighborhood. Do you have a burglar alarm system that can be set? Are there neighbors living close by that you know and trust? Are you next door to a high school, video arcade, or a tavern that attracts unsavory characters? Be honest with yourself. Don't overlook a bad situation because you feel leaving your children home alone is your only choice. If something bad happened to your children, you would realize that there were, indeed, other options.

5 Once you have decided that the situation is right for your child to be home alone, begin with short periods of time. Make certain you or another trusted adult who is close by are available by phone. Gradually increase the amount of time as you and your child become comfortable with the arrangement.

Remember to check for laws in your area that govern unsupervised children. You don't want to put your family in an unlawful position.

HOMEWORK, how to create a routine

SITUATION
Getting my kids to do homework is a big hassle and an energy drain. By the time report cards are sent home, I usually feel there should be a page that grades *me* for nagging, begging, coercing, and reminding. (I'm sure I'd get an *A* for effort but a *C* for results!)

THINK ABOUT IT
Your *A* for nagging, begging, coercing, and reminding makes it obvious that your children depend on this particular form of "guidance." If you'll put some effort into changing the rituals that you've developed, you'll find that your children can, indeed, become responsible for their own homework.

SOLUTIONS

1 Give your children responsibility and ownership of their homework. It should be clearly understood that homework is their job and one of their priorities. It's your job to create an environment that is conducive to getting homework done and to act as a manager and a coach. Don't hover or get overly involved with the actual work, because the more responsibility the parent takes, the less responsibility the children will assume themselves.

2 Establish a regular time and place for homework to be done. For example, immediately after the dinner dishes are cleared and the kitchen cleaned, the routine is to bring all homework to the kitchen table. To maintain the pattern, and thus create a habit, when the child has no homework, the time can be used to read or write letters or thank-you notes. If a sports or music lesson occurs at that time a few days a week, have a specific alternate time for those days.

3 Create a pleasant homework environment. Make sure the table is clean and clear, have ample supplies at hand, and include a healthy snack and a beverage. Avoid using this time to reprimand, nag, or complain. Some children work better with quiet music playing in the background or a window open for fresh air. Some kids are easily distracted and need absolute quiet. Try to figure out what works best for your children. It may not necessarily be your preference but choose the best environment to suit your child's personality.

4 Avoid homework-related rewards and punishments. These take the focus away from the learning process and create additional stress as your children try to avoid the punishment or earn the rewards. Or, even worse, your child decides the punishment isn't so bad or the reward isn't so great, so he continues to march to the beat of his own drummer.

HOMEWORK, not getting it done

See also ■ Dawdling ■ Homework, how to create a routine
■ Procrastination

SITUATION
My child knows all the homework excuses. "It's not due yet." "I don't have any." "I forgot it." "The dog ate it." The bottom line is that her grades have been affected because she's not getting her homework done.

THINK ABOUT IT
For many kids, doing homework is their fifty-sixth favorite thing to do. It comes somewhere between dropping a bowling ball on their toes and picking up the dog doo-doo in the backyard. In other words, given the choice, they'll avoid it at all costs. Your job, then, is to convince them that, regardless of their personal feelings, homework is important, required, and not a topic open for negotiation.

SOLUTIONS

1 Meet with the teacher so that you have a clear understanding of what is expected of your child and how much time homework should take. Make sure your child is doing well and keeping up in class and that the only problem is homework related. (Sometimes, reluctance to do homework is an indication of a bigger problem at school. It's best to rule this possibility out first.)

2 Set aside the "homework hour" to do your own paperwork, bill paying, or newspaper reading. Sit at the same table with your child. Be available to answer questions, but otherwise, stay focused on your own work. Your presence will "encourage" your child to complete her homework. If your child "doesn't have any homework," this doesn't excuse her from homework hour. Just let her know that you'll be happy to assign an extra-credit project to occupy her during the required homework time. She may remember an assignment that she can work on.

3 Provide your child's teacher with a stack of index cards. Ask the teacher to send home an index card each Friday with the simple notation, "Homework done (or not done) for this week," along with the teacher's signature. Let your child know that if the work has not been done for the week, then she'll have to complete all work Saturday prior to any playtime. (If your child is on a sports team, in a music group, or takes a Saturday class, this rule would apply to the time prior to or following the Saturday event.) Announce that if no index card is returned on Friday, you will need to assume that the homework was not done. If the paperwork is not at home, have your child complete a book report for you on the most recent book she read. (This requirement will encourage your child to remember the index card next Friday and is an excellent way to enhance her reading and writing skills!)

4 Hire an older child (perhaps a neighbor) to become your child's "homework coach." Often, a teacher can recommend a student from a higher grade at school. This older child can bring her own homework to your home (or vice versa) and sit beside your child during homework time. The "coach" is then close at hand to answer questions or provide guidance. Just be sure a parent is nearby so that this doesn't become a visiting session.

HOMEWORK, perfectionism

See also ■ Dawdling ■ Homework, how to create a routine
■ Perfectionism

SITUATION
My child takes an excessive amount of time to do her homework. She erases a lot and becomes frustrated over even the simplest mistakes. I don't want to encourage her to be sloppy, but I think there's a point when she should just get it done without obsessing over every little letter she writes.

THINK ABOUT IT
There are lots of reasons that children develop homework-perfection-itis. It can be helpful to try to pinpoint your child's reason. Is this typical of her personality? Has this behavior created undue attention? Is she in "over her head" and confused, or is she using the homework-perfection-itis to procrastinate doing work she doesn't like or doesn't understand? Whatever the reason, making and using a plan is essential to overcoming this behavior.

SOLUTIONS
1 If your child doesn't display these same behaviors at school, it's possible she is getting too much attention at home in regard to her homework. Let your daughter know that homework is considered "practice." Discuss with her the goals of her assignments. Talk to her about "priorities"; for example, her final book report needs to be especially neat, but the first draft can be less perfect. Be available to answer questions, but don't hover. If she asks for your help, provide simple, specific answers with no mention of the work she has already completed. If you aren't hovering, the only person affected by her dawdling is *her*. When she finds that she can actually complete her homework in less time, with less perfection, and still get good grades, she'll feel confident in moving a little more quickly.

2 Instead of saying things like "Stop taking so long!", provide an incentive for her to finish up by using the "If/Then" technique: "If you're done with your homework before 5:00, we'll play a game together before I make dinner."

3 Avoid "you" statements: "You don't have to erase that and do it over." Instead talk about yourself: "If that were my paper, I'd leave it just the way it is and move on to the next one." Or ask a helpful question that leads her to make her own discovery, such as, "Do you think it matters that . . ." or "Do you think your teacher expects . . ."

4 Find out from your child's teacher how much time the daily homework should take. Based on what you learn from the teacher, set a specific amount of time you will allow for homework. (Add a few minutes to the teacher's longest estimate so that your child doesn't get stressed over your limit.) Before your child sits down to begin homework, tell her you are setting the timer for thirty minutes. When it rings, homework time is over for the day. Ask her to take a few minutes to think about and plan how to best use that time. This exercise will help keep your child focused and on track. Remind her halfway through that she's got fifteen minutes left. Otherwise, don't nag!

HOMEWORK, sloppy or rushed work

See also ■ Carelessness ■ Homework, how to create a routine

SITUATION
My child rushes through his homework. The work is sloppy and careless. I know he's capable of doing a better job.

THINK ABOUT IT
Many kids see homework as an interruption of all the fun things they want to do after school. Some see it as a tireless repetition of things they already did at school. In either case, the result is that they rush to get it over with.

SOLUTIONS

1 Set a minimum amount of time for homework (based on the teacher's estimate of how much time should be spent on homework). Set a timer. Tell your child he cannot get up until the timer rings. If he finishes his homework, you can provide him with additional work to fill up the rest of the time. (Purchase educational workbooks from a bookstore, or get some from the teacher; create work sheets duplicating the types of tasks included in the homework, such as math problems; or ask your child to create sentences with vocabulary or spelling words.)

2 Convey an attitude of importance about homework. Review all your child's work when it is complete. Make positive comments about things that are done well. Show great interest, ask questions about the work, and let your child know that his work is important to you. Positive attention can often give a child the encouragement needed to improve the results of his work.

3 Children who are bored will often compensate by producing sloppy work. Meet with your child's teacher to see if this may be the problem. If it is, encourage the teacher to provide a slight variation on the homework to better suit your child. Avoid simply assigning *more* homework, because that just exacerbates the problem.

4 Children with too many extracurricular activities sometimes become overwhelmed and rush through work so they can fit everything into their day. If this is the case, have your child choose one outside activity to focus on and save the rest for summer vacation.

HUMOR, inappropriate

See also ■ Bathroom jokes ■ Clowning ■ Manners ■ Respect, teaching

SITUATION

My child repeats crude jokes, uses bathroom humor, and makes jokes at other people's expense. He sounds like a little stand-up comic on a

bad day! How can I curb this unappealing penchant for inappropriate humor?

THINK ABOUT IT

Many children go through a phase of experimenting with humor. Often, one accidental comment is perceived by friends as very funny and gives the child the feeling of power that we get from making other people laugh. The child then repeats this brand of humor, hoping to continue the positive response.

SOLUTIONS

1 The easiest way to move a child quickly through this phase is by teaching what is appropriate and what is not. When an inappropriate comment is made, simply look your child in the eye and say in a serious voice, "That's inappropriate." Or "That's not something we joke about in this house."

2 Try to avoid an agitated reaction to inappropriate humor. Your shocked response may be enough to keep your child interested in repeating the behavior. A better response is to give your child a look of distaste and displeasure, with a comment such as, "I can't imagine why people would think that's funny." If your child feels embarrassed by his comment, the behavior may not recur.

3 Pay close attention to the television and movies your child is watching. Often, kids pick up this kind of humor from the media. You can prohibit inappropriate shows or discuss them with your child.

4 Watch for adults who are modeling this kind of behavior. Sometimes, a family member or friend is receiving lots of attention by repeating crude stories. If so, try to limit what is said in front of young children. Because you can't prevent your older children from hearing such things, discuss your feelings with them about what you hear. Label inappropriate humor, and talk about the reasons people might use it. Discuss your family values, and identify what things are acceptable in your family.

INTERRUPTING

See also ■ Listening, not ■ Manners ■ Respect, teaching
■ Telephone interruptions

SITUATION

My husband and I haven't finished a complete sentence since last July! Our children interrupt our conversations constantly. Even while I'm asking them to wait until we're done talking, they're busy interrupting my request!

THINK ABOUT IT

Many parents admonish kids for interrupting, but in the same breath, they respond to the child's interrupted request! Interrupting is habit-forming. Like many annoying behaviors, once kids figure out that they can "get away with it," the behavior will continue.

SOLUTIONS

1 Teach your child how to determine if something warrants an interruption. Children often are so focused on their own needs that they don't really absorb the fact that they're being rude. Teach your child to wait for a pause in the conversation and to say, "Excuse me." When she does this, respond positively. If the interruption is of a nature that it can and should wait, politely inform your child of this and then continue talking.

2 Tell your child that if she wants something when you are talking to another adult, she should walk up to you and gently squeeze your arm. You will then squeeze her hand to indicate that you know she is there and will be with her in a minute. At first, respond rather quickly so your child can see the success of this method. Over time, you can wait longer—

just give a gentle squeeze every few minutes to remind your child that you remember the request.

 Pause, look your child in the eye, and say, "I'll be with you in a minute." Then turn your face, body, and attention away from your child. Do not engage your child with repeated pleas for her to stop. If your child continues to interrupt, motion to the person you're talking with to walk away with you.

Praise your child for using good manners, remembering to say "Excuse me," and for interrupting only for a valid reason.

JUNK FOOD EXCESSES

See also ■ Eating, disorders ■ Eating, overeating ■ Eating, picky eater
■ Vegetables, won't eat them

SITUATION

My kid thinks chocolate is one of the main food groups! She eats way too much junk food and not enough healthy foods. How can I help her develop better eating habits?

THINK ABOUT IT

Kids tend to focus more on immediate gratification than long-term benefits, especially when it comes to eating. It will take education and behavior modification to change your daughter's eating habits.

SOLUTIONS

1 Many children will eat junk if it's available to them. The first step, then, is to make junk less accessible. Clean out your cabinets and refrigerator. Keep only a minimum amount of treats on hand. If you absolutely must have your chocolate, keep it hidden from little eyes.

2 Kids aren't going to get excited about carrot strips and apple pieces! Keep a supply of *tasty* healthy choices available. Look for low-fat, low-sugar snacks that will appeal to your child. Many types of muffins, bagels, breads, fruit-based snacks, puddings, and crackers make good snack choices.

3 Habit is a powerful force. Children tend to have favorite foods that they eat over and over. Try to replace the old favorites with a similar but healthier choice. For instance, if your child often eats potato chips, try to find a salty, crunchy replacement, such as pretzels. If your child is hooked on candy, choose licorice, jelly beans, or hard candy in small quantities as a better choice. (Note: Do not give hard candy to young children, who may choke on it.)

4 Encourage your child to be more active. Bored kids who aren't staying busy may fill their time by eating. Enroll your child in a club or sports team or get her started with a hobby or craft activity. Replace old habits, such as munching in front of the TV, with a more productive activity.

LAZINESS, at home

See also ■ Carelessness ■ Sloppiness

SITUATION

When she's not watching TV, my child's favorite pastime is watching dust bunnies float through the sunshine. She's lazy and lacks motivation and energy. I'm not sure how to get her moving.

THINK ABOUT IT

It's a very rare child who is really "lazy." Most have just gotten into some bad habits. A gentle nudge will often lead a child in the right direction.

SOLUTIONS

1 Help your child find a hobby or craft activity that she enjoys. Interest and enthusiasm in one area usually boosts a child's energy level, which then carries over into other activities.

2 A child who is energetic at school but lazy at home needs more structure for her free time at home. Develop a specific routine and include chores, outside play, arts and crafts, or hobbies.

3 A child may seem lazy when in fact she's just watching too much television. More than thirty minutes of TV during the day can breed a habit of sitting in a vegetative state with the mind on "pause." Monitor your child's television time, and if you find an excess, review the ideas in this book under Television, watches too much.

4 Some children become lethargic as a result of too little exercise combined with poor eating habits. Monitor your child's eating habits to make sure she's getting a wide variety of wholesome, low-fat, low-sugar foods. In addition, encourage activity and movement through play and sports activities. (*See also* Eating; Athletics, poor sport.)

! A family counselor or psychologist should see a child who displays symptoms of extreme sadness, loneliness, or depression. A pediatrician or family doctor should see a child who typically displays normal behavior but suddenly becomes lazy and lethargic.

LAZINESS, at school

> See also ■ Homework, how to create a routine ■ Homework, not getting it done ■ Homework, sloppy or rushed work ■ School, behavior problems at ■ School, not wanting to go

SITUATION
My child lacks motivation and is lazy at school.

THINK ABOUT IT
Try to pinpoint the exact reasons for your concern, and identify the specific behaviors you would like to change. The more clearly you identify the problem, the easier it will be to solve it.

SOLUTIONS

1 Set an appointment with the teacher. Find out how your child is doing in class. One of the common reasons for this behavior is that your child is behind in class and struggling to keep up. An opposite but equally common reason is that your child is ahead of the class and bored with what is going on. Once you determine if either of these, or another reason, is the culprit for the current behavior, you can take steps to improve the classroom situation.

2 Your child may be uninspired because of a lack of proficiency in basic skills. If you suspect this is the case, enroll your child in a supplemental tutoring program or hire a student tutor.

3 Your child may simply be disorganized and need help managing his time. Purchase a daily planner and a wall calendar. Help your child plan the steps to completing his assignments. Help him get a clear picture of his goals for the year. If he has specific direction, he will be more likely to show interest in his daily activities.

4 Children have different personalities. Some are naturally more enthusiastic and self-motivated than others. Make sure your expectations are reasonable and not wishful thinking. Base your goals for your child's achievements on his actual ability, not on what you would like it to be.

LISTENING, not

See also ■ Arguing, with parent ■ Cooperate, won't ■ Introduction ■ Respect, teaching

SITUATION
My kid doesn't listen to me! I have to repeat myself over and over. Even then, he doesn't do what I've asked. When I remind him, he looks at me with that befuddled look that says, "Huh? You were talking to *me*?"

THINK ABOUT IT
Sounds like your child has what is commonly known as "Selective Hearing." (In other words, you can shout at him to take out the trash, and it's as if he has cotton in his ears; but if you whisper that you'll take him out for ice cream, his hearing becomes incredibly sharp!) The good news is that this malady is easily cured when you use the following solutions.

SOLUTIONS
1 When you make a request, be certain you have your child's attention by touching his arm or hand and making eye contact. Use a clear, simple statement. For example, do not call from three rooms away, "Time to go!" A better choice is to *go to your child*, look him eyeball to eyeball, and state a very specific request: "Fester, please put on your shoes and coat and get in the car."

2 If your child doesn't respond to your request, ask that he repeat back to you what you said: "Fester, what is it I want you to do?" Once the child has repeated your request, you know that he's heard you (and *he* knows that *you* know that he heard you), and he's more likely to follow through.

3 Make sure you are not encouraging the behavior by nagging or making requests that you don't follow through on. If you typically repeat yourself three or four or twelve times before you take action, your child will learn that he can ignore you the first few times, because all he'll suffer is having to listen to the drone of your voice.

4 Keep your requests brief and to-the-point. For example, say you want your child to get ready for bed. Don't launch into a ten-minute lecture on the value of sleep, the importance of getting up on time, the fact that Tuesday is a school night, and why you are sick and tired of going through this every night, and so forth. Limit yourself to a few important words, such as, "Nine o'clock. Bedtime."

5 Use action instead of words. Instead of complaining about the pile of dirty socks in the family room, simply pick them up and hand them to your child. Kids are remarkably perceptive when handed a wad of dirty laundry.

! Have a doctor check your child's hearing to be sure there is not a physical problem preventing your child from hearing you.

LOSING

See also ■ Athletics, poor sport ■ Competitiveness ■ Self-esteem, low

SITUATION
When my kid loses a game, the world knows it! Whether it's the baseball championship or a "friendly" game of tiddledywinks, if he loses the game, he also loses control. He gets extremely upset, accuses everyone

else of cheating, and finds all kinds of things that are "unfaaaiiiiirrr" about the game. How can I get him to lighten up?

THINK ABOUT IT

No one ever likes to lose. But learning how to lose *gracefully* is a skill that comes with time, maturity, and practice.

SOLUTIONS

1 Watch the messages your child is getting at home about winning and losing. Innocent comments such as "Last one in is a rotten egg" or "I bet I can finish before you can!" can send the wrong message about losing. Check your own attitude about losing, as well as that of other important adults who have influence over your child. Do you display great enthusiasm when you win but get grumpy when you lose? Do you show your disappointment or throw or slam game pieces when things aren't going your way? When your favorite sports team wins, are you euphoric, but when they lose, do you fall into a pit of despair? What messages are you sending about winning or losing?

2 Don't overprotect your child and let him always win when playing games with you. Losing in the safety net of the family environment lets a child understand he can still be loved and valuable when he's not the winner.

3 Validate your child's sad feelings about losing—no one *likes* losing! Then help your child move past the feelings by talking about the fun aspects of the game or what you enjoyed about it. Bring up a time when your child won to remind him that he can win, too.

4 Make sure no adult in the family is comparing the child to a sibling or friend who is a better player. Comments that validate the child's loss, which are often intended to make a child feel better, can actually make things worse, such as, "Frank never played this before" or "Lucy is the youngest player." Even subtle comments can make a child feel inferior instead of better.

LYING

See also ■ Promises, doesn't keep ■ Self-esteem, low

SITUATION
I've been catching my child in small lies of the "I didn't do it" variety. How can I stop this behavior before it starts to escalate?

THINK ABOUT IT
Children lie for a variety of reasons. They lie to keep their parents happy with them, they lie so they won't get in trouble, they lie to cover embarrassment or inadequacy, or they lie because they don't make the clear distinction between fact and fiction. Teaching your child the value of telling the truth takes time, persistence, and patience.

SOLUTIONS

1 Don't ask questions that set your child up to lie. When your child has chocolate on his face and the candy is gone, don't ask, "Did you eat that candy bar that was sitting on the counter?" Instead, make a statement of fact: "I'm disappointed that you ate the candy bar without asking. That will be your snack for today." If your child says, "I didn't," don't play twenty questions. Just state the facts: "The candy is gone, and there's chocolate on your face. Why don't you go up to your room for a while and come on back down when you want to talk about it."

2 Focus on finding a solution instead of assigning blame. "Regardless of how it happened, the lamp is broken. What are we going to do about it?"

3 If you're not sure if your child is lying, make an honest statement: "That doesn't sound like the truth to me."

4 If your child comes to you with the truth, resist the urge to lecture. Thank the child for telling you and then focus on finding a solution or imposing a necessary consequence, without anger. Don't make the mistake of saying, "If you tell the truth, you won't be punished." We all make mistakes, and owning up to them can be difficult, but we still need to accept responsibility for our actions. As an adult, if you're driving your car and hit someone's bumper in the parking lot, you are not "off the hook" if you own up to your mistake, but you can be in serious trouble if you are caught in a "hit-and-run." So avoid the trap of saying, "When you tell the truth, you'll be off the hook." Instead, think of it this way: "If you lie, you'll be in even bigger trouble!"

5 Kids sometimes lie because they feel they're not meeting your expectations, and they think it's easier to lie than feel like a failure. Take a look at how you respond to your child's mistakes or inadequacies, and make sure you leave room for imperfections.

6 Model truthfulness. When your child hears you telling those innocent "little white lies," you are teaching your child something about honesty. What "little white lies" do I mean? Having your child tell someone on the phone that you're not home so that you don't have to talk. Shrinking your child's age so that you can get the cheaper rate at the movies, the amusement park, or at a restaurant. You are teaching your child all the time, whether you plan it or not.

! If your child develops a pattern of lying, or lies about important things, and is persistent about continuing the lie even after the truth is discovered, it would be wise for you to seek the advice of a professional. Your pediatrician, school counselor, or hospital can help you find someone to talk to.

MANNERS, at home

See also ■ Arguing, with parent ■ Back talk ■ Disrespect ■ Interrupting
■ Respect, teaching ■ Tantrums, at home

SITUATION

My child uses bad manners at home. He's impolite to us and to his siblings and does and says things that would embarrass me if they happened in public.

THINK ABOUT IT

Your child doesn't run into the freeway, play with steak knives, or stick modeling clay in your VCR because in many ways you've made it clear that these behaviors won't be tolerated. In the same way, you must decide that bad manners won't be permitted, either.

SOLUTIONS

1 Make sure no one is laughing at his bad manners. Laughing encourages children to see bad manners as a source of humor.

2 Avoid that tired old response: "What do you say?" Instead, respond to your child by rephrasing what he's already said in the way you find acceptable: "What I'd like to hear you say is, 'May I please have more pancakes?'"

3 Teach; don't reprimand. Instead of saying, "That's disgusting! Don't act like a pig!", respond in this way: "It's impolite to belch at the table, and if you do, it's proper to say, 'Excuse me.'" If your child didn't know what the proper behavior was, you're teaching a valuable lesson. If he did, you're displaying *your* good manners as you correct him and possibly making him feel a bit foolish for acting in such a way.

4 If a child is using poor manners to show off or "get your goat," it's best to ignore him and walk away or pointedly ignore him by turning your back and focusing on something else. Later, find a time to talk with your child about appropriate manners.

5 Look your child in the eye and say, "When you can ask me using good manners, I'll be happy to answer you." Show your appreciation when your child uses good manners.

6 Model the behavior you'd like to see. It's easy for a parent to forget to use *please, thank you,* and *excuse me* when dealing with children. Remember your manners. It's good teaching, and it makes life more pleasant. So, replace "Go get me a hammer" with "Please get me a hammer."

MANNERS, at mealtime

See also ■ Disrespect ■ Eating, out with children ■ Respect, teaching

SITUATION
They say that having dinner together as a family is a bonding experience. Not so in my house! My kids have such atrocious manners that I spend the entire meal correcting, reprimanding, and pleading with them to act civilized! How can I get them to use good manners?

THINK ABOUT IT
Children aren't born with good manners; they must be taught. Your kitchen table is a great place for your children to learn.

SOLUTIONS
1 Be patient and teach. Don't nag and complain. Tell your child what you want, rather than what you don't want. Instead of saying, "Link,

don't eat with your hands!" tell him what you *do* want: "Lincoln, please use your fork." Maintain a positive mood during dinner. Focus on pleasant conversation, and don't use the time to reprimand or lecture. A happy environment is more conducive to teaching good manners.

2 Accept age-appropriate behavior. All young children spill their milk, splatter their ketchup, and leave an array of crumbs around their chairs. It takes time to acquire the motor skills required to be tidy and clean.

3 Every once in a while, have a formal meal at home. Use a tablecloth (an old one!), a full selection of silverware, and napkins. Pretend you're at a formal restaurant, and allow everyone to exaggerate his or her best manners. You may even choose to dress up and use candles. In addition to teaching good manners, it's a beautiful family ritual and will create wonderful memories.

4 Expect children to use the good manners they have been taught. If a child persists in purposefully demonstrating bad manners, pick up his dinner plate, have him follow you to another room, and tell him he'll be eating dinner by himself. (*Don't* put him in front of the TV!)

5 Be consistent. Require good manners every day, and over time you'll have to think about them less and less. For example, most children taught to say "please" during toddlerhood will be saying it automatically by the time they're four or five years old. Children who routinely practice using good manners will adopt those manners as good habits.

MANNERS, in public

See also ■ Disrespect ■ Gifts, rude response to ■ Gifts, thank-you notes
■ Gimmees ■ Interrupting ■ Respect, teaching
■ Rude comments ■ Tantrums, public

SITUATION
When we're out in public, my son seems to forget all the good manners he routinely uses at home. If we run into someone I know, he won't

even say a polite hello. He forgets to say "thank you" and "excuse me." The list goes on. How can I get him to remember to use his manners?

THINK ABOUT IT

As annoying as your child's lack of manners can be, resist the urge to reprimand him in front of other people. I've seen many parents do this. In a misguided effort to teach manners, they display some of the worst manners I've seen!

SOLUTIONS

1 Many children are not aware of their bad manners and must be taught not only what *not* to do, but what to do instead. For example, if a friend of yours speaks to your child, who looks down at his sneakers and ignores the comment, it's typically embarrassment and ignorance on the child's part that's causing the behavior. After the person leaves, make a brief comment to your child: "Casey, if an adult talks to you, it's polite to look him in the eye and say something back. When Mr. Nagamine commented on your new shoes, you could have said, 'Thank you. They're new.' People like it when you answer them like that."

2 If your child is acting in a rude way, lead him away from other people and quietly and briefly correct him. Give him a smile and a hug to show him that you love him. That way, you can send him back into the situation prepared to change for the better.

3 In advance of a social situation, brief your child on what manners will be expected of him. Younger children can benefit from a role-play at home previewing what they might expect.

4 Praise your child for using good manners. Believe it or not, children often feel embarrassed when they socialize with adults and use good manners. Because they have heard adults say things like, "Fine, thank you, and you?" they feel like impostors when they say it themselves!

MASTURBATION

See also ■ Nudity, during child's play
■ Sexuality, inappropriate personal behavior

SITUATION
My child has developed a habit of putting his hands in his underwear. This makes me really uncomfortable. How do I get him to stop?

THINK ABOUT IT
At some point, most children explore their genitals, just as they explore other parts of their bodies. Children need to be taught proper manners when it comes to this private activity.

SOLUTIONS

 1 If your child has his hands in his pants, simply ask him to stop, tell him that it's something he should do privately, and then encourage his interest in another activity.

Some kids don't bathe their private areas properly, which can cause dry skin or a rash. Check to see that your child isn't suffering irritation from a rash that's causing itching.

2 Some children masturbate when they are bored in front of the TV set. If this is the case, limit the amount of TV your child watches, and when he does watch, give him a snack or activity (such as a bead set or deck of cards) to play with while he watches or sit beside him while he watches. It's best if you don't even mention the habit as a reason for the change in the routine. After a few weeks, the habit will be broken.

3 If your child has been falling asleep masturbating, change the bedtime routine. Read a book to him, and when you turn off the light, stay in the room and talk quietly or give him a back rub. Once your child starts to fall asleep, you can leave the room.

4 If you have religious views that prohibit masturbation, don't resort to punishment or shame to stop your child, as this can backfire and force your child to hide this activity and then feel guilty and ashamed. Instead, calmly explain your feelings in words your child can understand. Let him know that it's normal to have a desire to masturbate, but then proceed with your thoughts and feelings about why you feel he shouldn't.

5 Purchase a book about sexuality and development. Read it yourself, first, because there's lots of stuff you may have forgotten and some things you may not even know! Share it with your child at an appropriate time. Let your child know that you're available to answer any questions.

MATERIALISM

See also ■ Gimmees ■ Money ■ Wastefulness

SITUATION
My child has an excessive focus on "things" and wants the latest popular brand names. She's much too focused on what everyone else has, what she doesn't have, and what she wants. How can I temper this materialism?

THINK ABOUT IT
Materialism is usually a direct result of the effect of television and other media on our children. Parents often compound the problem by giving children too much stuff. And if you aren't guilty of this, you can bet that many of your child's friends' parents are, and what your kids see and hear from their peers will affect them.

SOLUTIONS
1 A child who is going through this stage should be taught the value of money. Begin to use the word *budget* and label things with a dollar value. "I know you'd like to go back to McDonald's today, but the meal yesterday cost $20, and it's not in our budget to go twice in the same week." When your family makes a large purchase, put the cost into terms your child can relate to: "Our new hot water tank cost $800. That's equal to almost seven years of your allowance!"

2 Don't use the excuse "We can't afford it" when your child wants something you're not going to buy. (This response implies that if you *could* afford it, you would immediately buy that expensive designer jacket.) Instead, say, "That's not in our budget" or "We choose not to spend our money on things like that. Instead we'll fill the car up with gas and buy our groceries for the week."

3 Teach your child the difference between *needs* and *wants*. When buying something for your child, offer to purchase the best quality for the most reasonable price, thereby taking care of his *needs*. Allow your child to add the extra amount if he chooses to upgrade to a fancy name brand, thus fulfilling his *wants*. An alternative is to provide your child with a budget when shopping. For example, let him know how much you'll spend on school clothes. Demonstrate how he can purchase one name-brand pair of jeans or three store-brand pairs. He may decide on the popular name brand. If so, don't rescue him a few months later when he complains he doesn't have enough to wear; simply remind him of his original decision.

4 Teach your child about money choices during your daily routine. If you decide you'd like ice cream for dessert, explain that you can each get one ice cream cone at the local ice cream stand or you can buy enough for three cones each if you buy a gallon of ice cream and cones at the grocery store.

5 Help your children appreciate the things in life that don't cost money. Also, help them see that "things" don't bring happiness by pointing out and discussing people or situations that lend themselves to teaching this value.

MEANNESS

See also ■ Anger, child's ■ Arguing, with parent ■ Bully, your child is acting like a ■ Disrespect ■ Friends, doesn't have any ■ Respect, teaching ■ Self-esteem, low ■ Siblings, fighting, verbal ■ Siblings, hateful emotions

SITUATION

My child can be purposefully cruel and nasty. I don't know why he gets this way. It frustrates me, and I end up yelling at him. I know this isn't the way to change his behavior. What should I do?

THINK ABOUT IT

Children typically act in cruel ways for one of three reasons: to gain power, to get attention, or to cover their own insecurities. It's helpful if you examine your child's behavior and try to determine the reasons behind it and then make a plan to control the behavior itself.

SOLUTIONS

1 Teach a child that his feelings are acceptable, but his actions must be controlled. In other words, it's OK to be mad at your sister, but it's not OK to hit her or pull her hair. If you feel your child is trying to get attention, help your child learn new ways to achieve the goal, such as being helpful, learning a new skill, or asking for help.

2 Instead of telling your child what *not* to do—"Don't shove your sister"—tell him what you want him to do—"Scott, please be kind to your sister. If you want to get by, just say, 'Excuse me.'"

3 Watch for and praise even the smallest display of kind behavior. Give positive attention when your child behaves in the ways you want him to.

4 Make sure you are not being mean to your child. Sometimes, when a child behaves in a cruel way, parents respond with extreme harshness. This, obviously, doesn't model the kind of behavior you'd like to see from your child. As difficult as it is, it's critical that you keep your own temper under control. (*See also* Anger, parent's.)

5 Provide your child with opportunities to show how responsible he is, and thus build self-esteem. He will then have less reason to throw his weight around to feel powerful. Assign him jobs that will make him feel in charge and successful. For example, have him cook a meal, paint a chair, wax the car, bathe the dog, or rub the baby's back as she falls asleep.

6 Provide regular opportunities for your child to talk to you about his feelings and the important things in his life. One family with five children allowed each child his own day of the week to skip kitchen cleanup in favor of sitting on the porch talking with Mom and Dad. The time becomes a precious routine for the entire family. Children who have somewhere to turn to sort out their feelings are less likely to act out in unacceptable ways.

7 When your child behaves in a manner that is socially unacceptable, respond with an immediate time-out. Unlike the typical rule of thumb, which dictates a time-out of about one minute per year of age, meanness warrants a longer period of isolation. Because a toddler or preschooler is not capable of being truly mean, this behavior occurs with older children, and they can be awarded a time-out of about five to ten minutes per year of age, depending on the situation. For example, a ten-year-old who is purposefully mean can immediately be sent to his room for about an hour. This time should be followed by a calm discussion between parent and child. Outline what happened, why it was unacceptable, and what the child should have done instead. Children then learn that cruel behavior is not acceptable in our society, and they will suffer loneliness if they continue to act that way.

! If a child is continually mean, shows no regrets over his behavior, or displays other disturbing behaviors, such as depression, disturbed sleep, or lack of appetite, it would be wise to seek the advice of a professional.

MEDICATION, taking

See also ■ Cooperate, won't

SITUATION
When my child has to take medication, she fusses, whines, and complains. If I do get her to put it in her mouth, she usually lets half of it drip down her chin. Without resorting to torture, how do I get her to cooperate?

THINK ABOUT IT

Kids think they're invincible. They're convinced that if you'd just leave them alone, the problem would go away on its own. They don't see any logical reason for choking down the foul-tasting stuff that you're offering.

SOLUTIONS

1 When medication is prescribed, explain the reasons to your child in terms she can understand. For a younger child, liken the medicine to a warrior who is going to fight her illness. Express your understanding that the medicine doesn't taste good and is no fun to take, but, nonetheless, it must be taken. Use a matter-of-fact approach. Tell your child that you know she is a responsible person and will choose to take the medicine to get well. Don't apologize: "I'm sorry you have to take this." Instead, display an attitude of thankfulness for modern medicine and its ability to heal your child.

2 When possible, give your child choices about medicine. Chewable or liquid? Taken before breakfast or after? Taking it with juice or with milk?

3 Mix the medicine with a spoonful of chocolate syrup or other appealing food. (Check with your doctor first to be sure that this is OK, because some medicines cannot be mixed with food.) An alternative is to allow a child to have a jelly bean or other small treat right after taking the medicine. Hold up the dropper of medicine in one hand, the treat in the other. Say, "First this, and then this." If your child balks, tell her that the quicker she takes the medicine, the sooner she gets the treat.

4 Take advantage of your doctor as an authority figure. Ask the doctor to explain to the child directly the reason for the medicine and how it should be taken. Children enjoy being talked to like an adult, especially by an authority figure such as a doctor, and will often respond well to this technique.

5 Allow the child to put the medicine in her mouth by herself. Many kids resent having an adult shove an offensive-tasting elixir down their throats.

MESS, kid's constant

See also ■ Bedrooms, cleaning ■ Chores, how to get them done
■ Sloppiness

SITUATION
My child leaves toys, dirty clothes, dishes, and everything else lying around and expects the housecleaning fairy to clean up after him. How do I get him to clean up his own mess?

THINK ABOUT IT
Sorry to say we accidentally set ourselves up for this one. One day we have a newborn who requires our constant and total care; the next day we have a six-year-old who's never had a compelling reason to want life any other way. Trust me; if I had a live-in maid who followed me around and tidied up all my messes, I'd be pleased to let her do it!

SOLUTIONS

1 Create a daily routine for cleaning up. One day's mess is usually manageable, but a mess that adds up day after day becomes insurmountable! It's best to pick a scheduled time that you can adhere to every day, such as after dinner or before putting on pajamas. Be consistent. At first it may be helpful to join in during the cleanup time to make it more pleasant. After a few weeks, the cleanup routine becomes habit, and the kids will cooperate with little fuss. (Please notice I didn't say *no* fuss!) *See also* Chores, complains about; Complaining.

2 If kids have too much junk, they tend to make too much mess! Take a good look at the things that litter the carpet. How much of it would really be missed if it disappeared? Pick a day when your kids are away from home. Sort through all the toys and stuff, and get rid of all the excess. (Either pack it in a box in the attic or give it to charity.) Organize the remaining things into boxes, laundry baskets, or tubs, each one labeled for its use: books, Legos, stuffed animals, and so forth. Have a tub for each child's school and sports supplies. Install hooks for jackets, and racks for shoes. If everything has a place, it will be easier to keep the house clean.

3 Get a big box. Put it in the garage. Using a black marker, write "jail" on the side of the box. At the end of each day, pick up all the junk that's lying around the house and put it in the box. Tell the kids they have to pay a twenty-five-cent fine or do a chore for you to release things from jail. Be calm. Be firm. It's amazing how much less stuff you'll find around the house once the kids have to pay to get back their backpacks, soccer shoes, homework, and comic books! (If you don't like the idea of a fine, simply keep the box hidden and bring it out on each Saturday for emptying. Tell the kids that whatever is left in the box at the end of the day will be thrown away or given away.)

4 Go on strike. If your kids are older than ten, tell them you will no longer be picking up other people's messes. They will have to be responsible for their own things. Add this important rule: If the house is a mess, there will be no friends allowed over, nor will you be allowed to leave to visit a friend. It's amazing how quickly a room can be cleaned up soon after the telephone rings!

MONEY

See also ■ Allowances ■ Gimmees ■ Materialism

SITUATION
My child thinks I have bottomless pockets. Every time I turn around, he's asking for money. Yesterday, when I said I didn't have any, he suggested I use my credit card! I'm really tired of this attitude, but I'm not sure how to stop it.

THINK ABOUT IT
When your child asks for money, you sometimes say yes, sometimes say no, and sometimes gripe, complain, and moan loudly and *then* say yes. As long as things continue this way, your child will keep playing the money game because it *is* profitable for him to play.

SOLUTIONS

1 Review your child's money needs, and start paying a specific allowance. Help the child create a budget and saving and spending plan.

2 Open a "family bank" and have rules about loans. Require written requests for money including the intended use and payback schedule. Include interest and even take collateral for larger loans.

3 Start buying your child the things he *needs* and letting him earn the things he *wants*. You can create extra household chores or suggest that he start a paper route or search the neighborhood for odd jobs.

4 Start teaching your child about *cost* and *value*. Let your child see the grocery receipt. Let him pay the cashier for lunch at the fast-food restaurant so that he can see the cash going away. Help him place a more accurate value on the things you typically pay for without comment by getting him involved in some money decisions. "Yes, I could give you $5 to rent a movie. Or you could use it to cover part of the cost of the new CD that you want."

5 Be consistent. Decide how you want the money issue to be resolved, let your child know the new rules, and then follow through.

MOODINESS

See also ■ Complaining ■ Self-esteem, low

SITUATION
My daughter is so moody! One minute she's happy and content, and the next, she's grumpy and irritable! It seems that even microscopic issues can set her off. How can I help her?

THINK ABOUT IT
Many children go through moody phases. Some come into the world with a predisposition to moodiness. A child's moodiness usually has a more potent

effect on a parent than it does on the child—in other words, it makes the *parent* even crankier than the child!

SOLUTIONS

1 Trying to force a child to be happy by saying things like "Don't be such a grump" usually only makes things worse. The child will see herself in the way you label her and just get grumpier to prove that you're right. Let her explore her emotions, and help her learn how to identify her feelings and overcome them. Take a minute to assess the situation and then make a helpful statement that describes what you think she's feeling. Add a comment about how *you* would handle the situation. (This approach is usually much better received than if you start out with "*you* should . . .") For example, you might say, "It must be frustrating when you can't decide what to wear to school. If I can't decide, I usually wear one of my favorite sweaters; it always makes me feel better." Beyond a short statement, it may be easier to talk with her during a "happy" time, rather than trying to deal with her during a moody period.

2 Ignore the irritability and try to cheer your child up by distracting her or getting her involved in an activity. Act as if she's going along with you with a pleasant attitude, and soon she will be.

3 Watch for a predictable pattern of moodiness. See if it can be attributed to hunger or tiredness. If so, plan a snack or quiet rest time during that part of the day. Sometimes moodiness is caused by stress. Perhaps she becomes stressed before each basketball game. If so, help your child handle stress in a more productive way, perhaps by practicing in the driveway or by talking about the game plan on the way there. Help your child understand her feelings and find ways to bring herself out of a slump.

4 Get your child involved in some kind of daily exercise. Children who are too sedentary and spend too much time watching TV can get moody. Sign your child up for a sports activity or set up some fun things to do in your backyard. Limit your child's use of the TV to thirty minutes per day. Get her involved in a craft or hobby. Encourage her to start a collection. Children who are focused on learning something new and being involved in some kind of activity tend to be happier and less inclined to sulk.

5 Determine if your child is having a hard time mastering a skill that's important to her, such as playing the piano, learning the multiplication tables, speaking a new language, or playing soccer on a new team. Sometimes, if children can't perform according to the image they carry in their mind, their self-esteem is affected. Instead of showing frustration, they display moodiness. If this description seems accurate for your child, help her see the positive growth she has displayed. She may be so set on mastery that she doesn't realize how much she has already learned. Help her lighten up by practicing with her and making it fun, not a chore. If she seems obsessed with the activity, try to draw her out by involving her in other things.

6 Sometimes moodiness is just a symptom of a child's growing independence. In other words, she's really enjoying the family outing but it wouldn't be cool to admit it. Simply treat her normally, and avoid getting into a power struggle over something you cannot control.

! Determine if the moodiness is a drastic change to your child's usual personality. If it is, or if the behavior continues for more than a few weeks and is combined with changes in sleeping or eating behaviors or extensive solitude, there may be problems you're not aware of. You should seek the advice of a professional.

MORNING CHAOS

See also ■ Chores, how to get them done ■ Cooperate, won't
■ Listening, not ■ School

SITUATION
I have honestly thought of making a tape recording of myself to play to the kids in the morning: "Get up, get dressed, eat breakfast, hurry up, hurry up, hurry up." I get tired of listening to *myself,* and the kids

still don't seem to get ready on time. How can I get control of the morning chaos?

THINK ABOUT IT
Weekday mornings present a frustrating challenge to many parents. The key to control lies in these areas: planning, assigning responsibility, organizing, and creating routines.

SOLUTIONS

1 Begin preparing for the morning routine the night before. Select and set out clothes, pack lunches, sign permission slips, and even set the breakfast table after you clear the dinner dishes. Put backpacks, shoes, and coats by the door. The more organized you are in advance, the easier things will go in the morning.

2 Create a morning chore chart for each child. List all tasks that need to be done in the order they will occur. A great way to do this is to write the list on a dry-erase board with *permanent* marker. Use the *dry-erase* markers to check off items on the list each morning. Then, keep the kids on track by asking every once in a while, "How are you doing on your chart?"

3 Wake your children thirty minutes earlier. Some kids are useless for the first twenty or thirty minutes when they wake up. It helps to have a cushion of time when they can wake up slowly before having to rush into the morning routine. (A sneaky way to accomplish this goal is to set the clocks in the kid's bedrooms ahead thirty minutes. Who knows? This idea may even get them to bed a little sooner.)

4 Get yourself up earlier. It's amazing how much more peaceful the morning goes if you are showered and dressed before you wake the kids. Ask yourself, "What's more important? A scant thirty minutes more of sleep or a peaceful morning?" It's definitely worth making the extra effort. You may even fit in some time for a cup of coffee and the morning paper!

5 Have a box or laundry basket for each child near the door. This is the place to keep backpacks, permission slips, lunches, and anything else that must be taken to school. Once everyone gets in the habit of using the boxes, you'll have an easier time keeping track of all the important things.

6 If you have young children, dress them the night before (honest!), and let them sleep in their clothes. Most children's clothes are wrinkle proof, and it saves about fifteen minutes per child in the morning.* If you have more than one under the age of five, this technique is a true lifesaver! (Just don't tell your mother!)

 * (Look for clothing that has the same flame-retardant label as found on children's pajamas.)

! Make sure your child is getting enough sleep. Kids who aren't getting adequate rest are often cranky and slow-moving in the morning.

MOVING, child is depressed after

See also ■ Self-esteem, low

SITUATION
We have recently moved, and my child is having a difficult time adjusting to the move.

THINK ABOUT IT
As happy as you may be over the move, your child may feel great sadness and loss. Loss of friends, loss of the familiar environment, loss of a comfortable school setting. Your child may also be fearful. He may be scared of getting lost, worried that he won't make new friends, or afraid he won't like his new teacher. Most children have these emotions to some degree. If your child is having a hard time, you can help him adjust by being loving, supportive, and gentle during the next few weeks. And by following some of these suggestions.

SOLUTIONS
1 As tempting as it is to change everything to meet the demands a move creates, try to maintain family routines and rituals as much as

possible. The simple things, like a usual dinner hour or a regular bedtime routine, can be very comforting to your child. Arrange your child's bedroom in the same way it was arranged at your old home. You might even consider arranging the furniture in other rooms in familiar ways. You can always rearrange later.

2 Acknowledge your child's unhappy feelings about leaving your old home and his friends. Allow him to talk about his feelings and to be sad and even mad. Try not to get defensive if your child makes harsh comments, such as "You're ruining my life!" Children often have a hard time understanding the logical reasons behind a move. Try to understand from your child's point of view, and help him sort out his feelings. Be careful, though, not to let him dwell on these feelings. Instead, help him to face them and then move past them. You might even talk about some of your sad feelings, followed, of course, by your feelings of excitement and adventure.

3 Help your child build a bridge from the old home to the new. Encourage him to invite old friends to visit, and help him "show off" his new home. Allow him to call or write old friends and tell them all about the new neighborhood. At the same time, encourage him to befriend children in the new neighborhood and to explore the new area. As busy as you are after a move, it's important that you make time for fun. Find a little time each day to connect with your child and refresh yourself. Visit a new park, eat at the new pizza restaurant, or take a walk. The bonding time with a parent can help your child deal with the changes that are going on around him.

4 Give your child specific tasks to do that will keep him busy while helping him to make the transition to the new home. Try to make the jobs fun and interesting; for example, have him paint the mailbox post, water the flowers, or hang a bird feeder.

5 If you are feeling depressed about the move, try not to expose too many of your negative feelings when your child is around. Make the phone call to cry on your friend's shoulder when your child is out of the house. It's OK to admit that there are lots of adjustments to be made, but your child will absorb your negative emotions. Take care of yourself. Make

sure you're taking the time to make some new friends, to meet the neighbors, and to find the good things in your new neighborhood.

MOVING, planning in advance

SITUATION
**We're planning a move and want it to go smoothly for our child. What
ways can we soften the blow of this major transition?**

THINK ABOUT IT
Assume the best. Most children adjust quickly to a move, especially when
the parents plan in advance.

SOLUTIONS

1 If possible, visit the new home, the new neighborhood, and the new
school a few times. When your child has a clear image of where you're
headed, she'll be more comfortable. If you're moving out of state and if you
visit the new city, take plenty of pictures. Visit or write the local chamber of
commerce or ask your real estate agent to do this for you. Obtain brochures
and information that you can peruse with your child. Gather information or
call for brochures from the local zoo, amusement park, water-play park, public swimming pool, theaters, youth groups, or any other sites your child
might like. It's especially important to find out about those things that your
child is most interested in. For example, if your child loves to roller blade,
find out where she can do this. If she loves horses, find out about the local
stables. Plan to visit a few of these places soon after your move.

2 Pack your child's bedroom last, and unpack it first. Don't use this
time to "spring clean" your child's bedroom or toss old toys. Kids
tend to panic if they get to the new home and can't find any of their old,
familiar junk. Children adjust easier if they find their familiar belongings at
the new home. If possible, put the room together right away, including pictures on the wall. Your child will then have a haven in the middle of all the

chaos. (You can hide there, too, if you want!) Arrange your child's room the same as it was at your old home, so it will be familiar. If your children are old enough and interested, allow them to help unpack and arrange their bedrooms. Relax a few standard rules; for example, let her put posters up on her walls, build a fort over her bed, or set up her train set around the borders of the bedroom.

3 If possible, let your child spend the actual moving day with a relative or friend. Many kids find it difficult to see everything pulled from the house and loaded onto a truck. Reassure your child that everything inside your home is going to be moved to the new one. Young children seem to have a hard time understanding this. It may help to walk around the house and talk about what you are taking with you: the refrigerator, the sofa, and the lamps.

4 Let your child have a box or suitcase with all her most important things as a carry-on instead of packing these things in boxes. It can lend a real feeling of security for her to have her favorite toys and clothes with her.

5 Stay positive and upbeat. Your child will pick up on your attitude. If you are stressed and fearful that your child will have a hard time with the move, she just may follow your lead. Often, parents become so busy and stressed during a move that they don't realize how short-tempered they are with their children. Try to be sensitive to your child's confused emotions right now. Focus on the good aspects of the move. If you find that you just can't be Pollyanna right now, be kind to your child and let her spend some extra time at a family member's or friend's house.

MUSIC LESSONS, age to start

SITUATION
I would like to have my child take music lessons, but I don't know the right time to start.

THINK ABOUT IT

Adding music to your family life can add much joy. Take the time to explore the many possibilities available to you and your children.

SOLUTIONS

1 Begin lessons when your child is eager to learn. For some children, this happens at five years old; for others, thirteen; and for some, the desire will never be there. Keep in mind, though, that children who are never exposed to music or to watching someone play an instrument or sing will not be eager to try something they know nothing about. Begin by introducing your child to music via instruments in your home, informal and formal concerts, and hands-on experiences. When your child expresses an interest in an instrument or in singing, allow her to develop the interest though lessons.

2 Determine why you want your child to take music lessons. List the reasons: developing good habits, learning to appreciate music, developing good motor skills. Don't focus on the end result but instead on the process of learning to play. Review the list and decide if music lessons are the best way to address these needs. If so, allow your child to become involved in choosing the instrument and in any other aspects of the lessons, such as how often and how long the lessons should be. Children who are involved from the beginning will be more willing students.

3 Select a teacher who has an easygoing nature and who has experience working with children. Choose someone who has an enthusiastic, positive attitude and with whom your child has a good time.

4 If you have a child who displays a gift for musical ability, it is wonderful to help her develop her gift. Instead of idly waiting for her to set the pace, encourage her through a variety of interesting choices for musical involvement. Such activities can include purchasing an instrument for the home or becoming involved in a children's choir. Take the time to attend musical events of different kinds to expose her to the many choices available.

MUSIC LESSONS, not wanting to continue

SITUATION
My child is currently taking music lessons but complains about them and wants to quit.

THINK ABOUT IT
Take a few quiet minutes to think about the reason behind your child's complaints. If you understand where the complaints are coming from, you'll be more likely to choose the correct solution.

SOLUTIONS

1 Often, a child will hear someone playing an instrument—for example, a violin—and fall in love with the music and the idea of playing it. When he starts lessons, however, he doesn't sound anything like the violin he heard, and he learns it's hard to get even a few notes to sound right. Discouragement, then, is the real reason many children want to quit. It helps to have a teacher who is creative and willing to try the unusual or unexpected to spark a child's interest. Often, teachers will have a child learn a simple melody by rote even before he can read music so he can feel the joy of playing a tune. Take a close look at the class environment and the teacher to determine if your child is in the right place.

2 Make a deal with your child. He must give lessons his best effort for a specific amount of time, for example, six months. (Make sure the time frame is long enough for the child to develop some skills.) After the set amount of time, your child can make a decision to continue or quit. Usually, by that time a child has enough skills to make an educated decision about whether to continue. During that time, take your child to a professional concert and to a concert of talented children so that he can see what the goals of lessons are.

3 Let your child finish out the term and then skip one term and try something else. Give him several options to take the place of the current music lessons, perhaps allowing lessons for a musical instrument that is easier to learn and thus providing more immediate results.

4 Make sure your child isn't overwhelmed with activities. Most children can handle schoolwork and chores plus one outside activity. Some can handle two extracurricular activities—perhaps music lessons and one sports activity. Anything more than that, such as adding Scouting, art classes, or chess club, can cause a child to feel stressed. If this is the case, allow your child to choose one activity and take a break with the others.

5 Problem solve with your child to determine the real reason he wants to quit. Be willing to listen and ask helpful questions. Does he like the teacher? The songs he's learning? The practice schedule? The recital opportunities? Once you have figured out the problems, brainstorm solutions and give them a try. It's best to have this session immediately after a recital or a group experience that was enjoyable. Often, a child enjoys the actual process, so it will be easier to find real solutions when the sessions are fresh in his mind.

6 Are you an accomplished musician, and does your child feel inadequate compared to you? You can help him overcome these feelings by talking about your early days of lessons. Mention your own struggles and mistakes.

7 Determine why it's so important that your child continue lessons. Maybe the reason is that *you* always wanted lessons but were not able to take them or that you quit as a young child and wish you would have continued. If this is true, and music is not one of your child's talents, it's probably best if you don't burden your child with your desires. Instead, *you* should take music lessons, and enjoy them now!

MUSIC LESSONS, not wanting to practice

SITUATION
My child is currently taking music lessons but finds practice boring and tedious. She really does enjoy her instrument, but she has to be begged, bribed, and forced to practice.

THINK ABOUT IT

When a child is learning how to play a musical instrument, it takes as much *patience* as it does *practice*. Kids see the end result and want to get there quickly. Kids won't really understand the value of practice until they have done enough of it to enjoy the results. Until then, you're in charge.

SOLUTIONS

1 Begin to treat music lessons in the same way you treat homework. Your attitude will convey itself to your child. If you feel music lessons are nonnegotiable and must be done, your attitude will be reflected in your behavior. Create a specific routine, such as thirty minutes of practice immediately after dinner. Follow though every day. Encourage your child and give positive reinforcement after the practice session is over.

2 Problem solve with your child to determine the real reason she doesn't like to practice. Be willing to listen and ask helpful questions. Does she like the songs she is learning? The practice schedule? Is her seat comfortable? Are other children playing outside during her practice time and causing her to wish she were somewhere else? Once you have figured out the problems, brainstorm solutions and give them a try.

3 Practice sessions *can* be very boring. Find ways to make them more interesting. Perhaps allow her to decorate the area where she practices. Put up a wall calendar, and allow her to put up a sticker each day after she practices. Move the instrument to a sunny part of the house. Sit with her on occasion, and be an alert, encouraging audience (wear earplugs if you must!). Have a routine snack immediately after practice that she can look forward to. It may help to break the practice into two shorter sessions or change the time of day so that she is more alert and energetic during practice time.

NAGGING

See also ■ Arguing, with parent ■ Complaining ■ Cooperate, won't
■ Listening, not ■ Whining

SITUATION
My kid is persistent to the point of being exasperating. If he wants something, he's willing to fight to the bitter end. If I say no, he'll nag me until I'm ready to scream! How do I stop him?

THINK ABOUT IT
A gambler puts coins in a slot machine because every once in a while he wins a little pot of gold. Your child learned long ago that nagging sometimes pays off: "All right, all right already! You can have it; just leave me alone!" The key to eliminating the nagging, then, is to eliminate the payoff.

SOLUTIONS
1 Don't ever reward a child who nags by changing your mind, even if you have. Doing so encourages your child to continue his behavior in the future. Once you say *no*, stick with it. If you feel yourself crumbling under your kid's version of Chinese water torture, separate yourself from your child by putting him (or yourself!) in time-out.

2 Use the broken-record technique. Calmly repeat your first answer as many times as necessary until the child stops nagging.

3 Keep your "nos" to a minimum. Say yes when you can. Say maybe if you're not sure. Give your child a "qualified yes" answer when you can think of one, such as, "Yes, you may have a cookie . . . right after dinner."

4 Have a standing rule: "If I say 'maybe' and you ask me again, the answer will automatically be 'no.'"

5 After you have given your answer once, ignore your child's continued nagging. It's best to walk away if you can or turn your back to the child and hum or whistle, which means "I'm not listening." When you respond to your child each time he nags, you're opening the door for more conversation, as I'm sure he'll have a retort for each of your objections.

NAIL BITING OR NAIL PICKING

See also ■ Habits, bad

SITUATION
My daughter bites her nails. It's very annoying, and her nails look terrible. How can I get her to stop this?

THINK ABOUT IT
Nail biting is often done to relieve anxiety and bring comfort. Once it becomes a habit, it is very difficult to stop. Nagging or reprimanding your child won't stop nail biting, and in fact, may make it worse.

SOLUTIONS
1 Have a talk with your child and bring her attention to the habit (she may not be aware of how often she does it). Explain the reasons you'd like her to stop. Ask how she feels about it. Agree to a subtle, gentle reminder that you'll use to ask her to stop, such as a tap on her arm or a code word.

2 Notice the times your child demonstrates the habit most, such as when she's sitting in the car, watching TV, or in social situations. During those times, give her an alternative object to keep her hands busy, such as a string of beads, Silly Putty, or a smooth rock.

3 Enlist your child's cooperation by talking gently with her about the nail biting. Don't just assume she would like to quit! Once she has agreed to make an effort, your encouragement and consistent, gentle reminders will do more good than nagging or embarrassing her. Use a sub-conscious "trigger" to help your child: have her reach her hands to her mouth and then say "no" as she quickly clasps her hands in her lap. Repeat it ten times; then, repeat it several times during the day. Surprisingly, after practicing, this trigger will then initiate itself without your child realizing it (like a habit!).

4 Set up an incentive for abstaining. Agree to a specified time period and a specific behavior modification. One plan is to give your child ten nickels (or pennies or dimes, depending on your child's age) first thing in the morning. Tell her that any time you see her biting her nails, you'll ask for a nickel. At the end of the day, she can keep any of the nickels that are left. An alternate reward for girls is to offer a professional manicure and a bottle of nail polish when the habit is gone.

NAME-CALLING

See also ■ Friends, inappropriate choice of ■ Manners, at home
■ Manners, in public ■ Respect, teaching ■ Teasing

SITUATION
There are several kids in the neighborhood who frequently call each other nasty names. I've heard my child do the same thing a few times as well. How do I put the brakes on this behavior?

THINK ABOUT IT
Kids who are called names are obviously hurt, but those who use name-calling to attack others are hurting themselves as well. For the benefit of both children, it's best to be persistent in putting an end to name-calling.

SOLUTIONS

1 Avoid confronting the child in front of others and embarrassing him with a reprimand or lecture, because you'll force the name-calling to be used secretly. Instead, interrupt the children immediately and say, "May I see you in the kitchen for a minute?" Take the child aside for a private discussion. Firmly state your position on name-calling and set specific limits.

2 Many children call names to express anger. Give your child an alternative by specifically teaching what can be said when angry. For example, teach what words express anger in a more respectful way; discuss other options, such as walking away. Explain the benefits of these techniques versus name-calling.

3 Have a standard consequence for name-calling. Usually, when a child calls another a name, it's because he's angry. A very appropriate consequence is to require that the child rephrase his comments in three different ways that are respectful. So, for example, if you hear a child yell, "Give me my marker, you poo-poo head!" you can respond, "Ok, Newt, you know the rule. No name-calling. How can you say that nicely, three different ways?" If your child is reluctant to reply, offer a choice: "You can tell us now, or take a break and write it down on a piece of paper."

4 In a private conversation, teach the child who is being called names a few good comebacks, such as, "I'm rubber and you're glue; whatever you say bounces off me and sticks to you." Or "Whatever you say, you *are*." Or "And how long has this been bothering you?" Or "Perhaps your memory needs help; my name is Sarah." A few good retorts and the name-caller will lose interest in the game.

NAP, won't take one

See also ■ Bedtime ■ Cooperate, won't

SITUATION
My child needs a daily nap but refuses to take one without a major battle. By the time I settle her down, *I'm* ready for a nap!

THINK ABOUT IT
Who needs your child to go down for a daily nap? Examine your motivation here. Are you the one who really needs the break? It's perfectly OK for you to want a few minutes to yourself. Once you give yourself permission to have this time for yourself, you can open your mind to some creative ways to solve this problem.

SOLUTIONS

1 The idea of being forced to take a nap is truly offensive to many active children, and they will assert their independence by refusing to cooperate. Abolish the word *nap* from your vocabulary. Create a daily "quiet time" instead. Let your child know that during this time, she must remain lying down on her bed. She may read a book or cuddle a stuffed animal or listen to quiet music. Set a timer for the length of quiet time, and let your child know she can get up when it rings. If your child is really tired, this quiet period will easily turn into a nap, and if not, it will give you a specific amount of quiet time for yourself.

2 Go to your local library and rent children's books on tape. Introduce a "story hour" when your child can lay in bed and listen to a book. Choose restful stories that will create a calm environment. Once the story is over, your child will be rested, and so will you. A tired child will often doze off peacefully.

3 Many kids worry that they will miss something important if they sleep. Let your child know what you'll be doing during rest time. Make it sound boring and then promise a fun activity when rest time is over.

Increase your child's physical activity in the morning, and make sure she's eating healthy food. Some children seem to need a nap by their agitated and grumpy behavior when actually they need more exercise and a healthier diet. (*See also* Eating, picky eater; Junk food excesses.)

 Children's need for sleep varies, often even day-to-day. When your child has a quiet, less physically involved day, she may not need a nap. Or your child may be ready to give up a daily nap. Many children from age two on up do just fine without a daytime nap. Try letting your child go without a nap or shortening nap time. A little of the sleep time can be made up with an earlier bedtime or a later rising time.

NIGHTMARES

See also ■ Dark, fear of ■ Night terrors

SITUATION
My child sometimes wakes up crying and frightened from a nightmare. What's the best way to handle this?

THINK ABOUT IT
Children believe in all manners of fairy tales. They need to achieve a level of maturity to understand the difference between dreams, fantasies, and reality. In the meantime, keep in mind that your child's dreams are very real to him.

SOLUTIONS

 Most children's nightmares are about being attacked or abandoned. They need reassurance that they're safe. Comfort your child with calm words: "It's OK. Mommy's here. It was just a dream. You're safe." Offer a favorite stuffed animal or blanket and turn on a night-light. Stay with your child until he is calmed down and drifting off to sleep.

 The morning following the nightmare, casually ask if your child remembers the incident. If so, allow him to tell you about it. Talk about what dreams really are (thoughts in your head). Compare real things to thoughts. Say, "Think about a big black bear. Can you imagine what it looks like? Can the bear in your head right now hurt you? That's like a dream. Now, put a dress on the bear and a bow on his head and make him dance. That's like a dream, too." With practice, some children can even learn to change their dreams while they are having them.

3 Limit violent or scary television shows, movies, and books for several hours before bedtime, or for more sensitive children, eliminate them all together. Some children can be affected by a scary movie for weeks or even longer, replaying the scenes that scared them most in their minds and in their dreams.

! If your child has frequent or intense nightmares, they may be the result of stress or fears. If you think this may be possible, consult your family doctor or local hospital for advice.

NIGHT TERRORS

See also ■ Nightmares

SITUATION
This is the second time that my child has awoken with a very strange nightmare. She sits up in bed and cries inconsolably for five to fifteen minutes. Her eyes are open, but she acts like she's still asleep and doesn't respond to me at all.

THINK ABOUT IT
Your child isn't actually dreaming at all and isn't aware of what's going on; she's experiencing a "night terror." Night terrors are different from nightmares. Night terrors are a state of sleeping semiconsciousness.

SOLUTIONS
1 Comforting a child during a night terror has no effect. Night terrors are frightening for a parent to watch, but the child is still asleep and

will have no memory of the event. Stand close by and make sure she's safe. (If she seems OK with it, you can hold her or stroke her and murmur comforting words, but usually your actions are more soothing for you than for your child.) Sometimes, your child will awaken at the end of the episode. It's best if you're close by to ease her back to sleep. Wait until your child has gone back to sleep. Tuck her in and give her a kiss.

 After your child has settled down, get yourself a glass of warm milk and go back to bed!

3 If night terror episodes are frequent or severe in intensity or length, or if they are accompanied by sleepwalking or body tremors, talk to your doctor.

NOISE, excessive

See also ▪ Roughhousing ▪ Yelling and screaming

SITUATION
My child is in the habit of using a very loud voice, which is usually accompanied by constant motion. It seems as if he's always been this way. He's heard it repeated so often that I believe he thinks his name is "Be Quiet."

THINK ABOUT IT
Some children have a natural abundance of energy and a loud voice. It's typically not a conscious choice but a personality trait. The silver lining is that he'll never be a wallflower who's pushed around by his peers!

SOLUTIONS
1 This kind of kid will do well when given an outlet for all that enthusiasm. It's helpful to have a place where he can be noisy without disturbing others. You might consider a playroom or bedroom as one option. Put weather stripping around the door to reduce the escape of the noise. Whenever your child's volume increases, direct him to that room.

2 When your child's noise level increases and it bothers you, interrupt his current activity and redirect him to a quieter pursuit. Get him started on a puzzle or drawing or a building activity.

3 Children are great at modeling the communication styles they see around them. Is there an adult in your child's life who speaks loudly or yells often? Do you find yourself raising your voice to your child to get his attention? Do family members yell to each other from other rooms? Make it a family rule to find another person and talk to that person eye-to-eye rather than shouting from another room.

4 As easy as it is to do, do not *yell* at your child, "*Settle down!*" Instead, use a gentle, calm voice to bring your child's level down to yours. Often, if you get your child's visual attention and begin to whisper, he'll quiet down to hear what you say. If you engage him in a quiet moment, often the effect will last for a while.

! If, in addition to your child's loud voice, you find yourself complaining that "He never listens to me" or find that you have to nag repeatedly before he does what you ask, your child may have a hearing problem. Another sign of a hearing problem is an inability to speak clearly and correctly or speaking in a nasal or flat tone with little voice inflection. A child with a hearing difficulty will frequently say, "What?" Also, if your child has a history of frequent colds and ear infections, they may have temporarily affected his hearing. If you suspect your child may have a hearing problem, take him for an evaluation with a hearing specialist as soon as possible.

NOSE PICKING

See also ■ Habits, bad

SITUATION
This is embarrassing to talk about, but it's an annoying habit. My child picks her nose. I don't even want to tell you what she does with the stuff

she finds in there. I can't stand to watch her do this, and I've been tempted to tell her to put it back in her nose where it belongs!

THINK ABOUT IT

Nose picking is often done to relieve anxiety and bring comfort. Because the nose is always at hand (excuse me, I couldn't resist!), picking is an addictive habit.

SOLUTIONS

1 Nagging or reprimanding your child won't stop the habit and will just embarrass her. Have a talk with your child and bring her attention to the habit (she may not be aware of how often she does it). Explain the reasons you'd like her to stop. Have her watch herself pick her nose in a mirror so that she can see how offensive it looks. Agree to a subtle, gentle reminder that you'll use to ask her to stop, such as tapping on her arm, handing her a tissue, or using a code word.

2 Notice the times your child demonstrates the habit most, such as when she's sitting in the car, reading, or watching TV. During those times, give her an alternative object to keep her hands busy, such as a string of beads, Silly Putty, or a smooth rock.

3 Enlist your child's cooperation by talking gently with her about the habit. Once she has agreed to make an effort, your encouraging her and using consistent, gentle reminders will do more good than nagging or embarrassing her. Use a subconscious "trigger" to help your child: have her reach for her nose and then say "no" as she quickly clasps her hands in her lap. Repeat it ten times; then, repeat it several times during the day. Surprisingly, after practicing, this trigger will then initiate itself without your child realizing it (like a habit!).

4 Set up an incentive for abstaining. Agree to a specified time period and a specific behavior modification. One plan is to give your child ten nickels (or pennies or dimes, depending on your child's age) first thing in the morning. Tell her that any time you see her picking her nose, you'll ask for a nickel. At the end of the day, she can keep any of the nickels that are left.

NOSINESS

See also ■ Interrupting ■ Manners, at home ■ Manners, in public
■ Respect, teaching

SITUATION

My kid has to know everything that's going on. It doesn't matter if you're sitting next to him or if you're in the next room, he's listening to every conversation and asking questions about everyone else's business.

THINK ABOUT IT

Some children are naturally inquisitive about everything, including the adult conversations going on around them. These children are often very bright and eager to learn new things. Your goal as a parent, then, is to encourage the natural curiosity but teach appropriate manners.

SOLUTIONS

1 As annoying as this behavior can be, avoid the temptation to growl, "Mind your own business!" A better alternative is to look the child in the eye and say, "This is not something you need to ask about. Please go find something to do while we talk."

2 Have a conversation with your child to compliment his inquisitive nature and to explain that there are times when it's inappropriate to get involved in other people's conversations. Role-play a few examples. Try to use your child's viewpoint as a way to help him understand the lesson. An example: "What if you and your best friend, Ray, were in your room talking about yesterday's baseball game, and you were making plans for the play-off game. What if I came in your room and started asking lots of questions and interrupting your conversation. How would that feel?"

3 Agree to a hand signal or code word that means "This is not your business." Let your child know that when you give the signal, it means that he's out of line and should not be concerned with the business at hand. For example, a gentle squeeze on the arm or saying "Would you please get me a tissue," accompanied by a wink, may be enough to disengage him from the conversation.

4 Let your child know that if he has questions about a particular issue, he is welcome to ask you for more information later; but he will not be allowed to interrupt an adult conversation unless he is invited to do so.

NUDITY, during child's play

See also ■ Masturbation
■ Sexuality, inappropriate behavior with friends

SITUATION
My daughter and the little boy next door were discovered playing with their clothes off. Now what?

THINK ABOUT IT
Satisfying their curiosity about their bodies by removing their clothing is developmentally appropriate behavior for children from about age four to six. Kids aren't thinking the same things you are about the naked body. They're just innocently curious.

SOLUTIONS
1 The best approach is a calm, even tone of voice and an appropriate comment, such as, "Your clothes need to stay on when you play. Please get dressed right now." Then help the children dress and redirect their play.

2 Siblings of the opposite sex who have a close relationship may explore each other's private parts with the same innocence that they tickle each other's feet. A simple statement such as "That is your brother's private part. Any part your bathing suit covers is private. We don't touch each other's private parts."

3 Nude play may indicate that it is time for beginning sex education. It may be a good idea to share a basic child's book about sex, such as *Where Do I Come From?* Keep the information simple, and answer your child's questions honestly but simply. Let your child know that you're the one to come to for answers to questions.

4 Pay close attention to the television and movies that your child is witness to. Young children are great mimics and will imitate what they see adults do, even when they don't understand the significance of what they are imitating.

5 At a later time, have a discussion with your child and explain the boundaries in easy-to-understand terms, such as, "It's OK to take off your clothes when you're changing or having a bath. It's good manners and appropriate behavior to keep your clothes on and your bathing-suit areas covered up at all other times." This is a good time to address the issue of appropriate and inappropriate touching.

! **If your child continues to be involved in nude play or demonstrates a deeper understanding of the significance of the play, it is wise to seek the advice of a professional. A doctor or counselor can recognize or rule out any inappropriate acts on the part of any adult in the child's life or any other underlying problem.**

NUDITY, in family environment

SITUATION
We've always been casual about family nudity. But now that our children are getting older, we're wondering if we should modify our behavior.

THINK ABOUT IT
A relaxed atmosphere about nakedness is common in many families when children are babies. The questions usually arise as children begin to get

older. It's normal for parents to reevaluate their policies about family nudity at that time.

SOLUTIONS

1 It's best to follow your instincts in this situation. If your child is beginning to stare at or touch a parent's private parts, then it's a good time to introduce more modesty. Create rules about privacy, such as knocking before entering a bedroom or bathroom and keeping yourself covered in front of others. Teach in a calm, easygoing manner, as you would teach anything else to your child.

2 Teach your child that some things that are acceptable in the privacy of your home are not OK in other places. An example: "Carissa, it's fine to play at home in your underclothes, but when we're at Grandpa's, you need to get dressed before you come downstairs. That's using good manners." Explaining the difference between what's acceptable and what's not will also help your child make an appropriate decision if she's ever confronted with an inappropriate situation of adult nudity. An easy way to teach the boundaries is to explain that any area covered by a bathing suit is considered your private area. Discuss who can see her private areas and under what conditions. (Remember to include information about the family doctor in this discussion.)

3 Respect your child's growing need for privacy. A child you've bathed since birth will suddenly become modest somewhere between age six and twelve. It's fine to allow an older child more privacy. Let her know that you understand that she's growing up and that you respect her need for more privacy. Along with this, encourage communication by freely discussing her questions about her development and sexuality.

OTHER PEOPLE'S CHILDREN, friends

See also ■ Birthday, bad behavior, other children as guests
■ Other people's children, neighbors
■ Other people's children, relatives

SITUATION

I have a close friend that I've always enjoyed spending time with. The problem is that her children are undisciplined and annoying. It really puts a damper on our time together.

THINK ABOUT IT

You love your friend. She loves her kids. This is a sensitive issue. Chances are she doesn't see her kids the same way you do. Tread lightly. And remember, kids grow up quickly.

SOLUTIONS

1 Arrange for visits to occur during times when the children are in school or otherwise occupied. Try to meet for a meal away from home, or arrange your visits to take place at adult-oriented activities, so she'll be led to leave her children with a sitter.

2 Allow your friend to deal with her children's behavior (or not deal with it, as the case may be). Get involved only when something involves your children or your property. Make your comments nonconfrontational and friendly.

3 When you have a problem with your friend's children, don't try to change her life. Focus only on the issue at hand. Find a solution to the current problem, only to the extent necessary to get through the visit.

4 Using your enthusiasm as a starting point, invite her to accompany you to a parenting class or to attend a lecture. Share a copy of your favorite parenting book or tape with the opening comment that you love it and you're sure she will, too.

5 Pick your battles. Ignore the petty little things and be thankful your own children are better behaved.

OTHER PEOPLE'S CHILDREN, neighbors

SITUATION
My children like to play with the neighbor kids, but some of these children are poorly behaved.

THINK ABOUT IT
It's nice to have kids close by for yours to play with. Often, friendships will form simply because of convenience. There are ways you can monitor the time when they're together. And who knows? Maybe you'll play a role in improving the neighbor kids' behavior and, consequently, their lives.

SOLUTIONS
1 Invite the kids to play in your yard or at your home. Follow the rule, "My house; my rules." Let all the kids know exactly what your expectations are and what the house rules are. Be kind and friendly but firm. Surprisingly, when you are specific and consistent, even kids who misbehave at home will behave appropriately at your house.

2 If a child is misbehaving, don't stew and mumble about it, and don't yell at the kid in front of others. Simply take him aside, and in a very polite and calm voice, explain what it is you would like. Many children who are shown respect and asked politely to cooperate will gladly do so.

3 When you have a problem with the neighborhood children, don't try to solve all the discipline problems of their family. Focus on the specific issue at hand. Find a solution to the current problem, but only to the extent necessary to make things run smoothly where your children are concerned. Make your comments friendly and informal. Don't accuse or place blame; simply state the problem and create solutions.

4 If a specific child is so undisciplined that you don't want him around your children, you can gently interrupt the friendship. This approach takes a few weeks but will have effective results. Simply find excuses to say no whenever this child calls or drops by to visit. If he's usually around at a specific time of day—for example, right after school—find other things to do during that time. Over time, the child will find someone else to play with and will be around less often. (This approach is far more effective than trying to forbid your children to play with this child, as he then becomes "forbidden fruit" and may actually become more intriguing to your children.)

OTHER PEOPLE'S CHILDREN, relatives

See also ■ Grandparents

SITUATION
I have relatives with unruly, disruptive children. I can't believe that the parents would run such an undisciplined household. Our visits with them are strained, and I'm always one inch away from exploding.

THINK ABOUT IT
Memorize this line: "They're not my kids. It's not my problem." Use it as your mantra during your visits with them. Until such time as they move into your house, don't obsess about their behavior. (I saw you shudder! See? It could be worse!)

SOLUTIONS
1 Avoid the temptation to discipline the kids yourself. Allow the relative to deal with her children's behavior (or not deal with it, as the case may be). During moments of stress give yourself a "time-out" by using

the bathroom or making a pot of coffee. If the problem involves your children or your property, handle it in a quick, calm manner.

2 Don't expend energy thinking you can change the way your relative's family lives with a few well-placed comments. Focus on finding a solution to the current problem but only to the extent necessary for things to run smoothly at that moment. To prevent the parents from becoming defensive, make comments about "all the kids" (instead of targeting *your* kids). Make friendly suggestions: "Gee, because Norton's so excited about hitting everyone with that brick, maybe we can find something else for him to play with." Or solve the problem by distracting the problem child or getting him involved in another activity: "Norton, could you do me a favor and water the flowers? Here's a watering can."

3 Share ideas about child rearing in a friendly "guess what I learned" sort of way. Instead of pointing out your relative's children's shortcomings, focus on sharing an exciting new idea that you just learned about. You may want to invite the relative to attend a parenting class with you, using your excitement as a reason for the invitation. Many people don't realize that their children are so undisciplined, and you don't have to point it out! Approach this person in a conspiratorial "we parents are all in this together" way, and you may get some good results.

4 Use these visits as a reinforcement of your own commitment to good parenting—and a peek into what life would be like without rules and discipline. Learn to ignore the little stuff. Try to enjoy visits with the relatives and overlook the petty issues. Focus on the things you enjoy about the family or on finding some things to enjoy!

PARTIES, bad behavior at

See also ■ Birthday ■ Gifts, rude response to ■ Manners, in public
■ Public behavior, defiance

SITUATION

Every time I take my son to a party, his behavior embarrasses me. It's as if he leaves his manners at home! I'm even starting to turn down invitations because of the way he acts. Please help!

THINK ABOUT IT

Children are not born with social manners; they must be taught. Some kids get so caught up in the unusual atmosphere of a party that they forget all they have been taught about manners.

SOLUTIONS

1 It's best to use "preventative" parenting when possible. In other words, if you're invited to a party, spend some time before you arrive at the event to review what behavior is expected of your child. You might even make a list of party rules and review them before leaving the house. While you're at the party, if his behavior starts to slide, remind him of the rules.

2 If you have a younger child, role-play a few parties at home. Having a "pretend" party will allow you to practice the manners your child will be expected to use. It helps to exaggerate your manners so that they are very obvious to your child.

3 Avoid correcting or reprimanding your child in front of other guests. Take your child into a private room, such as a bathroom, for a discussion. Keep your comments brief and to-the-point. Don't just point out what he has done wrong; give specific instructions about the behavior you want to see instead.

PARTIES, doesn't want to go

See also ■ Birthday, bad behavior, your child as guest
■ Friends, sleep overs ■ Manners, in public
■ Shyness, around adults ■ Shyness, around children

SITUATION

My daughter has been turning down invitations to parties and social events. Why is she doing this? Should I force her to go?

THINK ABOUT IT

As you ponder this problem, don't isolate it. You'll come up with the right solution if you evaluate your daughter's life as a whole picture. Is she doing well in school? Getting along with her siblings? Eating well? Sleeping normally? Does she have interests and activities she enjoys? The answers to these questions will determine your best approach to this dilemma.

SOLUTIONS

1 If your daughter turns down only one or two events, don't over-analyze this issue. She's not going to turn into Howard Hughes overnight. Kids have valid reasons for not wanting to attend a specific party. Maybe the guest of honor is someone your child doesn't get along with, and she was invited because "everyone from the class" was. Perhaps your child hates bowling and doesn't want to be embarrassed by her lack of skill.

2 Some young children (up to about age seven) are very uncomfortable in a party environment. For most children, this phase passes; and by about first or second grade, they will be enjoying parties of all kinds.

3 If your child consistently turns down invitations, try to discover the real issue behind your child's decision. Does she have a shy temperament? Does she prefer smaller, more intimate gatherings? Is there one particular classmate who has been bullying her or embarrassing her? Did something happen at a party that is preventing her from repeating the experience? Ask a few helpful questions to find out. Brainstorm a few ideas to help her deal with her fears.

4 Gently encourage your child to attend an event. Give her as much information as you can about the event in advance so that it's not an unknown. If the party is at a public place, such as a skating rink or bowling alley, arrange to visit the location in advance. If a friend is also invited to the party, offer to let the friend drive over with you, so your child won't have to arrive alone.

5 Help your child plan a party of her own. The experience of coordinating an event and enjoying the results may give her a different perspective about parties.

PERFECTIONISM

See also ■ Homework, perfectionism

SITUATION
My child has to get everything just right or she becomes very frustrated and cries and even gives up. She seems overwrought about succeeding at everything.

THINK ABOUT IT
In our achievement-based society, perfectionism often rears its ugly head at a very young age. It will take some gentle coaxing and teaching to help your child learn to relax.

SOLUTIONS
1 Help your child learn to prioritize. Perfectionist children tend to give the same amount of importance to every task thereby making them

feel overwhelmed. Help her understand that some things are important and require a great amount of time and care, like her final book-report project, but some things can be done quickly, like sharpening her pencils.

2 Let your child see you make a few mistakes and observe that you handle them with aplomb and a sense of humor. "Darn, I burned the chicken. Well, I guess you lucky kids get to have cereal for dinner!" This kind of modeling helps a child learn to be more tolerant of her mistakes. Demonstrate that you can enjoy something even if you're not good at it. For example, let your child see that you enjoy a game of tennis even though you've never played before and miss half the shots.

3 Look carefully at the message your child is getting from the important adults in her life. Do you display disappointment when she strikes out? Do you acknowledge the *B* in math by asking why she didn't get an *A*? Do you call her "careless" when she spills her juice? Learn to compliment her good efforts and positive attitude, and help her focus on the process instead of the finished product. Help her understand that mistakes aren't bad—they're just a step toward learning—and that she doesn't have to be perfect in everything she does.

PET CARE

See also ■ Chores

SITUATION
My son begged us for a dog. He promised he'd take care of it. We finally got him the dog, but getting him to take care of his pet has become a daily battle.

SOLUTIONS
1 Children younger than age twelve simply don't have the mental and physical ability to care for a pet on their own. They have good intentions, and a lot of love for their pets, but when it comes to daily care, it's a

big responsibility. View this as an opportunity to teach your child responsibility. Accept that you will have to be a hands-on manager and that your son will take over the pet care, little by little, as he gets older.

2 With your help, have your child create a pet-care chart. List everything that needs to be done on two separate lists—a daily list and a weekly list. Copy the lists neatly on a large piece of poster board, each item followed by a series of boxes for check marks labeled by days of the week. Hang the poster in a conspicuous place, such as on your child's bedroom door. Have him check off each box every day after the chore is completed. The chart serves two purposes. It gives your child a written "to do" list so that everything is remembered, and it provides the basis for developing a routine habit.

3 Tie pet-care chores to other daily rituals to make them easier to remember. For example, feed the pet before dinner. That way, you can easily remind a child by saying "As soon as the dog is fed, you're welcome to have your dinner."

4 Use logical consequences when a child forgets his pet chores. If your child forgets to feed his guinea pig in the morning, don't allow him to take it out of the cage and play with it after school. If your child doesn't pick up the dog poop in the yard, have him take the time to do it before he heads out to play. Teach your child that a pet's care comes before playtime.

5 Let your child know in advance that if his pet-care chores are not done when he leaves for school, you will do them for him. *Then,* when he comes home from school, he can do a few of your chores. For example, if the dog's food and water dishes are empty after your child leaves for the day, you fill them. When he returns home from school, show him the laundry basket full of socks and towels to be folded.

 If you're already handling a majority of the pet care and have to nag and plead for the kids to handle the rest, a simple change may get everyone's attention. Announce that the pet is now going to be yours. Say something like this: "I have decided that Blackie is now going to be my dog. I will feed her and walk her and pick up her poop. If any of you kids want to play with her or walk her, you'll need to ask me first. She will start sleeping in my room, beginning tonight." When the kids cry and complain, tell them that five days from now you would be willing to reconsider. Spend the next five days being very possessive of Blackie. Take her with you when you leave the house, play happily with her in front of the children, and deny the kids the right to take her for a walk, saying, "No, thanks, I'll do it myself." After five days, and a major attitude adjustment on the part of the children, go back to using the above solutions to get them more involved in pet care. If this idea backfires, and the kids don't seem to care, you'll need to make a decision. Do you really want Blackie to be your dog? Or do you want to find her a new home? If you decide to sell the pet, don't use this as a threat, simply announce that you feel it would be best for the dog to find it a new home, and then do it. Don't be swayed by tears and promises if you've been through all of the above ideas and still find pet care to be a major issue.

PRIVACY, of children

See also ▪ Bedrooms, privacy between siblings ▪ Masturbation ▪ Nudity, in family environment ▪ Sexuality

SITUATION
My child complains that he doesn't get any privacy. He doesn't want us to walk into his room any time we want to and has even asked for a lock on his door.

THINK ABOUT IT
As children grow, many start to feel a need for a private space. This is a normal part of development. Your child's right to privacy, though, should be earned by the demonstration of trustworthiness and responsibility.

SOLUTIONS

1 This is a good time to discuss the rules you feel are important regarding privacy. It's OK that everyone in the family has to ask before getting into another's dresser drawers or to knock before entering each other's rooms. Children, however, must be taught to ask, "Who is it?" and if the answer is Mom or Dad, they need to say, "Come in." Don't allow your child to say, "I'm busy," or some such answer. You are knocking as a *courtesy*, not to gain permission to enter. (In reverse, however, they *are* asking to gain permission to enter a parent's room. This is one of those times when what's good for the goose is *not* good for the little ganders.)

2 Many children begin to assert their developmental independence by desiring more authority over their bedroom, which they perceive as the only part of the house that is truly theirs. If you have a basically responsible child, it's OK to turn over his bedroom to him, with a series of clear rules. These rules should cover housekeeping issues (food in the room, how often the room must be vacuumed and the sheets changed, and so forth) and design issues (how you feel about posters on the wall and other decorations). Let your child know that he can earn the privacy in his room by showing that he is responsible enough to follow the rules. If a child abuses this trust by doing things in his room that violate your house rules (such as playing with matches or eating treats after you have said no), let him know the door must remain open until he has earned the privilege of privacy once again. If your child continues to break the rules, simply remove the door from the hinges, store it in the garage, and set a time frame for following the rules that will result in the reinstallment of the door.

3 Explore the reasons your child is wanting more privacy. Is this just normal development, or does he have something he's trying to hide? Most likely, if the reason is the latter, his behavior will appear secretive in other ways, too. He may make whispered phone calls or answer questions about what he's up to in vague, disjointed ways. If so, try to get information by asking direct questions. Maybe he's planning a surprise or spending time reading a book such as, Lynda Madaras's *What's Happening to My Body? For*

Boys. It's also possible that your child is exploring his body or masturbating. If you talk with your child and aren't satisfied with the answers you get, it's time to talk to a family counselor or other professional.

❗ If your child is spending excessive time alone or is displaying other unusual behaviors, such as constant moodiness, anger, or secretiveness, please talk to a family counselor about your concerns.

PRIVACY, of parents

See also ▪ Manners, at home ▪ Nudity, adults' around children ▪ Respect, teaching

SITUATION
Our daughter demands entry into our bedroom and bathroom at all times and won't allow us privacy without a major fuss. It's becoming very annoying.

THINK ABOUT IT
Children need to learn proper etiquette when it comes to privacy. They don't learn what's proper by osmosis, particularly when they have been granted unlimited access to us since they were babies.

SOLUTIONS
1 The remedy may be as simple as a discussion about privacy, what closed doors mean, when to knock, and the other subtle nuances of good manners. Be consistent, and remember, some brief reminders will still be necessary, but over time your child will learn the rules.

2 Make door-handle signs similar to the ones found in hotels, one side saying "Enter" and the other saying "Privacy Please." Allow every person to hang one on their bedroom doors, and teach every family member to respect the signs. (Parents, of course, may request entry to a child's room even when the privacy sign is hung.)

3 Don't feel guilty about wanting some privacy. You don't have to be accessible to your children twenty-four hours per day to be a good parent. In fact, you may be a better parent if you allow yourself a few minutes of peace while you shower, dress, or use the toilet!

PROCRASTINATION

See also ■ Complaining ■ Cooperate, won't ■ Forgetfulness
■ Promises, doesn't keep

SITUATION
My child puts things off until the very last minute and then moans and complains while doing them.

THINK ABOUT IT
Some procrastination is normal. After all, what kid would actually *choose* to do the dishes when his new computer game awaits his attention?

SOLUTIONS
1 Teach your child how to manage his time. When an assignment is given, take the time to sit down with your child and outline the steps of a project. Next, assign a time frame to each step and a date by which the project must be completed. Help your child create a "to do" list and a calendar. Check in with him regularly to see how he's doing keeping up with his goals.

2 Don't make a global statement, such as "Clean your room," which can present itself as an overwhelming project that your child will avoid at all costs. Instead, help your child break down the task into smaller, manageable chunks. Make a check-off list: "Clothes in closet, books on shelf, Legos in box, vermin outside," and so forth. Viewing one item on the list at a time can make a large job seem more manageable.

3 Clearly establish routines that your child can follow for specific events. Homework can be done at a specific time and place every day and chores done at another specific time. When a routine is followed, it becomes habit, and regular tasks will be done without procrastination.

4 Don't torture your child by forcing him to spend long periods of time on a task he finds unpleasant. For example, if your child resists his hourly piano practice, try breaking it down into three twenty-minute segments.

5 Don't rescue a child who procrastinates until the very last minute. Doing so will not allow the child to learn from the mistake. Don't lecture or harass a child, either! Your reaction will change the child's focus from the task at hand (and the struggle he has created from his procrastinating) to your anger at him. When this change happens, the opportunity for him to learn a lesson will disappear.

! If a child continues to procrastinate, and does so with a very negative attitude, there may be an underlying problem. It may be that procrastination is his way of resisting your authority over him, or it may be a sign of fear or anxiety over the issue that he is reluctant to begin. Examine the issue from a "whole child" approach, and if you suspect a hidden agenda, spend some time discovering and dealing with the real problem.

PROMISES, doesn't keep

See also ■ Cooperate, won't ■ Forgetfulness ■ Lying ■ Procrastination

SITUATION
If I hear my child say "I will; I promise" one more time, I think I'll scream! She always says she'll do things, but then she doesn't follow through.

THINK ABOUT IT
All children lack follow-through from time to time, but if your child shows a consistent pattern of this behavior, it's important that you take the time to teach her the value of keeping her word.

SOLUTIONS

1 Don't make general statements that label your child, such as, "You *never* keep your promises." Instead, call your child's attention to specific issues, and assume that she will follow through: "You promised you would pick up your mess after lunch. I expect you always to keep your word." You can teach your child to see herself as someone who always keeps her promises.

2 Make sure you keep *your* promises. Often, parents make promises and then very valid reasons come up to prevent them from keeping their word. For example, you say, "I'll play ball with you after dinner," but then a neighbor stops by asking for your help, and you never get around to playing ball. Avoid these situations by choosing different words, such as, "We'll see" or "If possible" or "If all goes according to plan." Another option is to keep your thoughts to yourself, and announce what you'll be doing at the time you're ready to do it.

3 Point out when your child makes a promise. Often, kids say they'll do something without giving it much thought. Let your child know you're hearing what she says as a promise: "Angelique, I'm hearing you say you'll start cleaning your room tomorrow. I'll trust you to remember and to keep your word."

4 Suggest that when your child makes a promise, she writes it down and posts it in a safe place so that she'll remember to follow through.

PUBLIC BEHAVIOR, defiance

See also ■ Arguing, with parent ■ Back talk ■ Cooperate, won't
■ Disrespect ■ Respect, teaching ■ Tantrums, public

SITUATION
My child can be very rude and will defy me in front of other people. This behavior is frustrating and embarrassing.

THINK ABOUT IT

Parents sometimes become so involved in their own feelings of being judged by others that they react in abnormal ways, shouting or saying things they wouldn't usually say. The first step, then, is to understand that at some point all parents have to deal with the dreaded out-of-control-kid-at-the-grocery-store syndrome. You're not alone. My guess is that many of the people watching are thinking, "Thank goodness it's not *me* this time!"

SOLUTIONS

1 Focus on the actual behavior instead of how others may be judging it. Decide how you would handle this situation if it occurred in the privacy of your home, and respond accordingly.

2 Don't let the situation escalate into a public war. Immediately take your child aside. Let him know that you're angry and that you will deal with the consequence of his behavior later. Tell him that if the behavior continues, he'll be "digging his hole bigger" with every action. Later, when you have time to calm down, make a rational decision. Decide how bad the behavior actually was, and determine what an appropriate consequence should be. These decisions are easier to make when you've put some space and time between the situation and deciding how it should be handled.

3 Learn from the situation. Why did your child respond as he did? Did you bark an order or embarrass him in front of others? If so, be more sensitive to your responses to your child in public. Correct him, or issue a command, privately. Offer choices, and give warnings prior to announcing that he must do something.

4 Prior to your next public outing, give your child specific guidelines about what behavior you will expect. Let him know how long you'll be there and what you will be doing. The more you can outline your expectations in advance, the more likely your child will behave according to your wishes.

5 Be realistic in your expectations. It's too much to expect a three-year-old to be on her best behavior when you're spending hours shopping and she hasn't had her lunch or her nap. It's pushing your seven-year-old to his limit if you stop on the way to the playground for a twenty-minute chat with a neighbor. Of course, this kind of thing *will* happen, so try to view it from your child's point of view and do what you can to make the situation more tolerable.

6 Before you leave home, give your child three tokens. Tell him that if he misbehaves, you'll ask for a token. If he has any left when you get home, he can trade them in for a movie, a snack, and a board game with you. If he has none left, he'll not get any of those things, plus he'll have to take a time-out in his room. (Tell him that arguing about losing a token will cause him to lose a second token for the argument.)

7 For your child to behave appropriately in *public*, he needs to behave in *private*. Sometimes, the same things are happening at home, but you're not noticing because you don't have an audience. If you think this situation may be what's happening to you, reread the Introduction to this book.

PUBLIC BEHAVIOR, leaving peacefully

See also ■ Cooperate, won't ■ Doesn't come when called
■ Listening, not ■ Tantrums, public

SITUATION
When it's time to leave (the park, a party, a fast-food restaurant), my child refuses to listen to me. She won't leave without a tremendous amount of pleading, yelling, threatening, and bribing.

THINK ABOUT IT
What kid in her right mind would want to leave the excitement and fun of a birthday party only to go home and finish her homework? This request is going to take a bit of convincing and a very consistent parenting plan.

SOLUTIONS

1 Practice "preventative parenting." In advance of your outing, let your child know what to expect. Explain where you are going, what you'll do while you're there, and how long you will stay. If a child has a clear expectation, she'll be more likely to cooperate when it's time to go.

2 Get in the habit of using a "warning to go" routine. Let your child know when it's "Five minutes 'til we have to leave." Make another announcement at three minutes and a last warning at one minute. Stay consistent with this five-three-one pattern, and your child will become familiar with it and come to anticipate when it's time to leave.

3 Don't call to your child from forty feet away. Go to your child, get eye contact, and make a specific request for cooperation. "Trevor, it's time to leave. Please get your coat and follow me to the car."

4 Be careful that you're not in the habit of saying that it's time to go and then getting sidetracked for long periods of time. If you do so, your child will come to expect that you'll announce that you're leaving four or five times before you actually mean it.

READ, doesn't want to

See also ■ Homework, not getting it done ■ Laziness, at school ■ School

SITUATION

My child doesn't like to read and will only do the bare minimum required to get though his homework. I know that fluency in reading is important to his success in school. How do I encourage him to read more often?

THINK ABOUT IT

You're right to be concerned. Reading is the key to success in all school subjects. With a bit of creativity, you can help your child enjoy reading more and spend more time doing it!

SOLUTIONS

1 Purchase or borrow a stack of "fun" books. Choose books that will be relatively easy for your child to read, in other words, those that are slightly below his level of reading ability. Choose topics based on your child's interests: baseball, horses, sleep-over parties, wild animals, insects, and so forth. Pick a mystery, a joke book, books about current movie stars or athletes, even comic books. Don't comment on the books; simply leave them on the table where your child is sure to see them. To become a great reader, a child needs lots of practice. If you can find the types of books your child will be interested in reading, he'll get the pure practice he needs to make other, more complex reading easier.

2 Allow your child to get his own library card. Take him to the library, and teach him how to use the computers and the wide variety of resources available. Many libraries offer classes to teach kids how to use the resources. Make a routine visit to the library, and make sure you go when you're not rushed, so he can take time to explore.

3 Take advantage of your child's love of computer games to purchase software that requires a lot of reading to play the game, such as interactive stories, travel games, mysteries, and so forth. Avoid those that are simply computerized video games.

4 Buy your child a bedside reading lamp or a tiny book light. Tell him that from now on, he must be in bed by a specific time (for example, 8:30) and that he can either sleep or read. Most kids will do *anything* rather than go to sleep, so there's a chance you'll create a new bedtime reading habit.

5 Many children will read when they are sitting alone having a snack. Put a box of books and magazines near the kitchen table so that reading material is accessible.

6 Read to your child. Often, once children learn to read independently, parents stop reading to them. This change of routine causes great sadness to a child who has come to love falling asleep as you read. Even a teenager will enjoy being read to if you pick books that pique his interest. Select books together, and make sure they're ones you enjoy as well, so your enjoyment will come through as you read to them.

! Some children don't like to read because they have poor eyesight or an undetected learning disability. Look for signs that there is a problem. Does your child rub his eyes after reading? Complain of a headache? Become easily frustrated or angry while trying to read? If you notice any of these problems, make an appointment with your pediatrician to have your child's health checked out or with an optometrist for a complete eye exam.

RESPECT, teaching

See also ■ Arguing, with parent ■ Back talk ■ Disrespect

SITUATION
How do you teach a child to be respectful to parents, siblings, and other people?

THINK ABOUT IT

I wish more parents would take the time to ask that question, as it implies a commitment to good parenting. We seem to be surrounded by kids who have not been taught the first thing about respect. Because you are aware that respect is something you need to teach, you're already on the way to having a respectful child. Here are some specific ideas that should be helpful.

SOLUTIONS

1 Model respectful behavior. Children learn easiest by following your example. When you are respectful to your child, even in times of anger, you can rightfully expect the same behavior from him. (In contrast, if you yell, threaten, and belittle your child, call her names, or react in disgust when she misbehaves, you will be modeling the exact behaviors you want to prevent your child from displaying.)

2 Do not allow your children to treat each other disrespectfully. The ways they treat each other are often practice for the ways they will treat other people. To learn how to encourage healthy sibling relationships, read the various entries in this book under Siblings.

3 Children need to be taught the intricacies of social respect. Sometimes, they act in ways we perceive as disrespectful out of ignorance. Teach in a quiet place, one-on-one, rather than make a loud correction in front of other people. A slight blunder can be ignored and discussed at a later time, but a bigger mistake warrants taking the child aside and quietly pointing out the error *and* giving direction on how to recover in a respectful way.

4 Point out the respectful or disrespectful things you see as you go about your day. Comment on the acts of a cashier, friend, or the people you encounter. Point out the respectful and disrespectful acts shown in a TV show or movie.

ROUGHHOUSING

See also ■ Bully, your child is acting like a
■ Bully, your child is a victim of a ■ Noise, excessive
■ Yelling and screaming

SITUATION

My children play so roughly together! They wrestle, jump, and run. They're noisy and tend to knock things over and hurt each other. I don't have the patience for this behavior, and I usually end up yelling at them.

THINK ABOUT IT

It would be nice to have that much energy, wouldn't it? The reality is that although active play is a riot for the kids, it's nerve-racking for the parents. Here are a few ideas to help you settle things down a bit.

SOLUTIONS

1 Typically, the problem is the *location* of the play. When you see the kids begin to get physically active, move them outside or create a safe room for horseplay—a large rec room or playroom, perhaps.

2 Create a set of rules for rough play. For example, both kids must agree to play, there must be no touching another's face, no weapons of any kind are to be used, and so forth. Have a code word that means "stop" that either child can use if things get too heated up or that you can use if things get too rowdy.

3 Stop the play before it gets out of hand. Typically, a parent will repeatedly admonish the kids to "be careful" or "settle down," but will wait until something is broken or someone is hurt to stop the action. Instead, step in when you sense that things are headed in the wrong direction and divert the kids to another activity.

4 If something gets broken or someone gets hurt, hold both children equally responsible. Do not allow either to place blame on the other.

5 Sometimes, kids get involved in horseplay if they are bored and not being creative about finding something to do. Put together an easily accessible "activity closet" with games, crafts, puzzles, art supplies, and other activities that can help to absorb their energies.

RUDE COMMENTS, intentional

See also ■ Disrespect ■ Gifts, rude response to ■ Manners
■ Respect, teaching

SITUATION
My child can be very rude and hurtful with some of the things he says. How can I stop him from blurting out these kinds of comments?

THINK ABOUT IT
A child who is learning appropriate social behavior has not yet developed the understanding and sensitivity to discern the true impact of his words. Often, children blurt out statements as a way of protecting their own feelings or as a clumsy way of expressing their true emotions. Knowledge and maturity will help.

SOLUTIONS
1 The best response is one of teaching and rephrasing: "Ahmed, I think your words hurt Nathan's feelings. If you're done playing the game, just let him know you'd really like to play something else."

2 Say "Excuse us" to the person to whom the comment was directed. Take your child aside and privately and quickly let him know your feelings about his comment. Ask him how he can fix the situation. If he doesn't know, tell him specifically what to say. Later, have a discussion about the situation and impose a consequence if the comment was intentionally hurtful. A possible consequence for an obviously rude comment is a short note of apology.

3 Take a closer look at the influences for your child's behavior. A friend with bad manners? A favorite TV show that creates humor based on rudeness? An influential adult with a penchant for poorly directed humor? A sibling who teases endlessly? If you can find a cause, you can work at correcting the situation.

RUDE COMMENTS, unintentional

See also ■ Gifts, rude response to ■ Manners

SITUATION
My child makes offensive statements by being painfully honest. In the post office yesterday, she announced, "Mommy, that lady has a mustache." I could have died!

THINK ABOUT IT
It takes experience and maturity to tell the difference between telling the truth and being hurtful. Consider these moments as great teaching opportunities. (Either that, or hide out at home for the next few years!)

SOLUTIONS

1 It's best to take your child aside and give a quick lesson in restraint, such as, "It's best to keep comments about other people to yourself. It can hurt a person's feelings to hear something like that." Talk later, privately, about the specific person's trait and about talking about people in general.

2 You can often ward off the embarrassing comments in advance if you notice your child looking at an approaching person. Lean down and whisper, "That man only has one leg. It's polite not to stare. We'll talk about it later." Do make sure you remember to talk later about the differences in people, as well as what makes us all alike.

3 After an embarrassing comment, it's best to quickly distract your child and deal with teaching a lesson later. If you can find the courage, look the stranger in the eye, smile, and say, "Sorry about that." You can't take your child's comment back, but you can acknowledge that you feel bad about it.

SCHOOL, behavior problems at

See also ■ Cooperate, won't ■ Listening, not ■ Respect, teaching
■ Self-esteem, low

SITUATION

I just got a call from the teacher, who told me that my child is misbehaving in the classroom. He's a good kid! I'm really upset about the call and not sure what to do.

THINK ABOUT IT

It is extremely difficult to be told of your child's poor behavior. It's a normal reaction to defend your child and to look for blame or excuses. Make the effort to separate the facts from your emotions. Ask the teacher for specifics so that you can deal with actual facts rather than general complaints.

SOLUTIONS

1 Suggest a parent-teacher-*student* conference. This arrangement is preferable to the standard parent-teacher meeting, because it identifies the fact that your child is responsible for his own behavior. Prior to the conference, take the time to sit down with your child and write out a list of questions, comments, and possible solutions.

2 Avoid the reactive response, which is to punish your child. Punishment typically doesn't solve the problem, but makes your child defensive and angry. Instead, enlist his cooperation to solve the problem. Discuss the facts and set a plan for solving the problem. Create a contract between you and your child that outlines specific expected behaviors. Include consequences for failure to meet the contract terms. Have your child sign the agreement, and post the contract in a conspicuous place. Have a weekly discussion to review his progress.

3 Talk with the teacher about using a daily or weekly report system. (The determination of weekly or daily is dependent upon your child's behavior, age, and the input from the teacher on this suggestion.) Create a simple form that says, "Steven's behavior in class today was ☐ acceptable or ☐ unacceptable." Photocopy a stack of forms and give them to the teacher. Request that the teacher sign one at the end of each day (or week). (Ask the teacher to include a positive comment on acceptable days.) Tell your child that he alone will be responsible for bringing home a form each day (or each Friday). If the form was forgotten, it will be assumed to be an "unacceptable" day. Each "acceptable" form will result in your child keeping all his usual privileges. Each unacceptable form will result in a loss of privilege. You can set up the loss of privileges so that each negative report will add to the previous. For example, if you are doing daily forms, you might announce that the first unacceptable report would result in your child losing the privilege of using the telephone for the rest of the week. The second would result in loss of the use of his bicycle. The third, the loss of television-watching privileges. Each Monday would begin anew. This method is intended to be a teaching device. Once your child's behavior has improved, you can discontinue use of the forms. (If things start to slip again, you can repeat the process.)

4 If your child is having similar problems at home, it's time to evaluate your parenting plan. Have you established control in your relationship with your child? Do you have specific consequences for misbehavior? Does your child clearly understand what is expected of him? Take a minute to reread the Introduction to this book. Perhaps it would help if you took a parenting class or joined a parent-support group. Look for these at your local school, church, or hospital.

5 Sometimes misbehavior is a sign of another problem. Is your child able to keep up with the work? Or, conversely, is the work too easy? Is there a problem relationship with a classmate? Is your child struggling with an unusual situation at home, like a recent divorce or remarriage or the addition of a new sibling? Once you've thoroughly examined your child's situation, you may be able to come up with a specific plan to curb misbehavior.

 Take advantage of your school's guidance counselor or principal to help you evaluate and solve this dilemma.

SCHOOL, bus behavior

SITUATION
My child has been misbehaving on the school bus.

THINK ABOUT IT
Stick forty kids in a small contained area with no escape, twice a day, during their most difficult parts of the day. Add the fact that although some of the kids are friends, many are not. Stir in one adult who is totally distracted and focused on something other than the children. What do you get? Trouble, with a capital *T*.

SOLUTIONS
1 Personally take your child to the bus stop. Plan a time to talk with the driver, perhaps via a telephone call or, if yours is the last stop, at the end of the day. Ask her to explain the specifics of the behavior in question. Ask what she thinks would be a good solution to the problem. A possible suggestion is to have your child sit in the front seat behind the driver for better supervision.

2 Try to determine if there is another child on the bus who is motivating your child to misbehave. Sometimes, kids will influence each other to behave in ways that aren't typical for them. If this seems to be the case, ask the bus driver to require that they sit in different sections of the bus, perhaps one in the front and one in the back.

3 If your child enjoys taking the bus to school and your schedule allows you some flexibility, drive your child to school for a specified period of time. Charge your child a "fee" of one chore per day to drive him. The chore can be washing your car, folding laundry, or some other household chore.

Use this driving time to discuss the bus behavior problems and agree to a plan for better behavior. When your child returns to the bus, check in daily with the driver for a while to be sure things are going well.

4 The driver may not have specific rules for the children and may be unaware of how to deal with children who misbehave. Take the time to create your own list of rules and review them with your child. Many kids will respond better if they have specific expectations to meet.

SCHOOL, not wanting to go

See also ■ Bully, your child is victim of a ■ Clinging ■ Fears, of real things ■ Friends, doesn't have any ■ Morning chaos

SITUATION
My child says she hates school. She complains about mysterious headaches and stomachaches or finds other excuses for not going to school.

THINK ABOUT IT
By observing your child, asking subtle questions, and talking with the teacher, you may be able to determine the reasons for this behavior. There are a variety of typical reasons for a child not wanting to attend school. It may be that a school-yard bully is picking on your child. Maybe she doesn't have any friends, or she is having a difficult time with a specific project or subject or has a personality conflict with the teacher. If your child is reluctant to talk, use the safety of the "some kids" comment and take your best guess about what you think the problem might be: "Some kids are afraid

they might get lost in such a big school building. How do you feel about finding your way around?" Once you have pinpointed the problem, you can acknowledge and validate her feelings. Then problem solve with your child to find an acceptable solution.

SOLUTIONS

1 Make an appointment with a pediatrician for a checkup. Poor eyesight, a hearing problem, or other hard-to-detect learning disabilities can make school a very unpleasant place for a child. A checkup can pinpoint or rule out a physical problem.

2 Don't encourage your child's anxieties by overprotecting him. Saying things like "I'm just a phone call away if you need me" or "The teacher or principal is there to help you with any problems" can confirm a child's fears. She may think, "If my parents are worried, then I should be, too." Instead, have a relaxed, supportive attitude. Convey the message that all children go to school, and it's a normal, routine part of life. Make school more fun by participating in school events and showing great interest in your child's schoolwork and activities.

3 Help your child overcome her fearful emotions by letting her rehearse or practice for the situations she finds daunting. If she has a hard time speaking out in class, practice having her raise her hand and ask a question at the dinner table. When she does, say something like "That's a very good question!" If she is struggling with making friends, teach her a few opening lines, such as, "Hi, my name's Heather. Want to play catch?" If she's afraid she might get lost in the hallways, visit the school after-hours and walk around together, letting her point out her classroom, the art room, the gym, and the cafeteria.

4 If your child is having trouble with the teacher, have a discussion with her to clarify exactly what the problems are. If the problem is a very specific one ("She never calls on me"), problem solve with your child about how to find a solution. It may help if you assist your child in rehearsing the exact words she can say to the teacher, such as, "I would like to answer more questions in class. Could you please call on me more often?" If the problem is more complicated, set an appointment with the teacher. If you find the teacher is not helpful, talk with the principal or school counselor.

5 Have specific rules for staying home from school, for example, a fever of 100 degrees, vomiting, and so forth. Establish strict sick-day rules. A healthy child who must stay in bed all day and forgo any evening activities will often "recover" quickly.

6 For a low-intensity, whining complaint about having to go to school, simply respond, "It's the law. All kids have to go to school."

! If your child appears to have extreme fears about going to school, there may be something more complicated causing these fears. It's important that you talk with a professional. Call the school or your local hospital for a recommendation.

SCHOOL, teacher, doesn't like

SITUATION
We just started a new school year and already my child is complaining about his teacher.

THINK ABOUT IT
Don't immediately assume there's a problem. Many children complain at the start of a new year because the teacher is making them work after a summer of leisure or because they've overheard negative comments about the teacher. Give the relationship some time, and encourage your child to focus on his friends and schoolwork and let the relationship with the teacher develop. Let your child know that if he's polite and a good listener, he can make the best of the situation.

SOLUTIONS
 Present the attitude that it's normal for people to have differences, that differences can usually be worked out, and that it's more productive to try to make things work than to complain about them. Don't

make negative comments about the teacher to your child, because this just validates your child's complaints and takes away any incentive to work on the relationship. Ask helpful questions to determine the reason your child dislikes his teacher. It may be a specific issue or a general personality clash. Through discussion with your child, you can often pinpoint the real problem and can then try to find a solution.

2 Get involved at school so that you can be in the classroom, even for a short period of time. Having a firsthand look can often give you some valuable information about the teacher and her relationship with your child.

3 If there is a specific problem, don't rush in to fix it without thinking it through and having a plan. First, outline the reasons you feel there is a problem and describe the situations that have occurred. Next, try to come up with some possible solutions. Finally, set an appointment with the teacher and present the information in a calm, nonaccusatory manner.

4 If you have worked with your child, met with the teacher, and the problem still exists, it may be time to reach for more help. First, understand that if the problem is a minor one, you can make it worse by focusing on it. (Making a mountain out of a molehill!) If you feel that the problem is interfering with your child's schoolwork or is affecting his emotional development, those are good reasons to seek help. Schools respond best if you move up the hierarchy; in other words, don't approach the district superintendent unless you've worked with the teacher, the school counselor, and the principal, with no positive results. Use the steps outlined in Solution 3 as you approach each person for help.

! Move your child to a new classroom, or a new school, only as a last resort. Doing so could send a message to your child that he is not capable of solving problems or that something is wrong with him. It also may teach your child to run away from problems. If the problem is so severe that you have no choice but to move your child, write a specific letter of complaint to the district superintendent so that any other children will be spared the same problem.

SELF-ESTEEM, low

See also ■ Friends, doesn't have any ■ Moodiness ■ Siblings, jealousy
■ Sports, reluctance to play

SITUATION

I'm beginning to suspect that my child's negative behavior is due to a lack of self-confidence and low self-esteem. How do I help him feel good about himself?

THINK ABOUT IT

It's routine to teach kids how to read, write, and even how to paint or how to run the dishwasher. It's not customary to teach kids how to nurture their own self-esteem, though it's the most important thing they can learn.

SOLUTIONS

1 The foundation for healthy self-esteem is the feeling of unconditional love and approval a child feels from his parents. As children navigate the rocky road to adulthood, they need large, obvious doses of this kind of love. Make sure you're showing your child love on a daily basis. Say it with your words, your actions, and your heart.

2 Help your child discover his talents and the things he's good at. Allow him to try various sports, hobbies, and activities. Encourage him to apply himself to those things he seems skilled at and enjoys. Accomplishment builds self-confidence. Self-confidence builds self-esteem.

3 Assign your child household chores. Chores help a child feel like a capable, responsible member of the family. Chores promote a feeling of being trusted, skilled, and important. (*See also* Chores.)

4 Don't hover, protect, and rescue your child. Let him learn through his trials, his struggles, and his mistakes. A child's greatest sense of accomplishment comes through personal effort and personal success.

5 Compliment your child daily using sincere and specific praise. A child creates an image of himself largely through input from others, especially his parents. When you notice something worth praising, use descriptive statements to compliment your child, such as, "You sure stuck with that project until it was complete. That takes persistence and stamina!"

6 Choose your words carefully. You may have heard *your* parents say, "What is the matter with you?" or "Can't you ever remember?" and now you repeat it to your child without much thought to the punch behind the words. But think about what your words mean, and find alternatives that more clearly describe your intended meaning.

7 Help your child develop a more positive way of looking at life. Gently correct his pessimistic statements. When he says, "I can't do it," respond, "Take your time and try again, I have confidence in you." If he mutters, "I'm so clumsy. I'll never learn to roller blade," say, "It's tough to learn something new. Remember how much you fell when you first put on skis? Now you're a better skier than I am!"

SELFISH BEHAVIOR

See also ■ Manners, at home ■ Manners, in public ■ Rude comments, intentional ■ Self-esteem, low ■ Sharing ■ Siblings, jealousy

SITUATION
My child is overly possessive of her things and won't share. She seems too concerned with her own needs and feelings and doesn't display much empathy for others.

THINK ABOUT IT
Babies and young children are naturally self-centered. The ability to see beyond one's self is a process that comes with time and maturity. Some children develop empathy earlier than others. Help your child develop an awareness of others' needs in loving ways.

SOLUTIONS

1 Some children are fearful of losing the things they have or of having their things broken or damaged. They need to learn that people are more important than possessions. This lesson is taught more easily through modeling than lecturing. Be willing to share your things with your child, and point out the fact that you are willing to share because of your love for her. In addition, provide a safe place for your child's most special treasures. When her important things are safe, encourage her to share other possessions.

2 At times in a child's life, her self-esteem may flounder. Some children become so overly anxious about their own self-worth that they appear to be selfish. This child needs to know that she is loved for who she is, unconditionally. She needs private one-on-one time with the important adults in her life on a regular basis. Once she becomes more secure in her feelings about her position in life, she will display fewer selfish actions.

3 Encourage your child to share or show concern for others. Involve her in a volunteer project, such as working with the elderly, disadvantaged families, or even the local pet shelter. Praise and compliment her when she does this, and let her overhear you telling others about her thoughtful actions.

4 Make certain you aren't overindulging your child. If a child's every need and wish is fulfilled, and she's used to getting what she wants, she'll tend to act in selfish ways. For ideas on how to monitor this, check the entries under Gimmees, Materialism, and Money.

SEPARATION ANXIETY

See also ■ Clinging ■ Shyness ■ Work, doesn't want parent to

SITUATION

My child is afraid to leave my side to try new things or play with other children.

THINK ABOUT IT

It's a big world out there. Some kids jump right in, and some need to test the water with their toes before they're comfortable wading in. (And then they wade very slowly, of course!) Be patient. With some gentle guidance your child *will* leave your side. (I mean, honestly, have you ever seen a ten-year-old superglued to his mother's side? Me neither.)

SOLUTIONS

1 Don't force your child to jump into situations he's nervous about. Allow him to watch from the sidelines for a while to absorb the goings-on and get a feel for how he'll fit into the picture. Let him know he can sit and watch for as long as he wants to before joining in. Many children relax when they know they have permission to take their time getting involved.

2 Provide opportunities for your child to take small steps toward independence. For example, take your child to a familiar park, and once he's involved in an activity, move a short distance away, sit on a bench, and read a book. Every once in a while, touch base with him by waving or making a comment: "Wow! You're sure swinging high."

3 Don't overprotect your child. Saying things like "Don't worry; I'll be right here if you need me" imply that your child really does have something to worry about. Instead, make your comments positive in nature, and get the message across that what he's about to do is no big deal. For example, when he's leaving your side to attend a birthday party, let him leave on a positive note: "Have fun, honey! See ya in a little while."

4 Acknowledge his feelings, and help him understand them. Then, reassure him and help him deal with the feelings and learn to get by them. "I can see you're a bit nervous about joining the party. That's OK. Take your time and let's see who you know. There's David! Why don't you go over and show him your new watch?"

5 Talk about the event in advance. Let your child know what to expect, how long he'll be there, what he'll do, and when you'll be back to get him. Information like this will help your child feel more comfortable about your separation.

6 Give your child choices. "You've been invited to sleep over at Brandon's house Friday. He's really excited. He said you'd go roller-skating and then make homemade pizza. Would you enjoy that?" Ask your child helpful questions to see why he doesn't want to go. Perhaps there's something specific that would help him be more comfortable—maybe knowing that he can call you to pick him up if he changes his mind. Your child may not be comfortable and choose not to go. That's OK. There will be many opportunities for your child to spend time with a friend. Some more-tentative children will pass on an invitation and be comfortable with their decision. Typically, in time, the child will outgrow this separation anxiety.

SEXUALITY, inappropriate behavior with friends

See also ■ Nudity

SITUATION
I found my child comparing private parts with a friend. They said they were playing "doctor." How should I handle this?

THINK ABOUT IT
If you found the kids eating candy before dinner, or playing with a baseball in the house, you'd handle the situation easily. If, however, they were eating candy or playing ball *with their clothes off,* you'd suddenly feel confused and concerned. That's because you're viewing the situation from an adult point of view. Most times, childhood nudity and mutual curiosity is normal and natural. You just need to teach kids what's appropriate and what's not.

SOLUTIONS

1 If you actually walk into a room and catch children playing with their clothes off, it's best if you can remain calm. Make a statement such as "It is not appropriate to play with your clothes off." Help them get dressed and find something else for them to do. Later, at a quiet time, have a brief conversation with your child about what is and is not appropriate. Teach that they must always keep their private areas (bathing-suit areas) covered. If this happens with the same two children more than once, don't let them play together unsupervised. (Don't make a major announcement; just monitor their time together.)

2 Take the situation as a cue that your child is ready for more sex education. Spend a brief amount of time answering any of your child's questions. Let your child's interest and questions lead the discussion, and don't overwhelm your child with too much information. Give straightforward answers in accurate but simple terms. Address the issue of appropriate versus inappropriate touching so your child will learn how to be respectful of his own and others' privacy.

3 Purchase a book about sexuality and development. Read it yourself, first, because there's lots of stuff you may have forgotten and some things you may not even know! Share it with your child at an appropriate time. Let your child know that you're available to answer any questions. Two outstanding books for this purpose are *My Body, My Self for Girls* and *What's Happening to My Body? For Boys,* both by Lynda Madaras.

4 Take a serious look at what television shows or movies your child has been watching. Children model the behavior they see, even if they don't understand it, so be careful what images they are being exposed to.

! **Excessive interest in sexual topics, or repeated occurrences of sexual play, may be a warning sign of other problems. There may also be cause for concern if one of the children is several years older than the other. Discuss your observations with a pediatrician, school counselor, or family therapist.**

SEXUALITY, inappropriate personal behavior

See also ▪ Masturbation ▪ Nudity

SITUATION

We were at the park, and my son kept putting his hands in his pants. Then, he did it again at the store. I was really uncomfortable about it, and I ended up yelling at him. How should I handle this?

THINK ABOUT IT

In today's world, children are exposed to sexual messages via television, movies, and other media at very young ages. It's important that you, as parent, teach your child about sexuality and development before he gets confusing messages from other sources. It's best if you talk to your child from a young age, beginning with short but accurate answers to your child's questions. As your child gets older, learn to be an "askable" parent. This is a parent who's available to answer even the most disconcerting questions in a way that leaves the door open for further communication.

SOLUTIONS

1 Try to keep your embarrassment under control so that you don't give your child confusing messages. If your child does something that you feel is inappropriate, make a simple, private statement. "Bryan, please take your hands out of your pants. That's not an appropriate thing to do at the park."

2 Don't confuse a child's innocent actions with adult sexuality. A child may have his hands in his pants because he has an itch, because his hands are cold, or because he doesn't have any pockets in his jeans. Don't jump to conclusions. Take a minute to observe and decide what's really going on before you take any action.

3 Talk with your pediatrician about children's sexual development or take a class that focuses on these issues. Many hospitals offer parent-child classes designed to educate and answer questions. It is helpful for a young person to see that the changes occurring in his body and his feelings about these changes are normal.

SHARING

See also ■ Siblings, borrowing things without permission

SITUATION

My child has a difficult time sharing. She's very possessive about her toys and belongings. But that's just the beginning! She doesn't even like to share the swings at the park, her seat on the bus, or "her" patch of sand on the beach!

THINK ABOUT IT

When you're a little kid, nothing *really* belongs to you. Sure, you may get a baton for your birthday, but when you hit your brother with it, your father takes it away. It may be your favorite sweater, but when you grow out of it, your mother gives it to your little cousin. It may be your special swing at the park, but when you arrive and a big kid is abusing it, your baby-sitter tells you to wait your turn. You may start to believe that you have to keep all your important things hidden away to keep them safe from loss.

SOLUTIONS

1 Set up nonthreatening situations that lend themselves to sharing so that your child has practice sharing her belongings for a short period of time. A few examples are games that require two people, such as badminton or checkers; puzzles where everyone is making the same thing; and crafts where children are sharing supplies, coloring with one set of crayons or markers, or building a Lego city.

2 Let your child know exactly what to expect prior to a sharing situation. For example, before a friend's visit, let her know how long the friend will be there, and reassure her that all her things will still be hers after the friend leaves. Allow your child to put away a few favorite things that do not have to be shared, but let her know that the guest will be playing with the other toys during the visit.

3 Share things with your child and point out what you are doing, for example, "Andrea, would you like a turn on my calculator? I'd be happy to share it with you."

4 Encourage your child to share toys with you. It's often easier for a child to share with a parent, because the child knows you'll be careful and that you'll give the toy back when you're done. It makes for good sharing practice.

5 Give your child choices instead of demanding that she share a specific toy, for example, "Sarah would like to play with some stuffed animals. Which ones would you like to let her play with?"

6 It's easier to teach your child about sharing at times when she's *not* in a sharing situation. In the middle of a tug-of-war over her stuffed rabbit she won't be very receptive to your thoughts on the value of sharing. There are lots of good children's books about sharing that can be used to teach, as well as lots of opportunities to demonstrate sharing at home.

7 Have very specific rules about sharing. You should have "joint ownership" rules for things such as board games, sports equipment, and other things that are owned by "all the kids" or the family. Have separate rules about things that are privately owned, such as toys that were received as gifts or those things that a child has purchased herself. Allow children to have a few important things that they don't ever have to share so that they will be more willing to share other, less-valued possessions.

SHOPLIFTING

See also ■ Stealing

SITUATION

I'm in shock! My child was caught shoplifting! She's a good kid, so I'm really puzzled. What's up?

THINK ABOUT IT

Many children will steal something at least once in their lives. If parents don't panic and overreact, it can be a time for teaching a valuable lesson. There are different reasons that children steal, and it helps to know your child's motivation so that you can address your child's belief directly. The bottom line, however, is this: Stealing is wrong and it's against the law. This is the primary message you want to convey to your child.

SOLUTIONS

1 If your child is age six or younger, she may have taken something simply because she wanted it, without a genuine understanding of the ramifications of her actions. This is a great time to teach your child about the rules of property and purchase. In most cases, it's beneficial to have your child return the stolen item, along with an apology, to the manager of the store. (Call the store first and ask what their policy is about children shoplifting. If you have a feeling that they would be overly harsh, you may choose to handle this situation yourself, without involving the store.)

2 If your child has stolen clothing, jewelry, or the like, the motive may be a desire to fit in with peers. A child who observes classmates wearing the latest fashions and whose own wardrobe consists of hand-me-downs or the functional basics may be trying to gain acceptance through her appearance. It's difficult for adults, much less children, to understand and accept the fact that while some people in our world have excesses, others are barely getting by. A shoplifting situation opens the door for extensive conversation about this aspect of life. It's important to talk about your child's good qualities, about not judging a book by its cover, and what "success" in life really is. In addition, it's realistic to acknowledge that it's wonderful to have nice clothes to wear. Help your child find ways to make the best of her current wardrobe. For example, find a secondhand store that sells quality merchandise, and help her develop a plan for earning money and saving it for those items that are most desired.

3 If you've discovered the stolen item at home, don't try to trap your child by asking sneaky questions, such as, "Where did you get this?" If you do, you'll only have to deal with lying in addition to the stealing, as most kids panic when caught red-handed. Instead, make a nonthreatening, factual statement: "Heather, the new CD in your room came from the music store last night. You didn't pay for it. We need to talk." Ask your child why she took the item, and discuss the ramifications of such an act. Make a plan for its return or payment.

! If your child continues to shoplift, or if this is accompanied by other disturbing behaviors or part of a pattern of antisocial behavior, seek the help of a professional.

SHYNESS, around adults

See also ■ Clinging ■ Manners, in public ■ Separation anxiety

SITUATION
My child is very shy around adults in social situations.

THINK ABOUT IT
Even the most vivacious, talkative child can suddenly become timid when faced with social situations around adults. Most kids will overcome this with time and practice. Some, however, are naturally more tentative with strangers and will always be more reserved in social situations.

SOLUTIONS
1 Allow your child to "practice" by involving him in unthreatening social situations, such as a small gathering of friends or family. Being comfortable in such settings comes easier with practice.

2 Don't force your child to be more socially outgoing than is comfortable for him. Teach and encourage polite manners, but don't force more than that. Accept the fact that your child may be more reserved, and understand that all people are different and that these differences are healthy and appropriate.

3 Sometimes shyness is actually embarrassment. Children often don't know what to say to adults, or if they do talk, they feel that they are saying the wrong things. It helps to rehearse appropriate responses and tell your child what kind of things to say, such as, "It's polite to answer an adult who talks to you. When Mr. Zither commented on your haircut, you could have said, 'I just had it cut yesterday.'"

4 Don't rescue or overprotect your child by jumping in with an answer or excuse to fill a quiet moment. Instead, let him learn through experience, even when it makes him a bit uncomfortable. Encourage and support your child when he makes an attempt to be social. A smile, a pat, or a gentle squeeze can let your child know you recognize the effort and think he's doing a good job.

5 Don't label your child as "shy." If anyone else makes this comment, correct him or her by saying your child is sometimes "quiet, thoughtful, or cautious."

6 Give your child a way out if he is really struggling. Teach him to say quietly to you, "P.H.," which means, "I'm having a hard time; please help." Just knowing he can count on you when the going gets rough may give him the confidence to hold his own in a conversation.

SHYNESS, around children

See also ■ Friends, doesn't have any

SITUATION
My child is very shy around other children and has trouble joining in the play.

THINK ABOUT IT

The actions we perceive as shyness are a sign of various situations. Some kids need more time to warm up to a group or a new peer. Some kids don't have enough practice in social situations to feel comfortable jumping right into the action. Some kids are tentative about new situations. And some are, yes, shy. Most of these situations can be overcome through practice and encouragement.

SOLUTIONS

1 Invite one child to your home at a time for a play date. After a time, invite two friends over. In the comfort of her own home, your child will usually feel more comfortable and get to know the other children. She can then transfer that comfort to other social settings.

2 Play alongside your child until she feels comfortable and interacts with another child. Gradually move away from the group but stay close enough for your child to still see you.

3 Involve your child in a physical activity, such as swimming, gymnastics, or a sports team. After the initial adjustment, the experience will build your child's confidence in group settings. (*See also* Sports, reluctance to play.)

4 Allow a child to watch other children for a while before joining in. Some children need to scope out the situation and absorb what's happening before they participate. Pushing a child to get involved before she's ready will make her more uncomfortable.

5 Teach your child specific approaches to use when she meets new kids. Practice these at home in a role-play situation. Acknowledge her uncomfortable feelings, and encourage her to practice and try out her new skills. Let her know that although she may be concerned with her own appearance and her own side of the conversation, the other kid is likely to be feeling the same way. Once she has successfully used her new skills, she will be more likely to try them again.

6 Some children are comfortable and content in their quiet way of interacting with the world. They have one or two good friends, are doing well in school, and are happy and self-confident. Make sure you aren't assuming a problem where one doesn't really exist!

! Spending time with a professional counselor or therapist can help a child who is painfully shy and suffers from it. A school counselor may be a good source of help.

SIBLINGS, bickering

See also ■ Siblings, fighting, verbal ■ Teasing

SITUATION
My children are constantly bickering. It's not dangerous or extreme, but it really gets on my nerves.

THINK ABOUT IT
Sibling bickering is as common, and as annoying, as mosquito bites in summer. Take heart, though. Siblings learn much about life from each other—how to negotiate, how to compromise, and how to understand (and learn to live with) the differences in people. (Sounds like great training for marriage!)

SOLUTIONS
1 Remember when you were a kid and your sister or brother was saying things you didn't want to hear? You responded in a very reasonable way—you plugged your ears and hummed. Use this same concept to cope with your children's bickering. Learn to ignore it. Turn up your music, call a friend on the phone, watch a little TV, vacuum, take a shower. If all else fails—plug your ears and hum.

 Sometimes the bickering is over something really preposterous, like whose shirt is greener. If this is the case, don't waste your breath trying to solve the problem: "Now, come on, kids. You *both* have very nice green shirts." Instead, ignore the topic causing the bickering, and distract and redirect your children with an activity, a snack, or a chore.

3 Siblings *do* need to learn how to deal with each other without your interference. They *do* need to learn how to communicate with each other, even when they disagree. But no rule says you have to submit yourself to the torture of listening to it! Tell them that if they have a disagreement, they can discuss it all they want, but they need to do it elsewhere. (In other words, ask them to leave the room.)

4 Walk out of the room for five minutes. Chances are, when you return, the bickering will have stopped. This exit plan often works because siblings sometimes bicker in hopes that you'll intervene and declare a winner, so without an audience, the issue will fade away on its own.

5 Tell the children to play separately for one hour. (Do not let either of them watch television or play computer games during the hour.) Their first response will likely be, "Great! I didn't want to play with him anyway." But when the solitary play becomes boring, they'll begin longing for each other's company once again.

SIBLINGS, borrowing things without permission

See also ■ Manners, at home ■ Respect, teaching

SITUATION
My daughter takes and uses her sister's clothes and belongings without permission.

THINK ABOUT IT
Many kids see something they like and they use it, without a thought to the fact that they don't have permission to do so. We must teach our kids proper

manners. We need to enforce rules to help them learn how to respect other people's property.

SOLUTIONS

 If a sibling is caught "borrowing" without permission, then a rental fee of a previously agreed-to amount is paid. If the item is damaged or lost, then the child must replace it with something of equal value or with money from allowance.

 The child whose item was taken can choose something of the other sibling's to use for one day. ("Lovies" or special belongings are excluded!)

 Whenever the child does ask permission, make a positive comment to show you appreciate it.

! Allow the sibling whose possessions are being invaded to put a keyed lock on his bedroom door. The parent needs to keep a key, too.

SIBLINGS, fairness

See also ■ Sharing ■ Siblings, jealousy

SITUATION

My kids are always complaining, "It's not fair!" They never seem to feel satisfied with their share—of things, space, food, love, attention, you name it. Believe it or not, the other day I actually *counted* out the M&M's—by *color*!—so that they would be happy with what they got. There was one extra red one, and they actually fought over *one little M&M*!

THINK ABOUT IT

Life *isn't* always fair. And when it is, *fair* does not necessarily mean *equal*. The sooner your children learn this, the happier they will be. Use some of the following solutions to guide your children through this learning process.

SOLUTIONS

1 Help your children focus on their own needs separately from their siblings' needs. For example, if your child complains, "You gave him more crackers than me!" *do not* proceed to defend the certainty that you gave each of them the same amount of crackers. *Do not* try to convince your child that it's appropriate to give more crackers to the bigger, older child. Instead, respond in this way: "I'd like to hear about *your* needs. Are you still hungry? Would you like more crackers?" When you consistently respond in this way, you help your child grow into an adult who *can* find happiness in his own life even though his *coworker* got the raise, his *brother* built the dream home, and his *neighbor* bought the new car.

2 Don't lump your children into one generic category. If one child in the family outgrows his shoes, don't feel compelled to outfit the entire family in new footwear. "All for one and one for all" tends to increase the cries of "Not faaaiiiiirrr!" Instead, respond to your children based on their individual needs. If one child is planning a birthday party, she'll need a bit more of your time. If one child is playing in the soccer championship series, she'll require more attention. If one child outgrows his shoes, he alone will need new shoes. If this concept is something new for your family, expect to hear a few complaints, but given time, the kids will adjust quite nicely to this new definition of *fairness*.

3 Acknowledge your child's feelings and let him know that his complaint is valid, when it is. For example, what if your child is pointing out this fact? "Why does Edwina get to go to *another* baseball game! I've never even gone to one game! It's not fair!" The best response is an empathetic "You're right." Follow this up by voicing the real issue: "I bet you wish you could go to the game tonight." Often, just knowing that someone else sees the injustice in the situation makes a child feel better.

4 Accept the fact that your kids won't always see things the way you do. As an adult, it's perfectly clear to you why your six-year-old should have an earlier bedtime than your twelve-year-old does. Your six-year-old, however, may not "get it" no matter how reasonably you present your case. At some point, you need to untangle yourself from your child's emotions and proceed with the decision you know is right. Your most important goal as a parent is *not* to make your child happy, nor is it to be sure she agrees with every decision you make.

5   Use humor or distraction to end the argument. Kids who are arguing over something so trivial as how much juice is in their cups are often easily distracted.

SIBLINGS, fighting, physical

See also ■ Bully ■ Car, fighting in the backseat
■ Siblings, fighting, verbal ■ Teasing

SITUATION
My kids fight all the time. What upsets me the most is when they get physical: hitting, kicking, pinching, pushing, and hair pulling. I usually end up screaming at them. Is there a way to stop the battles?

THINK ABOUT IT
Children are not born knowing how to negotiate or compromise. When they are frustrated, angry, or annoyed, they will sometimes strike out physically. If they aren't taught the skills they need to control their emotions and if they aren't given direction about how to negotiate and compromise, they may continue to resort to physical actions to get their way. It's our job to teach kids how to work through their disagreements in a socially acceptable way.

SOLUTIONS
1   When two children are physically fighting, immediately separate them into different rooms for a cooling-off period. When both have calmed down, sit them at the table together and arbitrate a discussion between them until the issue is resolved.

2 Have both children sit on a sofa at opposite ends or on two adjacent chairs. Tell them they may get up when they have resolved the issue. At first, you may have to mediate and guide the resolution. Over time, they will learn how to negotiate and compromise on their own.

3 Tell the children they may not play together for one hour. Banish them to separate rooms. (Do not allow either child to watch TV or play video games.) Their first response will likely be, "Great! I didn't want to play with him anyway." But after a boring hour playing alone, they will likely be better company for each other.

4 Have the aggressor do a chore for the injured sibling, such as make the bed or take out the trash. An alternate idea is to fine the aggressor a predetermined amount of money, such as twenty-five cents. The injured sibling gets to keep the payment. (Impose a penalty only if *you* see the aggressive action.)

5 With your help, have the children create a contract agreement between them. Spell out what actions are unacceptable and what the consequences are for failure to meet the contract terms. Have each child sign the agreement, and post it conspicuously. Follow through with the agreed consequences when necessary.

6 Don't always assume that the child who is doing the hitting is the only one at fault. Sometimes the "victim" has taunted, teased, insulted, and tormented the sibling to the point of wild frustration. Although it is never appropriate for one child to hit another, it would behoove you to be aware of any behind-the-scenes torture that may be testing your child's patience to its limit. If you discover that this is happening, begin to hold both children accountable for their behavior.

7 Catch them being good. Reward them with positive attention for getting along. When your children are playing together without fighting, make a comment of appreciation, such as, "I'm happy that you guys enjoy playing together." Giving attention when things are going well will encourage them to continue the positive behavior.

! If your children have frequent intense physical battles, it is a symptom of a much bigger problem. It would be wise to seek the advice of a family counselor or therapist. You may be able to find an appropriate specialist through your church, school, physician, or local hospital. This is a difficult issue to resolve on your own. Don't be afraid to ask for help. Asking for help is a sign that you really care about your children and their relationship with each other.

SIBLINGS, fighting, verbal

See also ■ Car, fighting in the backseat ■ Name-calling
■ Siblings, bickering ■ Siblings, fighting, physical ■ Teasing
■ Telephone interruptions

SITUATION
My kids' fighting drives me crazy! It's usually over some *extremely* important issue, like who gets to use the red Lego piece. (Never mind that there are fifteen more just like it in the box!) I get so tired of the yelling, screaming, and threatening—not to mention what goes on between the kids! Please give me some ideas to put an end to this bickering.

THINK ABOUT IT
Most of us brought our second baby home from the hospital along with visions of our children becoming lifelong friends. (Some of us even had a second child specifically so that our first would have a playmate!) When our children fight, it not only grates on our nerves, it tugs on our hearts. The most important advice I can give you is calm down and relax. Keep a level head and view your kids' arguments in a realistic way. The fight over the red Lego, as intense as it may seem, will be over and forgotten by the time one of them realizes he needs a blue one. Kids fight for lots of reasons. They fight because they don't want to share, because they want parental attention, because they each have a differing view about what's fair, or simply because

they have to share the same space, day after day after day. The vast majority of sibling battles are not destructive to the relationship between the children. All this considered, there *are* ways to survive sibling fighting. And there are ways to reduce the number of fights, and the severity of them, as well.

SOLUTIONS

1 It's a proven fact. Kids will fight longer, louder, and with more enthusiasm when they have an audience. Usually, it's because they hope you'll step in and solve the problem. (You can sometimes tell that this is happening because your son's comments are directed at his sister, but his eyes are on you!) Therefore, it stands to reason that if you leave the room, they will have to solve the problem themselves. A large amount of verbal battles will fizzle out without a parent's interference. If you think about it, you'll really love this solution. It gives you permission to follow the essence of the advice from a particularly appealing bumper sticker I've seen: "When the going gets tough, the tough go shopping."

2 Try to identify if there is a pattern to the kids' fights. Do they typically fight over one thing, for example, the computer or choice of TV shows? If so, make a schedule for computer or TV use. Do they always fight while you're making dinner? You could enlist their help in preparing the meal, feed them a healthy snack, or have a routine activity planned during that time, such as homework or chores. Do they always fight over who sits where at the table or in the car? Assign specific seats and rotate them monthly. Do they fight while they get ready for bed in the evening? Let them take turns using the bathroom, one at a time, for a specified time period. The idea here is to identify the "hot spots" between your children and to create a plan to prevent the problems from continually causing arguments.

3 Teach your children how to negotiate and compromise with each other. Have both children sit on a sofa at opposite ends or on two adjacent chairs. Give them a choice. Tell them you will "arbitrate or mediate." Of course, they will ask what you mean. Let them know that *arbitrate* means *you* make the decision and they will live with it; *mediate* means *they* make the decision, and you will help them come to the best conclusion. Over time, and with practice, they will learn how to settle arguments on their own.

4 If the argument is over a trivial issue, you can often defuse the tension with humor or distract the kids with another activity. For example, if one kid is complaining that his brother is "looking at him funny," there is no sensible reason for you to intervene. Instead, ignore it and ask who would like to help you make brownies. Or try humor. "Oh no! I once read about a boy who made a face like that and it froze in place. They had to mash up his food so he could sip his squashed pizza through a straw. He had such a hard time eating that he lost so much weight the cat thought he was a piece of string and batted him around the kitchen."

5 It happens. The kids are playing together nicely. "Oh, good," you think, "I'll have time to catch up on my paperwork." As tempting as it is, don't ignore your children when they are getting along well! This is the time to show up with a plate of cookies and a kind word of praise. Reward the behavior that you wish to have repeated, and you'll see more of it.

! If your children spend little time enjoying each other's company and are often saying cruel and hurtful things to each other, it would be wise to seek the advice of a family counselor or therapist. You may be able to find an appropriate specialist through your church, school, physician, or local hospital. Don't be afraid to ask for help. This is a difficult problem to solve. Asking for help is a sign that you really care about your children and their relationship with each other.

SIBLINGS, hateful emotions

See also ■ Anger, child's ■ Bully ■ Meanness ■ Respect, teaching
■ Siblings, fighting ■ Siblings, jealousy

SITUATION
My children fight with such intensity it breaks my heart. They are always telling each other, or me, how much they hate one another. Is there anything I can do to make their relationship better?

THINK ABOUT IT

Although you cannot make your children adore each other or even desire each other's company, you can teach them how to be respectful and kind to each other. Ultimately, respect and kindness may create friendship and a lasting bond between them.

SOLUTIONS

1 Create specific family rules about behavior. Outline what things will not be tolerated and list consequences for failure to abide by the rules. Follow through when a rule is broken.

2 Teach children how to negotiate and compromise with each other. Many intense negative emotions come from a lack of good communication skills. Give them guidelines to follow when they disagree. Avoid solving their sibling relationship problems by stepping in with solutions. If you do, you'll solve the immediate problem but teach them nothing about how to work things out with each other. Teach, coach, and encourage them to solve their own problems.

3 Try to discover interests that both children share and arrange times for them to pursue those interests. Perhaps they both enjoy chess or swimming or baseball. Find time to share these things with them as a family. Conversely, don't force children to spend great amounts of time together if they have vastly different temperaments and interests.

4 Be careful that you are not inadvertently feeding the negative feelings between them by showing favoritism or by comparing them to each other in negative, or even positive, ways. Do your best to treat each child as an individual and to see that each one gets a bit of private time with the important adults in the family. Children who feel loved and secure will be less likely to take out their anger on their siblings.

SIBLINGS, hitting of new baby

See also ■ Siblings, new baby

SITUATION

My usually pleasant toddler has welcomed his new baby brother in some obnoxious ways. He's thrown toys at him, nearly smothered him with a blanket, hit him, and bear hugged him so tight the baby's startled scream really scared me. I know that "rivalry" and jealousy is normal, but the physical aggression has got to be stopped.

THINK ABOUT IT

Before the baby entered your family, your toddler was told he'd have a wonderful little brother to play with and how much fun it would be. Then, the little brother is born, and your toddler is thinking, "Are you kidding me? This squirming, crying, red-faced lump that takes up all your time and attention is supposed to be *fun*?" He then "plays" with the baby in the only ways he knows how. He plays catch. You yell at him for throwing toys at the baby. He plays hide-and-seek. You screech that he's trying to suffocate the baby with the blanket. He gives the kid a hug, and you explode in fury. Is it any wonder that your toddler is confused?

SOLUTIONS

1 Your first goal is to protect the baby. Your second, to teach your older child how to interact with his new sibling in proper ways. You can teach your toddler how to play with the baby in the same way you teach him anything else. Talk to him, demonstrate, guide, and encourage. Until you feel confident that you've achieved your second goal, however, do not leave the children alone together. Yes, I know. It isn't convenient. But it is necessary, maybe even critical.

2 Whenever the children are together, "hover" close by. If you see your child about to get rough, pick up the baby and distract the older sibling with a song, a toy, an activity, or a snack. This action protects the baby while helping you avoid a constant string of nos, which may actually encourage the aggressive behavior.

3 Teach the older sibling how to give the baby a back rub. Tell how this kind of touching calms the baby, and praise the older child for a job well done. This lesson teaches the child how to be physical with the baby in a positive way.

4 Every time you see your child hit, act quickly. Firmly announce, "No hitting; time-out." Place the child in a time-out chair or room for about one minute per year of age. When the time-out is over, remind your child to "touch the baby gently."

5 Whenever you see the older child touching the baby gently, make a positive comment. Make a big fuss about the important "older brother." Hug and kiss your older child and tell him how proud you are.

SIBLINGS, jealousy

See also ■ Self-esteem, low ■ Sharing ■ Siblings, fairness

SITUATION
My son is constantly comparing himself to his brother and turning every daily event into a contest. No matter what his brother has or does, I guarantee you it's bigger, better, faster, and more exciting than what he has.

THINK ABOUT IT
Jealousy is defined as "feeling resentment against another person because of his success or advantages." That makes a sibling relationship *very* fertile ground for breeding jealousy. The mere existence of a sibling in the family signifies less for your child and gives him a constant source of things from which he can measure his own value. Our job, as parents, is to help each child feel good about himself and to feel content with his own successes while finding the courage to feel happiness for his sibling's successes at the same time.

SOLUTIONS

1 Acknowledge your child's feelings of jealousy. Once your child knows that you understand how he feels, he may not be so compelled to prove his point to you or to himself. Often, a younger child feels jealous over an older sibling's privileges. Instead of belittling him for his feelings, acknowledge his desires, for example, "I bet you wish you could ride a big bike like Bubba's. When you're twelve, what kind of bike do you think you'll have?"

2 Help your child focus on his own *needs* rather than what his brother *has*. If he says, "How come he gets a whole sandwich, and I only get half?" you can respond, "Oh, are you still hungry? Would you like more sandwich?" He may quickly figure out that half is all he wanted, anyhow. I remember watching my sister one day as she changed my baby nephew's diaper. He sneezed, and she sang, "Bless you bless you bless you" as she tickled his tummy. My then five-year-old niece said, "How come you never do that to me?" A few minutes later, my niece sneezed. My very wise sister went to her and tickled her tummy as she sang, "Bless you bless you bless you." Sarah immediately blushed, as she realized how silly she felt being treated like a baby. My sister then gave her daughter a few minutes of cuddle time, which was the attention that her daughter actually craved.

3 Avoid comparing your children to each other as a way of encouraging compliance. "Your brother's room is nice and clean. Can you get yours to look like that?" "Your sister always does her homework without a reminder." "Your little sister's not afraid to go down the slide." Comparisons breed jealousy and resentment because children feel that your love and acceptance is based on a competition between them.

4 Help your child see and appreciate his own strengths. Comment on the things he does well, praise him for a job well done, and encourage him to develop his own skills. If a younger sibling always feels in his older brother's shadow, try to direct them to different arenas. For example, if the older brother excels in baseball, sign up the younger one for soccer so he can develop his own abilities without comparing himself to anyone else.

SIBLINGS, name-calling

See also ■ Teasing

SITUATION

My son has been calling his brother some awful names. How can I get this behavior to stop?

THINK ABOUT IT

From a child's point of view, name-calling is a safe way to let a sibling know how unhappy you are with him. After all, you're not allowed to slug him one, so name-calling seems like a good alternative.

SOLUTIONS

1 Avoid confronting your child in front of his sibling and embarrassing him with a reprimand or lecture. Embarrassing him can only force the name-calling to be used secretly. Instead, interrupt the children immediately and say, "May I see you in the bathroom for a minute?" Take the child aside for a private discussion. Firmly state your position on name-calling and set specific limits.

2 Many children call names to express anger. Give your child an alternative by specifically teaching what can be said when angry. For example, if your son is angry and yelling, "Get out of my room, dog breath!" you can correct him by requiring that he restate his request more politely, such as, "I don't want you in my room without asking." Explain the benefits of this kind of statement versus name-calling (it clearly explains the problem, and the sibling may respond positively instead of just getting angry.) Also, encourage him to think up a solution to the problem, in this case, perhaps creating a "please knock" sign for his door.

3 Have a standard consequence for name-calling; for example, you must then say three nice things about the person, or you must restate what you just said in three different, respectful ways.

4 Charge a standard fine for every name called. The recipient of the name-calling is the one who gets the money.

5 In a private conversation, teach the sibling who is being called names to ignore it and walk away. Also teach the kid a few good comebacks, such as "Whatever you say, you *are*" or "How long has this been bothering you?" A few good retorts can end the name-calling.

6 Watch for any adults who are modeling name-calling. Is anyone making such statements as "You're acting like a wild animal" or "Don't be such a brat"? Are there any interesting names that are being taught to your children as you sit in traffic? Do you refer to the guy you didn't vote for by names other than his given one? Once you've eliminated any "home-schooling" program, check to be sure that your child isn't picking up this behavior from favorite TV shows or movies. If so, discuss the connection to your child's behavior and give a choice: "Either the name-calling stops, or you can't watch the show."

SIBLINGS, new baby

See also ■ Siblings, hitting of new baby

SITUATION
Our firstborn is showing extreme jealousy toward the new baby. She's obviously mad at us for disrupting the predictable flow of her life with this new challenger for our attention. How can we smooth things out?

THINK ABOUT IT
Take a deep breath and be calm. This is a time of adjustment for everyone in the family. Reduce outside activities, relax your housekeeping standards, and focus on your current priority—adjusting to your new family size.

SOLUTIONS

1 Acknowledge your child's unspoken feelings: "Things sure have changed with the new baby here. It's going to take us all some time to get used to this." Keep your comments mild and general. Don't say, "I bet you hate the new baby." Instead, say, "It must be hard to have Mommy spending so much time with the baby" or "I bet you wish we could go to the park now and not have to wait for the baby to wake up." When your child knows that you understand her feelings, she'll have less need to act up to get your attention.

2 Watch your words—don't blame everything on *the baby*. "We can't go to the park; *the baby's* sleeping." "Be quiet, you'll wake *the baby*." "After I change *the baby* I'll help you." At this point, your child would just as soon sell *the baby*. Instead, use alternate excuses. "My hands are busy now." "We'll go after lunch." "I'll help you in three minutes."

3 Increase your little demonstrations of love for your child. Say extra I love yous, increase your daily dose of hugs, and find time to read a book or play a game. Temporary regressions or behavior problems are normal and can be eased with an extra dose of time and attention.

4 Teach the older sibling how to be helpful with the baby or how to entertain the baby. Let the older sibling open the baby gifts and use the camera to take pictures of the baby. Teach her how to put the baby's socks on. Let her sprinkle the powder. Praise and encourage whenever possible.

5 Avoid comparing siblings, even about seemingly innocent topics such as birth weight, when each first crawled or walked, or who had more hair! Children can interpret these comments as criticisms.

SPITTING

See also ■ Biting, child to child ■ Fighting, with friends, physical
■ Habits, bad ■ Hitting, child to child
■ Siblings, fighting, physical ■ Siblings, hateful emotions

SITUATION

My son thinks it's real cool to spit. It was bad enough when he was spitting on the ground. But now I caught him spitting at his sister! Yelling at him hasn't made him stop. What are your ideas?

THINK ABOUT IT

Some kids watch their favorite baseball star or an esteemed older kid spit and suddenly they think it's a mature thing to do.

With a bit of practice, they find they can spit more and farther each time. Then, they begin to find a variety of uses for this creative sport. It's a parent's job to give a kid like this the correct perspective about spitting.

SOLUTIONS

1 Tell your child clearly that you will not allow spitting. Explain that it is socially unacceptable. (Except on a professional ball field?) Explain that spitting spreads germs. Decide upon a consequence for each time that you see him spitting and follow through without exception. An appropriate consequence, for example, if you catch him spitting while he's playing outside, is to have him come in the house for a fifteen-minute time-out. If he spits inside, have him get a bucket and sponge and clean the area—and maybe the whole floor, while he's at it.

2 Give your child an alternative for using his mouth in a creative way. Purchase him a harmonica, a whistle, a kazoo, or a recorder (a simple wind instrument similar to a flute). Consider letting him chew sugarless bubble gum, with the caveat that he keeps the gum in his mouth.

3 Teach your child how to handle his frustrations. Some kids spit as an immature method of swearing. Help your child learn to vocalize his feelings in a respectful way.

4 Require that each time he spits, he brush and floss his teeth. It's a good way to sneak in some extra dental hygiene, and the tedious repetition may help end the habit quickly.

SPORTS, reluctance to play

See also ■ Athletic lessons/practice, not wanting to continue

SITUATION
My child doesn't want to participate in any kind of sports. Should I force the issue, or just let him off the hook?

THINK ABOUT IT
There are many positive aspects of youth sports. Sports promote teamwork, healthy self-esteem, and mastery of skills. Participation in sports also promotes a healthy lifestyle that can combat the TV-computer–couch-potato mentality of many of our children. It's worth the effort to encourage your child to participate in some kind of sporting activity.

SOLUTIONS
1 Make sure you're offering sports that fit your child's personality. Some children are drawn to "ball" sports, such as baseball, soccer, and tennis. Others prefer swimming, horseback riding, gymnastics, or sailing. Analyze your child's strengths and weaknesses, and the things your child enjoys or avoids. Let your child try several different activities until he finds one that suits him. You may have played baseball all through your childhood and love the game today, but if your child is drawn to swimming instead, open your heart and mind and support the sport your child chooses, while gently encouraging him to try your favorite, too.

2 Take your child to a few professional-sporting activities of the types you would like him to consider. Often, when children see skilled athletes and feel the excitement of the event, they become more interested in trying the activity themselves.

3 Play sporting games at home or at the park with your child. Often, playing a casual game with the family, without the pressure of a coach or team, can encourage a child to learn a game and enjoy playing it. This activity also gives your child a role model to follow. (It's tough to require your child to become more physically active when *your* only sports activity is remote-control lifting.)

4 Find a sport activity you can enjoy with your child, such as martial arts, swimming, or tennis, and take lessons together. Children enjoy the attention from a parent and will learn to enjoy the sport in the process.

STEALING

See also ■ Shoplifting

SITUATION
Money has been disappearing from my wallet, and my daughter is suddenly buying things that she couldn't possibly afford on her own. I suspect that she's been taking the money from me, and it makes me wonder if this is the only incident of her stealing.

THINK ABOUT IT
Your daughter isn't yet a scoundrel on the low road to villainy. A lot of kids steal something at some point in their lives. Some kids steal simply because they want something and so they take it, without thought to the rightness or the consequences. Some steal to impress their friends. Some steal to "punish" their parents for not giving them what they want. Whatever your child's reason, now's the time to get control of the situation.

SOLUTIONS

1 Don't play Sherlock Holmes and try to "trap" your child into confessing. If you hint and question, "Bonnie, where did you get the money to buy that new shirt?" you'll have to deal with the inevitable lie that she'll respond with as she tries to protect herself. Instead, confront her with the evidence: "Bonnie, I see that you have an expensive new shirt on. Yesterday, after you left for the mall, I discovered $20 missing from my wallet. Let's talk." Try to determine what led to this behavior. Have a serious discussion about stealing. Hold your child responsible for her behavior. Require that she return the purchase to the store, if possible, and if not, require that she repay the money.

2 Children younger than about age six steal because they see something they want and they take it. They don't know the implications of their behavior. A first incident of stealing gives you a perfect opportunity to teach your young child some valuable social lessons.

3 First, deal with the stealing episode according to the above solutions. Next, take a look at your child's money needs. Determine if her allowance is meeting her basic needs or if an adjustment needs to be made. (*See also* Allowances; Money.)

4 Ask yourself if you've been an overindulgent parent. Children who are used to getting everything they want start to believe that they are entitled to have what they want. Maybe it's time to start saying no more often.

! If your child continues to steal, or if this is accompanied by other disturbing behaviors or part of a pattern of antisocial behavior, seek the help of a professional.

STUBBORNNESS

See also ■ Arguing, with parent ■ Back talk ■ Cooperate, won't
■ Doesn't come when called ■ Listening, not
■ Public behavior, defiance ■ Respect, teaching

SITUATION

When my kid makes up her mind to do something, or *not* do something, a herd of wild beasts couldn't make her change her mind! The more I say, "Yes, you will," the louder she says, "No, I won't."

THINK ABOUT IT

As frustrating as her unyielding behavior is now, there *is* something for you to look forward to. You can find comfort in the fact that your daughter won't grow up to be a compliant and submissive little mouse! Her assertive and persistent traits can protect her from being pushed into wrong decisions by peer pressure as an adolescent. It may also help her achieve great success as an adult.

SOLUTIONS

1 When possible, avoid giving your child a direct command. Instead, offer choices. The beauty of this approach is that you control the options, so you're pleased with whichever choice she makes. In addition, having an opportunity to choose satisfies your child's thirst for autonomy. For example, don't say, "Clean up this room right now!" as it will, of course, invite an argument. A better approach is to say, "What would you like to do first: put away your clothes or make your bed?" or "When would you like to start cleaning up your room? Before lunch or after?"

2 Allow your child to be part of the decision-making process. Ask her opinion so that she feels some sense of "ownership" of the decision. For example, you might say, "What do you think is the best way to organize all these sports supplies?"

3 Stubborn children often have an exaggerated opinion of right and wrong, fair and unfair. If they come to a conclusion, they feel compelled to defend it. The harder you try to convince them otherwise, the stronger their arguments become. An easier way to get them to cooperate with you is to acknowledge their position and display understanding for their feelings. Follow this up with your "however" statement: "I can see your point. It must be frustrating to have to clean up your room when you like it this way. It'll be fun to keep your room any way you want it when you grow up. However, it's a family rule that every part of our home be neat and clean."

4 Create a set of very specific family rules. Keep them simple, and post them in a conspicuous place. When the boundaries are clear and your child knows exactly what's expected of her, she'll be less likely to question your daily decisions.

5 Initiate very precise routines for everyday activities such as morning and bedtime activities, homework, chores, and cleanup. The more the routines become habit for your child, the less you'll have to deal with her stubborn behavior. For example, if she *always* does homework as soon as the dinner dishes are done, then you'll not have to engage in a daily battle about when to start homework.

6 Use clear, exact instructions that cannot be misinterpreted. Some kids will jump on any sense of ambivalence on your part as an opening to defy you. Abolish these phrases from your vocabulary: "Why don't you . . ." "It would be nice if you . . ." "Don't you think it's time to . . ." "I sure wish you'd . . ." and, the Grandmommy of them all, ". . . Ok???" So, instead of saying, "Don't you think it's time to get ready for bed?" make a clear, indisputable statement: "It's 8:30. Please put your pajamas on and brush your teeth."

SWEARING

See also ■ Bathroom jokes ■ Humor, inappropriate ■ Manners, at home
■ Manners, in public ■ Respect, teaching
■ Rude comments, intentional

SITUATION
I was appalled to overhear my child using foul language with his friends. What's the best way to handle this?

THINK ABOUT IT
Just as children learn everything else, they will learn that words are powerful and that some words are much more powerful than others are. Just as children explore and investigate other things they learn, they will experiment with these words as well.

SOLUTIONS

1 Young kids are great mynah birds. They will repeat things that they hear, even when they haven't a clue about what it means. If your child is young and doesn't know the definition of the word, but is using it because of mimicking someone else, simply make a statement such as "That is not a word children use. You may say *bologna* instead." (Substitute an acceptable word, and use the same tone and volume as were used for the swear word.)

2 If an older child swears, and knows the intended meaning, you can respond in a calm manner: "That language is unacceptable. I know you're smart enough to come up with an acceptable alternative."

3 Kids often swear for effect. You can burst the bubble by repeating the word in this way: "Sylvia, *damn* is not a word we use in this family." Often, hearing a parent repeat the word in this way can take the "punch" out of it.

4 Determine where your child is hearing swear words. A friend or family member? Movies? Peers? (Certainly not from *you*!) This is a good time to have a chat about the power and meaning of words, why people swear, and what you feel is acceptable. Give some appropriate alternatives to use when angry. Making a brief, calm comment about the word that your child obviously just heard a friend say, or a movie actor shout, can help your child sort out his feelings. An example, "I enjoyed that movie, and I really like the actor, but all the swear words were unnecessary and made Arnold seem dumb and crude."

5 Fine the child for each swear word you hear. The money can go into a pot and be given to your church or a local charity.

6 Swearing becomes a much more serious offense if it is directed at you. If this is the case, you need to act quickly and forcefully. Think about the privileges that are important to your child. Using the telephone? Visiting friends? Playing with the computer? Riding his bike?

Because you've thought about this in advance and made a plan, you can respond to the next offense with authority. The next time your child swears at you, calmly respond, "That is disrespectful and unacceptable. You have just lost the privilege of using the telephone for the next three days. Talk to me like that again and I will permanently remove the telephone from your bedroom."

TANTRUMS, at home

See also ■ Anger ■ Arguing, with parent ■ Cooperate, won't
■ Listening, not

SITUATION

Yes, yes, I know: temper tantrums are a normal childhood reaction to anger and frustration. Knowing this does not make it easier when my daughter's ballistic contortions are punctuated by her piercing screams. There has got to be a way to end this agony!

THINK ABOUT IT

You're right; it's normal for your child to have tantrums. But your response to them will determine if she keeps having them and having them and having them . . .

SOLUTIONS

1 Let your child know in advance that all tantrums will take place in one specific room, such as her bedroom, the bathroom, or the laundry room. When a tantrum starts, you can escort your child to the "tantrum room" with one brief comment: "You can come out when you're done." If she comes out of the room and she's still having the tantrum, just lead her back, repeating, "You can come out when you're done." At first, your child may spend the whole day in the tantrum room, but she'll quickly find out that tantrums are no fun without an audience!

2 If your child has tantrums and can't seem to calm herself down, it's best to teach her how to control herself. Do this by enveloping her in a hug and rocking her with soothing words: "It's OK. Calm down." When the tantrum is winding down, distract her by washing her face or giving her a drink of water. Do not give in to the child's original request, and stay calm yourself. At a quiet time, begin to teach your child what to do when she gets angry (what words and actions are appropriate).

3 As long as your child's tantrum is not dangerous to her or to property, feel free to say, "I'm leaving the room. Come and get me when you're done." And do just that. Busy yourself with something else, and wait patiently for your child to calm down.

4 Make an agreement with an older child who displays tantrum behavior that when she starts to lose control, you're going to ask her to go to her room to cool off. If she doesn't go immediately to her room when asked, she will lose a privilege (decide in advance what that might be—telephone, TV, or bike riding, for example) or she'll be assigned an extra chore. This is, of course, in addition to the fact that she *still* gets to go to her room to calm down.

5 When you see your child beginning to lose control, distract her before the tantrum can turn into a full-blown outburst.

6 Avoid tantrums by offering your child choices. Instead of saying, "Get ready for bed right now," which may provoke a tantrum, offer a choice: "What would you like to do first—put on your pajamas or brush your teeth?" In addition, you may be able to elude tantrums by avoiding the situations that most likely set your child off, such as allowing her to become overtired, overhungry, or overstimulated.

! If your child has frequent intense tantrums, it would be wise to talk with your pediatrician, a counselor, or a family therapist.

TANTRUMS, public

See also ■ Anger ■ Cooperate, won't ■ Listening, not
■ Public behavior

SITUATION

My child yells, stomps, screams, and throws his body onto the floor when he doesn't get his way. He doesn't do this at home, of course, but in public places, like the grocery store, toy store, or restaurant—anywhere there's an interested audience. I feel like my hands are tied when everyone's watching us.

THINK ABOUT IT

The first time your child acted this way in public, you were probably caught off guard. In your embarrassment, you did everything you could to stop the tantrum. If you had looked closely, you would have seen a little twinkle appear in your child's eye as he realized he discovered a new way to get what he wants.

SOLUTIONS

1 Use a preventive approach by reviewing desired behavior prior to entering a public building. "Eric, we're going into the toy store now. We are going to buy a birthday gift for Troy. We are not buying anything for ourselves today. If you see something you like, let me know, and I'll put it on your wish list. I want you to remember to walk beside me and keep your hands to yourself."

2 While you may be concentrating on your tasks, your child has been shoved in and out of his car seat and ushered from place to place enduring endless hours looking at grown-ups' knees. You may be able to prevent tantrums by bringing along a toy or snack to keep your child occupied. Also, get him involved by having him select groceries, find the shoe store, read the menu to you, or any other "busy work." The positive attention and focused activity will keep him too busy to worry about having a tantrum.

3 When a tantrum starts, put your face next to your child's ear and announce, "Stop now or we go out to the car." If he doesn't stop, pick him up or lead him to the car. Sit him in the backseat while you stand outside the door (or, in foul weather, sit in the front seat and pointedly ignore him). An alternative to the car is to find a secluded bench or quiet corner. If he doesn't stop quickly, and you can change your schedule, go home. Send him to his room for a specified time (about three minutes for every year of age, for example, fifteen minutes for a five-year-old.) The extra time it takes to do this once or twice will establish great credibility and can save you from many painful hours at the mall with an obstinate teenager.

4 Get eye level with your child and say, "Follow me." Break eye contact and begin to walk away. Walk slowly where he can see you. Many children will follow. If yours doesn't, stop a short distance away and wait, pretending interest in something else. After a few minutes pass, and your child has calmed down, you can approach your child, hold him by the hand, and say, "Let's go now."

5 Stand above your child with arms crossed and a stern face. Say nothing. When the tantrum is over, complete your errands. When you return home, announce that because your child had a tantrum while you were out, he will suffer a consequence now (forgoing dessert after dinner, staying inside, missing his TV show, or going to bed early). Do this once; then, use it as your "ace in the hole." At the next public tantrum say, "Stop now or you will stay inside when we get home, like you did last week." Your child will remember and know you mean business.

6 If public tantrums are a regular occurrence, plan a training session. Go to the grocery store. Buy a few staples and put a nice assortment of your child's favorite goodies in the cart (potato chips, ice cream, and cookies). Walk around long enough for your child to have the expected tantrum. Walk the cart over to the register and announce to the cashier that you'll have to leave the groceries and go home because your child is misbehaving. (Smile at the cashier and she'll probably smile back, happy to see at least one customer controlling her child!) Then go home. Your child will most likely comment on the loss of the goodies. Just say, "Oh well, some other time." Expect great, loud unhappiness but long-term value!

! After an unpleasant experience, plan an outing and leave your child at home with a baby-sitter. Explain that the tantrum he had the day before is the reason why he is staying home. Expect crying, screaming, and pleading, but be firm. Doing this once has an impact that lasts a long time.

TATTLING

See also ■ Siblings, bickering ■ Siblings, jealousy

SITUATION
I have one child who tattles with a vengeance. The infractions run from minor issues to major crimes and often cover incredibly ridiculous things, such as "She breathed on me *on purpose!*"

THINK ABOUT IT
Children tattle for various reasons. Some get hooked on the idea of saving the world from moral and physical wrongs, some have figured out that a parent's punishment is an effective way of dealing with an offender, and some hope to be labeled the good guy when others appear to be bad. It's helpful if you take a few moments to determine your little tattler's motivation.

SOLUTIONS
1 Acknowledge the tattler with a brief statement: "I'm glad *you* know the rule." (This will satisfy your child's need for attention and approval without rewarding the tattling.) Then walk away. If the situation is one that you need to address, casually walk into the room where the offense is occurring and deal with the situation as if you discovered it on your own. If you do decide to discipline the child committing the offense, make sure the tattler isn't witness to your action. Allowing her to watch will only encourage her to continue tattling.

2 It's better to tattle than to hit. If the tattler is frustrated or angry and showing restraint by asking for your help, it's OK to get involved. Try to stay neutral in your emotions instead of labeling a winner and a loser. Calmly state the rules and request compliance.

3 If the problem involves a dispute between two children, disengage yourself by summarizing the situation, making a subtle suggestion, and encouraging them to work it out. "I see the two of you are having trouble sharing the paints. Because there are *six* colors and *two* children, I know you guys can handle this."

4 If the child has a habit of tattling, take special notice of any time the child solves a problem without tattling and give lots of praise. This reinforcement will demonstrate that your child can get special attention without tattling.

5 Use humor to diffuse the situation. Respond to the tattler in an animated, exaggerated way: "Oh no! Are you serious? She did *that*? Wooaaah dude! Off with her head!" Typically, this response makes the offense seem rather petty, and the tattler feels kind of silly for coming to you.

6 Teach the child the difference between tattling and telling you something that you really need to know. For example, if she tells you that her brother is jumping on the bed, that's tattling. If she tells that her brother is setting the bed on fire, that's telling you something that you need to know!

TEASING

See also ■ Bully ■ Hate, expressions of ■ Manners, at home
■ Manners, in public ■ Meanness ■ Name-calling

SITUATION

My son's favorite indoor sport is "sister-teasing." If she doesn't like her new haircut, you can bet it'll be his favorite topic of conversation. If she

doesn't like a song he's learned, he'll sing it repeatedly, loudly, and with great enthusiasm. If she's sensitive about something, you can be sure he's well aware of it and uses it to torment her. What's the best way to handle this?

THINK ABOUT IT
Teasing is a child-sized weapon used to gain attention, create a feeling of power and superiority, or hurt the opponent without leaving visible scars.

SOLUTIONS

1 If the child being teased doesn't seem bothered, then it's OK to consider it harmless childishness. Just ignore the behavior, or leave the room for a few minutes.

2 Don't comment on the teasing, but immediately give loving attention to the child being teased and turn your back to the teaser. You may even want to leave the room and announce loud enough for the teaser to hear something that makes it obvious he's being left behind, such as, "Let's go upstairs and I'll read your new book to you."

3 Focus your children's attention away from the remark itself and onto its inappropriateness. Rather than trying to make one child feel better by discounting the teasing, point to the fact that the person who teases is being rude and unkind.

4 Give a direct command: "I do not allow teasing. Stop it now." And then change the subject and redirect the children's attention elsewhere.

5 Teach the child who is being teased how to protect herself. Discuss several options that she can use to discourage the teaser. For example, suggest that she laugh at the comment, ignore the teaser, or walk off to join a larger group of kids, leaving the teaser behind.

6 Make sure none of the adults in the family are teasing the kids. Often, adults think it's funny to tease and assume that the kids think it's funny, too. Children are sensitive to things other people, especially their

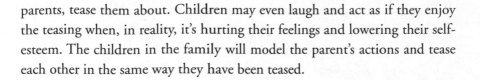

parents, tease them about. Children may even laugh and act as if they enjoy the teasing when, in reality, it's hurting their feelings and lowering their self-esteem. The children in the family will model the parent's actions and tease each other in the same way they have been teased.

7 Keep an eye on the television shows your child is watching. Some TV sitcoms' primary source of humor is putting people down. Your child may be picking up on this and adapting the technique to his own repertoire.

TELEPHONE INTERRUPTIONS

See also ■ Interruptions ■ Manners, at home

SITUATION
My child interrupts constantly when I'm on the telephone. It's never anything important, and it's extremely annoying, especially when it's a business call, because it makes me appear unprofessional.

THINK ABOUT IT
When you're on the phone, children cannot see or hear the other person; they only see a quiet, seemingly available parent. They assume it's a great time to get your undivided attention.

SOLUTIONS
1 Teach your child how to determine if something warrants an interruption. Make a two-column list showing things that are OK to interrupt for and those that are not. Children often are so focused on their own needs that they don't really absorb the fact that they're being rude.

2 Tell your child that if she wants something when you are talking on the telephone, she should walk up to you and gently squeeze your arm. You will then squeeze her hand to indicate that you know she is there and will be with her in a minute. At first, respond rather quickly so your child can see the success of this method. (Otherwise, your child's squeeze may escalate to the intensity of a blood-pressure band.) Over time, you can wait longer—just give a gentle squeeze every few minutes to remind your child that you remember the request.

3 Pause, look your child in the eye, and say, "I'll be with you in a minute." Then turn your face, body, and attention away from your child. Do not engage your child with repeated pleas for her to stop! If the interruptions continue and you have a long cord or a cordless phone, go into the bathroom and lock the door.

4 It can help to have several training sessions. Enlist the help of a friend or family member. Let your child talk on the phone, and tell her and the caller that you will demonstrate the annoyance of interruptions. Then, do so in an exaggerated way. (It's really quite fun!) Follow this exercise with a demonstration of good manners using the previously listed solutions. When the roles are reversed and your child is the person on the phone, she will clearly see the reasons behind your requests.

5 Have a "telephone toy box" of activities or games that can only be used when you are on the telephone. Be firm the first few times about putting them away when you hang up. The kids will be looking forward to your next call!

6 Before you make a call, let your child know what to expect. "I'm going to make a phone call. I'll be a while, so please find something quiet to do while I'm on the phone."

7 Praise your child for using good manners, remembering to say, "Excuse me," letting you talk without interruption, or interrupting for a valid reason.

TELEVISION, watches too much

See also ■ Video games, excessive use of

SITUATION

My kid is turning into the ultimate couch potato! I realized it was getting bad when he started planning his playtime around his favorite TV shows. I keep telling him to find something better to do with his time, but he just gets angry and defensive.

THINK ABOUT IT

TV watching is an addictive activity, and the more your child watches, the more he wants to watch. Like any addiction, simply demanding that your child stop is ineffective and a great way to start a major war.

SOLUTIONS

1 Start by deciding how much TV you think is appropriate, for example, one hour per day. Make a list of suggested alternate activities for your child's remaining free time. Announce that your new rule is one hour of TV per day. Give your child the suggested list. Be positive. Expect great unhappiness on your child's part. Be firm and loving. Stick to your guns. After about two weeks, you'll see a new, energetic kid emerge!

2 If your child has a typical TV-watching time, such as after dinner, begin planning more activities during that time. Arrange for a friend to visit, plan an outing to the store, or gather the family outside to rake leaves. If you're consistent about interrupting his pattern, he'll be weaned from the habit and be more likely to find other things to do on his own.

3 Move the TV to a less-desirable, less-comfortable area of the house, such as the basement. Move it far away from snacks and family camaraderie. Make it a lonely, uncomfortable place for your child to plant himself for hours on end. (You may, of course, keep a TV in your bedroom if you wish, one that is off-limits to the children.)

4 Take the TV to the shop for repair or tune-up. Leave it there for two weeks. Provide ample alternatives during this time to fill your child's time. By the time the set is returned, your child's addictive behavior will have ceased, and you may immediately initiate Solution 1 to prevent it from returning.

 Be selective about your own television viewing. Children will learn from and model your example.

TOILET TRAINING

See also ■ Bed-wetting

SITUATION
It seems like everybody's kids are toilet trained except mine. He's only interested in his potty-chair because the bucket makes a great helmet!

THINK ABOUT IT
When was the last time you saw a first grader wearing a diaper?

SOLUTIONS

1 No matter how much you want your child to be potty trained, it won't happen until he's ready. Look for these signs: a dry diaper for several hours. Letting you know he has to go or is going. Being uncomfortable with a wet or messy diaper. The ability to put on and take off his own clothes. An interest in the potty and the desire to be trained. Once you see that your child is ready, put your child in charge. Potty training is one of the few areas over which he has complete control. If you demand that he toilet train on your schedule, you will likely create a major power struggle. A low-key, no-pressure approach works best.

2 When you feel your child is physically and emotionally ready to be toilet trained, present the idea as an exciting opportunity to do something very grown up. Your idea will be much better received than if you indicate that this is something you want him, or need him, to do.

3 Teach your child how to use the potty in a very matter-of-fact, light-hearted way. Use the same approach you use when you teach your child how to cut with scissors, button his sweater, or put on his socks. Buy him some training pants that are a size too big so that they're easy to take on and off. Put him in pants with an elastic waist, or if its warm enough, just let him wander around in his undies for a week or so. Help him out the first few times, then pronounce him ready to take care of his own business. Shake his hand and stay out of his way. Be pleasantly encouraging when he does it right, but avoid doing a whoop-and-holler war dance. This low-key approach conveys a message to your child that potty training is no big deal and that he can easily learn this.

4 Accidents are bound to happen during the training period. Use the same approach you use when he buttons his sweater the wrong way. "Oops. Missed the potty that time. Don't worry; pretty soon you'll get it right every time."

5 There are lots of tricky contraptions on the market that can be fun and interesting to try. There are musical potty-chairs, dissolving toilet-training targets, creative videos, and books. Use any of these items if you like, but use them with an attitude of fun. After all, learning to use the toilet is just a practical step in the normal process of growing up.

! **If your child is physically and emotionally ready to be toilet trained but, for whatever reason isn't, try this I-hate-to-even-suggest-it-but-it-always-works idea. (I usually don't recommend bribery, but if you have a toddler reluctant to potty train, I know that at some point, you'll do anything to end this business!) Go to the toy store and buy about thirty little prizes. (Check the party aisle for a great selection of inexpensive trinkets.) Wrap each prize separately in wrapping paper. Put them in a clear glass bowl, and place the bowl on the counter in the bathroom. Don't say a word. When your child asks about it, respond in a matter-of-fact way: "Oh. Those are potty prizes. You'll get one each time you do your business in the toilet. But, no hurry. Whenever you're ready." Most kids are "ready" immediately, but don't be surprised if your child drools over the bowl for a few days before deciding to be "ready." Allow your child to choose one prize each time he goes. When the bowl is empty, the habit will be firmly in place.**

TOOTH BRUSHING

SITUATION

My kids always "forget" to brush their teeth. When I remind them, they fuss over having to do it or do a poor job.

THINK ABOUT IT

Kids don't have the wisdom to understand the long-term value of good tooth care. They see it as one of those boring things that you make them do.

SOLUTIONS

 Make the process more fun. Use an egg timer and have kids brush until the sand runs out. Invest in an electric toothbrush set. Buy a variety of different kinds of toothpaste and let the kids experiment by mixing flavors together.

2 Have a "Decay Detective Day." Bring an assortment of foods into the bathroom, such as licorice, chocolate, bread, and corn. Take turns eating something and inspecting teeth afterwards. Point out the food and tell your kids that if it stays in their teeth, it will cause decay. (Be graphic in your descriptions! Kids who are used to watching TV, movies, and video games are hardly frightened by the prospect of a tiny little cavity!) Brush thoroughly and inspect again. The visual process is very helpful.

3 Focus on a discussion of the impact bad breath and ugly teeth have on friendships and social situations. Kids aren't too concerned about the idea of having false teeth at seventy (much too far away!), but the idea of people noticing discolored teeth can motivate them into better tooth care.

4 Utilize your dentist as a tool for teaching tooth care. Many kids will pay more attention to an adult expert than they will to their parents.

 A child who refuses to follow your instructions for dental hygiene can be put on a frequent dental visit schedule, such as every three

months. Some children have teeth that are prone to cavities and would benefit from this more frequent cleaning schedule. It may also help to have the dentist put a cavity-resistant coating on their teeth.

TRIPS, airplane, boat, bus, train

See also ■ Vacations

SITUATION
My husband wants us to take a family vacation, and he has big ideas about a romantic train journey. We have three young kids, and I only have one word for him: "Fuhgeddaboudit!"

THINK ABOUT IT
Believe it or not, you can have a delightful trip with three young children. (Trust me; I've done it many times with my three.) There are three things you absolutely must do to make it work: prepare, prepare, and prepare.

SOLUTIONS

1 Boredom is one of the main culprits for cranky kids and misbehavior during trips. Prevent boredom by packing "fun bags." Use gallon-sized plastic bags (or small boxes) to create activity packs. The party aisle of your favorite toy store has lots of inexpensive ideas, such as tiny plastic animals, Silly Putty, stickers, drawing paper and markers, playing cards, comic books, View-Masters, Etch-A-Sketches, and miniature travel games. Cassettes with music and children's stories on tape and radio headsets are also great travel companions. To prevent a big mess and confusion, allow only one bag per child at a time. Require that the bag be returned intact before another can be taken out. If you stay organized, you can use the bags on your return trip, also.

2 Lack of freedom to move about is another of the main culprits for misbehavior during trips. Sometimes, there is little you can do to avoid this problem. The best solution is to keep the kids happy and occupied in their seats. (Reread Solution 1.) In addition, let the kids know in advance the amount of time they will be required to stay in their seats. Review as many details as you can so they know what to expect. On a long airplane flight, it is definitely worth the money to pay for the in-flight movie; just check in advance to make sure it's one that meets your standards for child-friendly viewing. Take advantage of the times when you're able to move about to take a few walks up and down the aisle. Another way to combat seat fatigue is to dress the children in very comfortable layers and allow them to remove their shoes.

3 Have a supply of "snack bags." Ask in advance about available children's meals and order them, but also count on your kids turning their noses up at any commercial food provided and on them being hungry only when all the food service is finished. Bring favorite snacks that are low-sugar and healthy, such as pretzels, dry cereal, popcorn, or crackers. Include juice drinks and water bottles. An absolute must is chewing gum and suckers—they take a long time to finish and on airplanes help prevent ear pain. (It's OK to break a few regular rules and buy some flavored bubble gum!)

4 If possible, travel during your child's "happy" part of the day. Don't count on excited kids, no matter how young, sleeping during a trip. (I once traveled by car at night, six hours, with my then two-year-old niece, who stayed awake the entire time!)

TRIPS, car, long

See also ■ Vacations

SITUATION
We're about to take a long car trip. If history repeats itself, the kids will fight, bicker, and whine, and *I'll* be the one asking, "Are we there yet?"

THINK ABOUT IT

If history repeats itself, it will be because you didn't change anything that happened the first time around. If you want to change something, you need to analyze what went wrong and create a plan for future success.

SOLUTIONS

1 Kids have lots of energy and find it difficult to sit still while strapped in the backseat of a car for hours on end. Inevitably, they become bored, and boredom leads to misbehavior. Prevent boredom by using gallon-sized plastic bags or boxes to create activity packs. The party aisle of your favorite toy store has lots of inexpensive ideas, such as magnetic checkers, tiny plastic people and animals, Silly Putty, sticker books, coloring books and crayons, simple crafts, playing cards, comic books, View-Masters, Etch-A-Sketches, and miniature travel games. Cassettes with music and children's stories on tape and radio headsets are great for long trips. To keep things organized, allow only one bag per child at a time. You can use the bags on your return trip and as rainy-day activities during your stay.

2 Plan to stop often for the kids to use the bathroom and stretch their legs. Giving them these opportunities for movement will keep them much happier in between stops. Use a seat-rotation system logged on an index card, and have children switch seats each time you stop. Rotation provides a change in view and environment.

3 Don't overpack the car. Kids who are squashed between bags and packages tend to get grumpy.

4 Let children know in advance what the travel plans are—how long the journey will take, expected time of arrival, how many packages of cupcakes they'll get to eat, and so forth. Give the kids a map, colored pencils, and a compass so they can follow and record the journey. Plot the starting point and ending point. Provide a calculator and paper, so when they ask, "How long 'til we get there?" you can teach them how to figure it out themselves!

5 Have a supply of "snack bags" in the car. Snacks serve multiple purposes. They keep the kids' blood-sugar levels even, the search for just the right snack is an entertaining activity, and kids who are chewing will tend to argue less frequently. Make sure most of the snacks are low-sugar and healthy, such as pretzels, dry cereal, popcorn, or crackers. Include juice drinks and water bottles. (If you have young children, be careful to avoid any snack that is a choking hazard.)

6 Car travel makes many children sleepy. Even older children enjoy a pillow and blanket. Dress the kids in comfortable clothes and allow them to remove their jackets and shoes—cozy kids are happier kids!

TRIPS, car, short

See also ■ Car ■ Car pool, bad behavior

SITUATION
My kids can't even make it up the driveway from the garage to the street without misbehaving in the car! It seems the minute we get in the car, I start nagging them to "Cut it out, behave, stop it, quiet down . . ."

THINK ABOUT IT
With all the taxiing a parent has to do, this is a situation you really can't live with. Nagging won't solve your problem, but some of these ideas will.

SOLUTIONS
1 Boredom is the main culprit for misbehavior during routine car trips. Prevent boredom by using the seat-back pockets, or hanging canvas bags on the backs of the front seats, or putting shoe boxes in the backseat, as activity sources. Fill the bags or boxes with books, comic books, car-bingo games, a deck of cards, and other simple, easy-to-use activities. Routinely circulate the items with different activities.

2 Set strict car rules. Write them down and keep them in the car. When your expectations are clear, simple, and exact, children will more often comply, for example, "Keep hands to yourself. Use a quiet inside voice. Clean up your own trash." Decide on consequences for breaking the rules, and follow through. A great consequence—one that is fair, related to the misbehavior, and is great fun for parents—is one that allows a rule breaker to wash or vacuum the car!

3 Keep "snack bags" in the car. Interesting enough, kids who are chewing tend to be better behaved! Make sure snacks are low-fat and healthy, such as pretzels, dry cereal, popcorn, or crackers. (Avoid any snack that may be a choking hazard for younger children.)

TRIPS, children alone on

See also ■ Vacations

SITUATION
My child is scheduled to be traveling as an unaccompanied minor. What can I do to ensure a successful journey?

THINK ABOUT IT
This is a big step. Don't treat it lightly. Prepare and organize as much in advance as you can. Cover all the bases. Make sure you check and double-check every part of the trip. When the adults at both ends of the trip are heads-up, everything will go smoothly.

SOLUTIONS
1 If possible, visit the airport or station in advance of the trip. (Going there to purchase tickets is often a valid reason.) When your child has visited in advance of the big trip, the event will seem less overwhelming.

2 Talk with officials from the organization your child is traveling with. Ask questions about their rules for unaccompanied minors. Ask about their procedures for late arrivals or what they do if the designated adult is not there on time for pick up. Make sure you're comfortable with the information you're given.

3 Discuss as much of the trip as possible in advance with your child. Cover as many of the details as you can. It can be frightening for a child to find herself in an unexpected situation, such as having to change planes in the middle of the journey.

4 Help your child pack a carry-on bag or large backpack filled with snacks, juice, gum, books, and activities to pass the time. Even a twelve-year-old can become bored and disruptive while traveling with nothing to alleviate the boredom.

5 Make sure your child has a variety of telephone numbers of people at both ends of the journey, along with specific instructions on how to make phone calls from the terminal. An early arrival can leave a child sitting alone for a long period of time waiting for someone to greet her. If your child is aware that this could happen, and knows how to handle it, she'll be calm if the situation does occur.

TRIPS, cruise

See also ■ Vacations

SITUATION
We took a cruise on our honeymoon that was the best vacation we've ever had. Now, we're considering going on a cruise with our children. What advice can you give us?

SOLUTIONS

1 As much as you love your kids, it's best to avoid taking a child younger than age six on a cruise, unless you're committed to entertaining your child for the entire trip. Even the best planning cannot guarantee that your young child will blend into the unusual routine aboard a cruise ship. There are, of course, exceptions to this rule, and families with young children who thoroughly enjoy their trip. You'll need to take an honest look at your expectations and think this through carefully before you plan the trip. If you're one of the lucky few who can take along a baby-sitter, make certain your expectations are specifically written out prior to the trip so that the sitter knows exactly what her responsibilities will be and how much time she'll spend with the children.

2 Shop for a cruise ship that is prepared to meet your child's needs and keep your child entertained. A hoity-toity, four-star cruise ship may come highly acclaimed but may not be prepared to meet the needs of a young child. (There's nothing worse than finding out too late that they don't have any diapers or baby food on board!) Don't take the salesperson's word for it! Ask for the name of a person or two who have traveled on the ship with children, and find out firsthand if the promises are kept. There are some cruise lines that cater to the needs of children while offering parents an enjoyable vacation as well. Shop carefully.

3 Even though a good cruise ship offers lots of activities, you should still bring along things to entertain your child. Rainy weather or bad moods can interfere with the best-laid plans. (For specific ideas *see also* Trips, car, long.)

4 Plan ahead for seasickness. If you can take a short boat ride prior to the cruise, you can determine if your children (or you!) are prone to seasickness. Even if you don't think it will be a problem, plan for it anyway! Talk to a doctor about the best medication to take along for your children.

VACATIONS, misbehavior during

See also ■ Anger ■ Cooperate, won't ■ Doesn't come when called
■ Listening, not ■ Siblings, bickering ■ Trips

SITUATION
Our last vacation was nearly ruined because of our children's unruly behavior. We're about ready to leave for this year's trip. What can we do to prevent a repeat of last year's catastrophe?

THINK ABOUT IT
Often, when parents get in a vacation mood, all the normal rules and routines fly out the window. Even though the workday routines don't need to be adhered to, a set of vacation rules and routines should be established.

SOLUTIONS
 Kids will respond much better if they know exactly what's expected of them. At the start of the trip, or even before you leave, write down a list of rules. (Add to them as necessary.) Review the rules together each morning as a powerful way to avoid power struggles during the day.

When misbehavior occurs, avoid the knee-jerk reaction of yelling. Instead, pull the child aside, look her in the eye, and remind her of the rule she is to follow. Instead of saying, "Don't," "No," or "Stop" and telling her what you don't want her to do, remind her of what you do want her to do. For example, instead of saying, "Stop yelling!" remind her of the rule, "Amanda, when in the hotel room, please keep your voice quiet."

Offer your child a choice. "You can either *X* or *Y*—you decide." If your child creates a third choice, simply repeat your first statement with a calm manner, "Zoe, you can either *X* or *Y*. If you can't decide, I'll choose for you."

4 Describe the problem and make a very specific request for compliance. "You keep wandering too far away from me. I would like you to go no farther than the lifeguard chair." Include a predetermined consequence: "If you wander farther than that, you will have to sit here on the towel next to me for fifteen minutes."

5 Use "Grandma's Rule," otherwise known as "When/Then," to establish priorities. "When you have put on your pajamas and brushed your teeth, then you may watch your movie."

6 Relax and pick your battles. Bending a few rules is OK when you're away from home. Don't worry so much about the little things, and focus on having a good time yourself. For example, if you're eating out at a restaurant, don't worry about how much your kids eat or if they finish their vegetables. Once your meals have arrived, focus on enjoying *your* food and encouraging interesting dinner conversation.

VACATIONS, preparing for good behavior

See also ■ Cooperate, won't ■ Introduction ■ Listening, not ■ Trips

SITUATION
We're planning a vacation trip. How can we make sure the children will behave properly during the time away from home?

THINK ABOUT IT
The fact that you're contemplating this question before you leave is half the battle. Reviewing a plan for keeping the kids under control is even more important than checking for tickets before the taxi arrives!

SOLUTIONS

1 Children get so excited about a vacation trip that their energy level is extremely high, and they lose all memory of the correct ways to behave. If you can give the children specific jobs to keep them focused and occupied, they will be less likely to fill the time with annoying behavior. At each step of the way, enlist their help with "jobs" that are fun and take lots of time to complete. For example, when you're packing, have them sort, separate, and bag the Legos. During the trip, give them a map and colored pencils to log the trip. When you arrive and are unpacking, give them the travel brochures, magazines, a pen, and paper, and have them note the fun things they would like to do during the vacation.

2 Discuss the details of the trip with the children before you leave. Let them know how long it will take to get there, where you will stay, and what you will do. Cover all the things you can think of. The more knowledge the kids have, the more content they will be. For younger children, you can even role-play the trip in advance. An example: using chairs, set up an airplane in your living room. Pretend your bedroom is the hotel room. Playact the trip, discussing what will happen when you're on vacation.

3 If you are one of the lucky few who get to take a baby-sitter along on your trip, make certain you have made your expectations for the trip clear. Write out the sitter's responsibilities and hours of duty to prevent any problems or resentments once you arrive.

4 Even if you're heading for a tropical island, there is always the chance that it will rain and you'll spend hours in the hotel room. Be prepared. Bored kids stuck in a hotel room are too scary to even think about! Bring along your rainy-day insurance. Pack small activities that bring long play value. (*See also* Vacations, rainy day ideas.)

5 Read a parenting book that focuses on good discipline techniques to prepare for the extra time you'll be spending with the children in close quarters. I'd recommend *Kid Cooperation* by Elizabeth Pantley as a good choice!

VACATIONS, rainy day ideas

See also ■ Boredom ■ Cabin fever

SITUATION

It never fails: when we're on vacation, the rains hit. We're all stuck in the hotel room, and inevitably, everyone gets grumpy. How do we keep the kids happy if this disaster strikes again?

THINK ABOUT IT

To quote the insightful words of William Shakespeare, "There is nothing either good or bad, but thinking makes it so." Hey, you're still on vacation, no one has to go to work or go to school, and you don't have to cook and clean. You can still find plenty of ways to enjoy the time.

SOLUTIONS

1 If you read this book before you left, you've packed some indoor activities. If not, venture out to a local store, and buy a selection. It will be the best money you spend on the trip. A few ideas are paint-by-number sets, Legos, balloons, headsets with music and books on tape, puzzles, clay, and hand-held computer games. One toy that's a hit for many kids from about age three to ten is a selection of plastic miniature animals or bugs. Many kids will play happily with these for hours. Many favorite games are made in small travel-sized versions, such as checkers, chess, and even Monopoly. Check out the local toy store.

2 If you're lucky enough to have a kitchenette in your room, allow the kids to play house. Let them use the dishes and supplies. Cleaning up the mess is worth it, because this activity will keep them busy for long periods of time. Even better, give room service an extra tip and let them take care of the mess.

3 Let the kids build a fort using tables, chairs, blankets, and whatever else they can find. Let them play, eat, and even sleep in the fort. Need I say it again? The mess is worth the hours of happy playtime.

Fill the bathtub with water. Toss in anything you can find that can be used as water toys, such as cups, plastic dishes, and empty shampoo bottles. Let the kids enjoy playing in the water and don't worry about the splashing.

 Play "Easter Egg Hunt" using coins. Hide them all over the rooms, and let the kids find them. Have a scavenger hunt or a treasure hunt.

 Set up a beauty salon. Let the kids practice hairstyles, paint each other's fingernails, and put on makeup.

 Let the kids play dress up with your clothes if you're comfortable with the idea. Have a fashion show. Put on a play. Have a concert.

Let them play in the rain! Just dry them off and give them some hot chocolate when they come in.

VEGETABLES, won't eat them

See also ■ Eating, picky eater ■ Junk food excesses

SITUATION
My child doesn't like vegetables and refuses to eat them. Every meal, we get into the same arguments, and I usually resort to begging and bribing.

THINK ABOUT IT
Children often assert their independence with food-related issues because it's one area they can completely control. Fascist tactics aside, you simply can't *make* a child eat. Avoid letting food become a battleground, and be creative in solving the problem. (And be honest: when's the last time you craved a nice big bowl of lima beans?)

SOLUTIONS

1 Serve your child frozen vegetables (such as peas and corn, right from the bag) or raw vegetables with yogurt or dressing for dipping, either of which is more appealing to many children than cooked veggies. Many children also enjoy dried vegetables, which crunch like chips but pack the nutrients of real vegetables. (Note: Don't give frozen or hard raw vegetables to children with braces or sensitive teeth or to young children, who could choke on them.)

2 Increase the amount and type of fruits your child eats to balance the lack of nutrients from vegetables. Also, give your child a daily multi-vitamin.

3 Sneak vegetables into other foods, such as chopped spinach in meat loaf or lasagna, carrot slivers in potato salad, grated zucchini in hamburger, peas in tuna salad, lettuce and tomato on sandwiches, or mashed broccoli in spaghetti sauce. Finely grated or chopped vegetables can be a hidden addition to many foods. Also, try making or buying reduced-sugar versions of zucchini or carrot muffins or other vegetable-based breads or snacks.

4 Let the kids help plant a vegetable garden. Children will eat and enjoy fresh vegetables that they have grown themselves.

5 Start calling green vegetables "brain food," and let your kids know that the green stuff will make them smarter and stronger.

6 For the under-five-year-old set, have your child nearby while you're preparing the meal, and play "Peter Rabbit in Mr. McGregor's garden." Tell your child that you're Mr. McGregor and that you hope Peter Rabbit doesn't hop by and eat your veggies. Your child will, of course, "steal" vegetables that you carelessly leave on the counter. Act surprised and puzzled every time another piece of your nice sliced vegetables disappears. Young children love this game and will eat tons of vegetables in the process.

VIDEO GAMES, excessive use of

See also ■ Television, watches too much

SITUATION

My child spends too much time playing computer and video games. He's so passionate about these games that when I suggest he's overdoing it, he gets angry with me.

THINK ABOUT IT

Your most important job as a parent is not to make your child happy. It's to raise a responsible, capable, thinking person. Therefore, not all your decisions will be popular with your son. Your goal should be to make the *right* decisions.

SOLUTIONS

1 Start by deciding how much time you think is appropriate for spending on these activities, for example, one hour per day. Make a list of suggested alternate activities for your child's remaining free time. Announce that your new rule is one hour of playing per day. Give your child the suggested list of alternatives. Be positive. Expect great unhappiness on your child's part. Be firm and loving. Stick to your guns. After about two weeks, you'll see a new, energetic kid emerge!

2 If your child has a typical video-playing time, such as after dinner, begin planning more activities during that time.

3 Use the "When/Then" technique: "When you have finished your homework and chores, then you may turn on the computer." Establish this routine as standard practice.

4 Take advantage of your child's love of the computer by using it as a teaching tool. Replace the mindless or violent games with the creative, exciting learning programs that are available. There are now many available that use exciting games and graphics to teach history, math, reading, and thinking skills. These are programs that you're only too happy to see your child happily engaged in for long periods of time.

WANDERING IN PUBLIC PLACES

See also ■ Cooperate, won't ■ Doesn't come when called
■ Listening, not

SITUATION
My child wanders away from me when we're shopping and at other public places, such as the beach or park. How can I make her stay close to me?

THINK ABOUT IT
In today's world, a child's wandering is a risky situation. A parent of a wandering child must have one important goal at all times: keeping track of the kid. This concern makes any excursion tiring and stressful. Try these ideas to get control of the problem.

SOLUTIONS

1 Before entering a public place, or as soon as you arrive, take the time to set clear limits and review them with your child. Be very specific about what behavior you expect. For example, as soon as you arrive at the beach, set clear boundaries: "Krista, do you see the lifeguard tower? Do not go past that place. Do you see the ice cream stand? Do not go past there." Have your child point out the boundaries and repeat them back to you. Include a predetermined consequence for not adhering to the rules: "If you go past the boundaries, you will have to sit here on the blanket with me for a time-out for fifteen minutes." Follow through and be consistent.

2 Just as you teach your child that you will not drive until everyone has a seat belt on, teach her that she cannot step into a street or parking lot without holding on to an adult. If you have your hands full, teach her to hang on to an end of your shirt or jacket. When developing the habit, your child may begin to step out of the car without you. Using a loud, clear voice, say, "Stop! Parking lot—grab a grown-up!"

3 Teach your child that she must always be able to see you. Every once in a while, or if she begins to wander out of your sight, remind her: "Can you see me?"

4 If you have a young child and you're going to a location that is crowded with people, it may be easier to use a stroller for that outing. Also, it's perfectly OK to tether her to you with an expandable leash or harness designed for that purpose. A few people may give you odd looks, but most people have become very accepting of these tethers as an excellent safety device for keeping track of young children in crowds.

5 Have a "training session." Take your child someplace she enjoys, such as a park or playground. Give her the boundaries. Tell her to stay where she can see you. Watch her carefully. The first time she steps outside the boundaries tell her the outing is over, explain why, and *go home*. Expect quite a bit of crying and unhappiness. Ignore it. If you have other children with you, they will suffer and complain that it's not fair. Just look at this as a great learning experience for all of them. The next time you go on an outing, you can remind them of what happened, and watch as they all help each other stay within the boundaries!

6 Be realistic about your expectations for your child to wait patiently while you shop or are otherwise occupied. A child who is bored standing and waiting will want to wander. Either break your errands into smaller portions or bring along something to occupy your child while she waits for you. Portable activities include Silly Putty, a book, a calculator, or a cat's cradle string. Another option is to keep your child occupied as she waits. For example, give her a list to check off as you shop, have her count the number of people in line, let her try on a few pairs of adult shoes.

7 Point out the times when your child stays close to you and reward her with praise and positive comments.

WASTEFULNESS

See also ■ Carelessness ■ Materialism

SITUATION

My child doesn't seem to have any concept of the value of his posses-sions, or anyone else's belongings. He doesn't care about tossing away an entire sandwich after a few bites or throwing away perfectly good paintbrushes because he doesn't want to clean them. He tends to be careless and wasteful.

THINK ABOUT IT

From the time your child was born, "things" just magically appeared when-ever he had a need for them. You'll now have to take the time to teach him about the value of possessions and call his attention to the things that are being wasted. Keep in mind that there is a difference between scolding, lec-turing, and teaching!

SOLUTIONS

1 Children don't understand the significance of waste. It can help to get the family involved in a charitable endeavor that exposes them to situations and people who don't have enough food or belongings to live comfortably. Serving meals in a soup kitchen or delivering blankets to homeless families can give children a sense of the abundance they have in their own lives. Resist the urge to preach, and instead, let the situation teach your child what he needs to learn.

2 Get your children involved in recycling projects. Set up a recycling sta-tion near your trash containers. Take a trip to a recycling plant to learn about and watch the process. Read a few books or articles about recycling.

3 Serve meals on smaller plates and give your child smaller servings. It's easy to get seconds, and you won't have an abundance of food left over, as you would on a large plate filled with too much food.

4 If a child has too many "things," he will tend to be wasteful. Stop buying your child everything he wants. Encourage good decision making before purchases. Involve your child in spending his own money for the things he wants. Offer to pay for a portion of the object of his desire, and let him pitch in to buy it. A child who spends his own money buying things will tend to be less wasteful with those things.

5 Start teaching your child about the value of the things you purchase. When you have a meal at your local fast-food restaurant, let your child know what it costs. When you go grocery shopping, let your child see the receipt. Keep your attitude positive; this is not meant to be a lecture but a lesson in learning about value. Compare the cost of things to your child's allowance as a way of helping him understand the comparative value: "Your new shoes cost $30. That's equal to six months of your allowance."

WHINING

See also ■ Complaining ■ Crying

SITUATION

My daughter is constantly whining. Every time she calls "Mommmy!" I have this great desire to change my name or run and hide under the nearest bed! Please don't tell me "she'll outgrow it," because if the whining continues, she may not make it to her next birthday!

THINK ABOUT IT

Talk about fingernails on a blackboard! Whining has got to be the ultimate in annoying childhood behavior. Because a whining child sounds worse than a frenzied siren alarm, we tend to do anything to make it stop. Thus, our little whiner discovers a great way to get our undivided attention.

SOLUTIONS

1 *Never ever* respond or give in to a whining request. Make an announcement: "When you use your normal voice, I will listen to you." Then turn your back to the whining child and make it obvious you are ignoring her by singing or reading out loud from a book held in front of your face. If the child continues to whine, repeat the same sequence without engaging the child any further. (Pleading or discussing will only increase the whining.)

2 Help your child by modeling what you want to hear: "I can't understand you when you use a whining voice. Please say, "Mommy, may I please have a drink?"'

3 Put a jar on the kitchen counter. Put ten nickels in it. Tell your child that every time she whines or fusses you will take a nickel out of the jar. Any nickels left over at bedtime will be hers to keep as a reward for remembering to use her "big girl voice."

4 Often children aren't really aware they are whining. Have a discussion about whining and demonstrate what it sounds like. (Put on a good show!) Tell your child you want to help her remember not to whine, so every time she does, you are going to put your fingers in your ears, say, "Yuck!" and make a funny face. That will be her signal to find her regular voice.

5 Tell your child that you're going to set the timer for three minutes. She can fuss for three minutes and then she must stop. Some children will complain, "That's not enough time!" Then ask, "How much is enough—four or five minutes?" Typically, of course, five will be chosen. Make a big production of setting the timer for five minutes, and announce that she must stop when the timer rings. Most kids will stop before the timer rings. If your persistent whiner doesn't stop after five minutes, you can put her in time-out, or put yourself in time-out, until the fussing ends.

 Make sure you aren't giving whining lessons, such as, "Will youuu pleeeze stop whyyyniingg! It's driving me craaazeee!"

 Praise your child's attempts at using a regular voice. "Ariel, I really enjoy hearing your pleasant voice!" Try to say yes to a request made in a regular, polite voice. For example, if your child normally whines about having a cookie after lunch and today she asks pleasantly, try to give her at least a piece of a cookie to reward her for her appropriate manners. Make sure you tell her that's why you said OK: "Yes, you may have a cookie. I'm saying yes because you asked in such a nice voice and you didn't whine about it. Lucky you!"

WORK, doesn't want parent to

See also ■ Clinging ■ Separation anxiety ■ Whining

SITUATION
My son fusses, whines, and complains every morning when I get ready to leave for work. I have to work, and I want to work, but my son's attitude makes me feel terrible. Also, this is a lousy way to start the day.

THINK ABOUT IT
Children easily pick up on a parent's ambivalence about going to work. If you have mixed feelings about leaving your child and going off to work, it's very possible your child is picking up on those feelings. If you're leaving your child with a competent caregiver, it's perfectly OK for you to go to work. As a matter of fact, some people are better parents because of the break that going to work provides them. Reconcile your own feelings so that you can start leaving for the day with a confident, cheerful attitude.

SOLUTIONS

1 Try to convey to your child a calm confidence about the situation. Leave for the day with a wave and a smile on your face. Let your parting comments be positive: "You can show me what you paint with your new paint set when I get home. I'll be looking forward to it. Have a great day!"

2 Keep your good-bye brief. Have a routine for leaving. Use the same sequence each time you leave. For young children, this routine might include pretending to give your child a "little tiny Mommy" to put in his pocket and taking an imaginary miniversion of your child to put in your pocket. Some kids enjoy being your "helper" and buttoning your coat, carrying your briefcase to the door, or unlocking your car. They can then send *you* on your way, which puts them in more of a position of control over the situation.

3 Let your child visit your place of work so he can see where you will be during the day. Allow him to sit in your seat, use your phone or computer, and meet the people you spend your time with. Then, let him check in with you, if possible, at a specific time of the day. You can then explain where you are and what you're doing, and he'll have a mental picture of your workplace. Many children feel better about letting you leave after this experience.

4 Acknowledge his feelings, and help him understand them. But, equally important, reassure him and help him deal with the feelings and learn to get by them. "I know you miss Mommy when I go to work. I miss you, too. That's because we love each other and like to be together. I do need to go to work every day. I like my work. You have lots of things to do when I'm gone. You can tell me all about your day when I get home."

YELLING AND SCREAMING

See also ■ Anger ■ Noise, excessive ■ Roughhousing ■ Tantrums

SITUATION

Playtime at our house puts a crowd at a football game to shame. My kids yell and scream until I'm tempted to stuff their mouths with old socks. Any better ideas?

THINK ABOUT IT

Your automatic response may be to yell louder than they are so that you'll be heard. Consider the ambiguity and humor of the situation next time you bellow, *"There will be no yelling in this house!"*

SOLUTIONS

1 Tell the children what you want of them in a calm, quiet voice. To be heard, you'll need to give up the luxury of correcting them from sixteen rooms away. Go to them. Hold them by the shoulders, look them in the eye, and talk clearly and quietly. Be specific. Instead of saying, "Stop yelling," clearly tell them what you do want: "Please use a quiet voice in the house."

2 Create house rules about noise. Write the rules down and post them in a conspicuous place. Include a described consequence for breaking the rules, such as a time-out in their bedrooms or loss of a privilege.

3 If two children are yelling at each other, walk over to them and stand between them. Look at them with a crumpled, disapproving face, with your hands on your hips. Don't say anything. Often, this is enough to remind them of the rules.

4 Some children have an abundance of energy and loud voices. Make sure these kids have an outlet for their boisterous inner voices. Sign them up for a sports team, or cheerleading squad, where they can yell in an appropriate environment. Get them involved in a choir. Take them to an indoor play arena or a large park often enough to exercise their lungs.

RECOMMENDED READING

ANGER

■ *Kid Cooperation—How to Stop Yelling, Nagging, and Pleading and Get Kids to Cooperate*
  Elizabeth Pantley
  New Harbinger Publications
  1996
Chapter 7: "Why Do I Get So Angry? How Can I Stop?" A discussion of the reasons why parents get angry with their children. A step-by-step plan to control angry feelings when you're in the heat of the battle.

■ *Love and Anger: The Parental Dilemma*
  Nancy Samalin and Catherine Whitney
  Penguin Books
  1995
A practical, optimistic book about dealing with the overwhelming anger that parents sometimes feel toward the children they love so much.

■ *When Anger Hurts Your Kids: A Parent's Guide*
  Matthew McKay, et al.
  New Harbinger Publications
  1996
This book is the result of a two-year study of 285 parents. It explains the typical reasons that parents get angry and offers solutions that can help you get control of your emotions.

ATHLETICS

■ *Victory Beyond the Scoreboard*
   John Devine and Cliff Gillies
   BookPartners
   1997
Two esteemed coaches reveal innovative ideas for making sports more fun and less stressful for both players and families.

ATTENTION DEFICIT DISORDER

■ *Attention Deficit Disorder: A Different Perception*
   Thom Hartmann
   Underwood-Miller
   1993
This book provides an inside view of how ADD persons think and function in society. It demonstrates that ADD can be associated with creativity and high achievement.

■ *The A.D.D. Book: New Understandings, New Approaches to Parenting Your Child*
   William Sears, M.D., and Lynda Thompson, Ph.D.
   Little, Brown and Company
   1998
This book offers an approach that will help parents reduce or eliminate the need for drugs. It includes strategies that empower children with ADD and teach them how to cope.

CHILD DEVELOPMENT

■ *Your One-Year-Old, Your Two-Year-Old,* and so forth. (series)
   Louise Bates Ames, Ph.D., et al.
   Delacorte Press
   1981–1995

An excellent series of books that explain typical behaviors at each level of development. Helps you understand your child's behavior as "normal" and suggests ways of handling the behavior.

DIVORCE/SINGLE PARENTING/ STEPPARENTING

■ *Putting Kids First*
Michael L. Oddenino
Family Connections Publishing
1995

A well-written book filled with excellent advice for divorcing parents. This book helps parents use positive solutions to create a more "child-centered" result during the divorcing process.

■ *The Single Parent Family: Living Happily in a Changing World*
Marge Kennedy and Janet Spencer King
Crown Trade Paperbacks
1994

Written by two single parents, this is an authoritative, supportive, and comprehensive guide, filled with specific, realistic advice.

GENERAL TOPICS

■ *Kid Cooperation—How to Stop Yelling, Nagging, and Pleading and Get Kids to Cooperate*
Elizabeth Pantley
New Harbinger Publications
1996

A book filled with real ideas for real families—practical things you can do to improve daily family life. Covers topics such as cooperation, discipline, sibling relationships, anger management, and building self-esteem. It even has a chapter on how to take care of yourself and your marriage, because a happier adult is a better parent.

■ *The 10 Greatest Gifts I Give My Children: Parenting from the Heart*
    Steven W. Vannoy
    Simon and Schuster
    1994
A pleasant book that helps put the joy back in parenting. Stories and thoughts that will encourage you to focus on what's most important in your life.

■ *The Discipline Book: Everything You Need to Know to Have a Better-Behaved Child: For Birth to Age Ten*
    William Sears, M.D. and Martha Sears, R.N.
    Little, Brown and Company
    1995
A book that clearly identifies "discipline" as a lifelong teaching process. Offers advice on how to prevent, as well as stop, problem behaviors.

■ *Smart Parenting: An Easy Approach to Raising Happy, Well-Adjusted Kids*
    Dr. Peter Favaro
    Contemporary Books
    1995
Clear, down-to-earth, practical ideas for raising responsible, self-assured, and happy children.

■ *Battles, Hassles, Tantrums and Tears: Strategies for Coping with Conflict and Making Peace at Home*
    Susan Beekman and Jeanne Holmes
    Hearst Books
    1993
Conflict resolution techniques for handling problems with children.

■ *Positive Discipline A–Z*
    Jane Nelsen, Lynn Lott, and H. Stephen Glen
    Prima Publishing
    1993
A handy reference tool with logical advice and practical solutions.

HOMEWORK

■ *Ending the Homework Hassle: Understanding, Preventing, and Solving School Performance Problems*
    John Rosemond
    Andrews and McMeel
    1990
A straightforward book to help you understand, prevent, and solve school performance problems. Rosemond's approach will help you disengage from homework hassles as you manage your children toward greater success in school.

HUMOR

■ *You Might as Well Laugh—Surviving the Joys of Parenthood*
    Sandi Kahn Shelton
    Bancroft Press
    1997
A light and cheerful book about parenthood.

■ *Guilt-Free Motherhood: How to Raise Great Kids and Have Fun Doing It*
    Joni Hilton
    Covenant Communications
    1996
Easy-to-read and fun-filled. A realistic book that contains some exceptional insights.

■ *I Didn't Plan to Be a Witch: and Other Surprises of a Joyful Mother*
    Linda Eyre
    A Fireside Book
    1988

When a parenting expert and mother of nine shares a few of her bad moments, it makes you feel a whole lot better about your own mistakes.

MARRIAGE/ADULT RELATIONSHIPS

■ *How Can We Light a Fire When the Kids Are Driving Us Crazy?*
    Ellen Kreidman
    Villard Books
    1993

A book of ideas to help you awaken those wonderful romantic feelings that may have been dormant since your children were born.

■ *How to Stay Lovers While Raising Your Children*
    Anne Mayer
    Price Stern Sloan
    1990

Ideas that rekindle the love, intimacy, and spontaneity you thought you lost when you brought your first baby home.

■ *Why Marriages Succeed or Fail and How You Can Make Yours Last*
    John Gottman, Ph.D.
    A Fireside Book
    1994

Good insights and realistic advice.

■ *Couple Skills: Making Your Relationship Work*
    Matthew McKay, Patrick Fanning, and Kim Paleg
    New Harbinger Publications
    1994

A book of tools to use that help you communicate with each other in more productive ways.

SEXUALITY

- *My Body, My Self for Girls*
- *What's Happening to My Body? For Girls*
- *What's Happening to My Body? For Boys*
  Lynda Madaras
  Newmarket Press
  1984

Straightforward answers to all the basic questions about sexual development and the emotional and physical experience of puberty.

- *Where Do Babies Come From?*
  Margaret Sheffield and Sheila Bewley
  Knopf
  1973

A book that explains conception, pregnancy, and birth in terms that a very young child can understand.

SIBLINGS

- *He Hit Me First: When Brothers and Sisters Fight*
  Louise Bates Ames, Ph.D.
  Warner Books
  1989

This book gives a detailed description of what parents can expect from sibling relationships and how to deal with the inevitable problems.

■ *Kid Cooperation—How to Stop Yelling, Nagging, and Pleading and Get Kids to Cooperate*
Elizabeth Pantley
New Harbinger Publications
1996
Chapter 6: "How to Nurture Sibling Relationships." Gives specific methods to reduce sibling conflict and encourage friendship between your children.

■ *Loving Each One Best: A Caring and Practical Approach to Raising Siblings*
Nancy Samalin
Bantam Books
1996
An invaluable resource that offers support and proven solutions for any parent facing the challenge of raising siblings.

■ *Siblings Without the Rivalry: How to Help Your Children Live Together So You Can Live Too*
Adele Faber and Elaine Mazlish
Avon Books
1988
A classic book about sibling relationships.

SLEEP

■ *Nighttime Parenting: How to Get Your Baby and Child to Sleep*
William Sears, M.D. and Martha Sears, R.N.
New American Library Trade
1995
Helps you understand your baby's sleep needs. Gives outstanding suggestions for parents who don't want to let their baby just "cry it out."

■ *Sleep: How to Teach Your Child to Sleep Like a Baby*
Tamara Eberlein
Pocket Books
1996

This book compiles what the experts from diverse schools of thought have to say about helping your child sleep through the night so that you can choose the methods that work best for your family.

STRONG-WILLED CHILDREN

■ *Raising Your Spirited Child: A Guide for Parents Whose Child Is More Intense, Sensitive, Persistent, and Energetic*
Mary Sheedy Kurcinka
Harper
1992

A reassuring and positive book that will help you understand and raise your child.

■ *Parenting the Fussy Baby and the High-Need Child: Everything You Need to Know—from Birth to Age Five*
William Sears, M.D. and Martha Sears, R.N.
Little, Brown and Company
1996

Sincere help and essential advice for the overwhelmed parent.

■ *The Challenging Child: Understanding, Raising, and Enjoying the Five Difficult Types of Children*
Stanley I. Greenspan, M.D.
Addison-Wesley Publishing Company
1995

Helps you identify your child's personality type and learn the kind of care that will be most successful with your child.

TEENAGERS/"TWEENAGERS"

■ *Stop Treating Me Like a Kid: Everyday Parenting: The 10 to 13-Year-Old*

   Robin Goldstein and Janet Gallant
   Penguin Books
   1994

An excellent book for navigating the "tweenage" years, from ten to thirteen. Practical answers to everyday questions.

■ *You're Grounded Till You're Thirty!: What Works—and What Doesn't—in Parenting Today's Teens*

   Judi Craig, Ph.D.
   Hearst Books
   1996

A good book to read if you're coming up on the teen years. Explains common struggles and helps you understand what's really going on with your teenager.

■ *Parent in Control*

   Greg Bodenhamer
   A Fireside Book
   1995

This straightforward book written by a former probation officer can be extremely helpful for parents of hard-to-control teenagers.

■ *Parenting Teens with Love and Logic: Preparing Adolescents for Responsible Adulthood*

   Foster W. Cline, Ph.D.
   Navpress
   1993

Commonsense ways to get kids to take responsibility for their own behavior.

VALUES

- *What Good Parents Have in Common*
  Janis Long Harris
  Zondervan Publishing House
  1994
  Based on interviews with successful parents, this book shares wisdom and realistic ideas. (Christian-based, but also an enjoyable book for parents of all faiths.)

ADDITIONAL INFORMATION

To obtain a free catalog of parenting books, videos, audiotapes, and newsletters available by Elizabeth Pantley:

Write to the author:

5720 127th Avenue NE
Kirkland, WA 98033-8741

Call the toll-free line:

(800) 422-5820

Fax your request:

(425) 828-4833

Visit the website:

www.pantley.com/elizabeth

E-mail the author:

elizabeth@pantley.com

ABOUT THE AUTHOR

Parenting educator Elizabeth Pantley is the president of Better Beginnings, Inc., a family resource and education company. Ms. Pantley frequently speaks to parents in schools, hospitals, and parent groups, and her presentations are received with enthusiasm and praise. She is a regular radio show guest and often quoted as a parenting expert in magazines such as *Parents, Parenting, Working Mother, Woman's Day, Good Housekeeping,* and *Redbook.* She publishes a newsletter, *Parent Tips,* that is distributed in schools nationwide, and is the author of one previous book, *Kid Cooperation: How to Stop Yelling, Nagging and Pleading and Get Kids to Cooperate.* She and her husband, Robert, live in Washington State with their three children, grandma, and assorted family pets. She is active in her children's school and sports activities. Ms. Pantley serves on an education advisory council and as the school PTA president.